FIERCE
Five Plays
for High Schools

FIERCE
Five Plays
for High Schools

plays by
Michael Kras
Dave Deveau
Ali Joy Richardson
Tanisha Taitt
Judith Thompson

FIERCE: Five Plays for High Schools
first published 2019 by Scirocco Drama
An imprint of J. Gordon Shillingford Publishing Inc.
© 2019 the authors

Scirocco Drama Editor: Glenda MacFarlane
Cover design by Doowah Design

Use of "Close-Up on a Sharp-Shinned Hawk" on page 277
by permission of Don McKay.

Printed and bound in Canada on 100% post-consumer recycled paper.
We acknowledge the financial support of the Manitoba Arts Council and
The Canada Council for the Arts for our publishing program.

Licensing Inquiries, please contact:

The Team:
Ian Arnold, Catalyst TCM, 15 Old Primrose Lane, Toronto, ON, M5A 4T1
ian@catalysttcm.com

Out in the Open:
Colin Rivers at Marquis Literary, info@mqlit.ca, www.mqlit.ca

A Bear Awake in Winter:
Ali Joy Richardson, www.alijoyrichardson.com

Admissions:
T. Taitt at meditaitt@gmail.com

Who Killed Snow White?:
Rena Zimmerman, Great North Artists Management, 350 Dupont Street,
Toronto, ON M5R 1V9, 416-925-2051; info@gnaminc.com

Library and Archives Canada Cataloguing in Publication

Title: Fierce : five plays for high schools / plays by Michael Kras, Dave Deveau, Ali Joy
Richardson, Tanisha Taitt, Judith Thompson.
Names: MacFarlane, Glenda, editor.
Description: Edited by Glenda MacFarlane.
Identifiers: Canadiana 20190186879 | ISBN 9781927922552 (softcover)
Subjects: CSH: Children's plays, Canadian (English) | CSH: Canadian drama (English)–21st
century. |
  LCGFT: Drama.
Classification: LCC PS8307 .F54 2019 | DDC C812/.60809283–dc23

J. Gordon Shillingford Publishing
P.O. Box 86, RPO Corydon Avenue, Winnipeg, MB Canada R3M 3S3

The Team by Michael Kras

Bobbie Brantwood has just returned to school after dealing with the suicide of her brother Ben, a former high school basketball superstar. As a way to process her grief, she's joining the White Oak Senior Girls basketball team as they prepare for a live-or-die battle to the championships. The crushing weight of expectations and issues of identity loom as each member of the team reaches the end of high school and stands on the precipice of her uncertain future.

Winner of the Herman Voaden National Playwriting Prize, 2017.

Out in the Open by Dave Deveau

Best friends Adam and Stephen are complete opposites: Adam is a rough-and-tumble outdoorsman, whereas Stephen is a clean-cut fashionista. When they get lost in the woods during a camping trip, it becomes clear how much gender stereotyping has forced them both into roles they aren't sure they fit. But in a moment of truth one of them reveals a secret they have been hiding for fear of losing everything they know as "normal."

A Bear Awake in Winter by Ali Joy Richardson

Dartmouth, Nova Scotia. A high school band. A teacher from Toronto wants to inspire his students but is afraid to come out to them. A boy bullies a girl until she takes matters into her own hands. Violence at a school dance fractures the community. This is a dark, funny, and difficult story about the fight to stand up for yourself.

Admissions by Tanisha Taitt

Trish, a Grade 12 student, is being tutored for a university program entrance exam by her best friend Carly. During their session, Trish notices something under Carly's sleeve, leading to a devastating revelation. Trish's response, however, is derailed by an inextricable complication that threatens to leave the friendship irreparably damaged.

Who Killed Snow White? by Judith Thompson

Who Killed Snow White? is a theatrical response to the rash of suicides by teens following sexual assault and relentless cyberbullying. The play is a reconstruction of events told to us by the teen's devastated mother; despite the dark centre of the play there are many moments of joy, humour, and finally, triumph.

Foreword
by Glenda MacFarlane, Scirocco Series Editor

When Scirocco publisher Karen Haughian and I first came up with the concept of compiling an anthology of plays for high schools, I knew the kinds of scripts we should include. I was looking for variety: a large-cast comedy, a sweet romance, a serious play about an issue, a non-traditional or experimental drama of some sort, and perhaps a musical or a one-person show. I called for submissions of professionally produced plays, received more than 100 manuscripts from across the country, and settled in eagerly to read them.

What I soon discovered was that the vast majority of the manuscripts submitted – and virtually all of the ones that resonated strongly for me – were dramas dealing with problems facing teenagers in the 21st century. I made the decision to abandon my preconceived notions of what a high school drama anthology should look like, and chose these five powerful scripts written by five extraordinary playwrights. Although the plays in *Fierce* feature unforgettable moments of hilarity, connection, and joy, each of them tackles complicated issues head-on.

The current generation is coming of age in an era fraught with anxiety: polarizing politics and a resurgence of extremism, income inequality and job insecurity, the increasing influence of technology, and accelerating climate change that threatens our very survival. As young people struggle to navigate this confusing landscape, they're also coping with private lives impacted by social media, changing gender roles, racism, issues of consent, and more.

Each of the plays in this book asks provocative questions. *The Team* by Michael Kras features a young woman grieving for her dead brother who is placed on the basketball team without having first paid her dues. It leads us to ask: what makes someone an outsider? How can you rebuild your life after suffering a devastating loss? What does it take to be true to your authentic self and claim your place in the world?

In *Out in the Open* by Dave Deveau, two young men are on a camping trip when one reveals something that threatens their long friendship. The characters, linked by history and a shared sense of humour, are forced to consider painful questions. Which is stronger: the bond between friends or the pressure to conform? What price do you pay for living honestly and courageously?

In Ali Joy Richardson's *A Bear Awake in Winter*, two band students with troubled personal histories are headed for a collision. When the situation builds to a shocking climax we are left to ponder what exactly went wrong. How do traumatic life experiences continue to impact us? What constitutes harassment? When is it acceptable to fight back?

Tanisha Taitt's *Admissions* lets us into the world of three high school seniors on the brink of independence. When a confession explodes like a bomb in the centre of a conversation, we wonder: can honesty be dangerous when loyalties conflict? How does a destructive relationship damage the spirit?

And finally, Judith Thompson's *Who Killed Snow White?* examines the kinds of pressures placed on young people and their parents in an era when everything is moving too quickly and situations spiral out of control at breakneck speed. Why are some young people singled out for persecution? How does a culture poisoned by toxic masculinity affect young men and women? How does internet culture impact vulnerable teens? What is society's responsibility to its young people?

The playwrights offer no easy answers to the thought-provoking questions they raise, because there are none. But the plays explore the issues with insight and courage, providing young people with new perspectives, inspiring in-depth discussions, and offering hope for the future. Whatever problems they encounter, these five writers contend, the young people of this generation can handle it. They're *fierce*.

The Team

Michael Kras

Michael Kras

Michael Kras is a playwright, actor, and director based in Hamilton, Ontario. He is the recipient of the prestigious Herman Voaden National Playwriting Prize for his play *The Team*, which was also nominated for the Tom Hendry TYA Award and the Safe Words New Canadian Play Award. *The Team* made its professional world premiere with Essential Collective Theatre, in association with Theatre Aquarius and the FirstOntario Performing Arts Centre. Other works include *The Year and Two of Us Back Here,* which premiered at the Hamilton Fringe Festival and made its international premiere at Iowa State University; *Lydia,* commissioned by the Frost Bites Festival; and *#dirtygirl,* which won the Audience Choice Award at the Hamilton Fringe Festival. Michael is a graduate of Humber Theatre School.

Photo by Megan Kras.

*For every extraordinary team of performers who put their heart,
brain, body, and guts into making this play what it is today.
You taught me so much about these characters.
Thank you for your generosity and empathy.*

Acknowledgments

The Team was developed at Theatre Aquarius, under the dramaturgy of Luke Brown and with support from the Ontario Arts Council and Theatre Aquarius Playwrights Unit. It received workshop presentations with safeword.theatre as a finalist for the Safe Words New Canadian Play Award, and at Queen's University as winner of the Herman Voaden National Playwriting Prize. The world premiere was produced by Essential Collective Theatre in association with Theatre Aquarius and the FirstOntario Performing Arts Centre, made possible by the support of The Ontario Arts Council, Niagara Investment in Culture, and the City of St. Catharines Cultural Investment Plan. Endless thanks to everyone who had a hand in this play's journey: Luke Brown, Colin Bruce Anthes, Rebecca Walsh, Lennon Bradford, Kaitlin Race, Emily Lukasik, Laura Welch, Kaylyn Valdez-Scott, Jo Pacinda, Ethan Rising, James McCoy, Michelle Mohammed, Marienne Castro, Katelin Richards, Julianne Dransfield, Cass Van Wyck, Brandon Crone, Stephanie Hope Lawlor, Vicktoria Adam, Caroline Toal, Kaleigh Gorka, Alyssa Nedich, Rebecca Benson, Ciana Henderson, Mahalia Golnosh Tahririha, Amanda Lin, Maryse Fernandes, Emma Hickey, Hannah Moscovitch, Nicolas Billon, Erin Shields, Andrew Lamb, Ian Arnold, Stephen Near, Ryan Sero, Jessica Anderson, Peter Gruner, Kevin Somers, Playwrights Guild of Canada, Mom, Dad, Megan.

Production History

The Team was written and developed with support from the Ontario Arts Council and Theatre Aquarius. The play made its world premiere in the 2018 / 19 season at Essential Collective Theatre in association with Theatre Aquarius in Hamilton, Ontario and the FirstOntario Performing Arts Centre in St. Catharines, Ontario from March 14th–23rd, 2019 with the following cast and creative team:

BOBBIE ....Lennon Bradford

ALICIA .... Kaitlin Race

MIRANDA ....Emily Lukasik

JENNA.. Laura Welch

JESS ....Kaylyn Valdez-Scott

Director – Colin Bruce Anthes

Assistant Director – Michelle Mohammed

Stage Manager – Jessica Campbell-Maracle

Costume Design – Jo Pacinda

Lighting and Set Design – James McCoy

Sound Design – Ethan Rising

Production Manager – Rebecca Walsh

Dramaturg – Luke Brown

Characters

BOBBIE

ALICIA

MIRANDA

JENNA

JESS

Setting

A high school gym. A locker room. A lunch room. A stairwell. Miranda's house.

Production Notes

On the characters
While these characters are teenagers, these young women are also dropped-in, grounded, complex individuals. Please avoid stereotype in all aspects of the work, including voice and body, even when it might feel like the text could be pushing you there.

On simultaneous dialogue
A slash (/) in the middle of a line of dialogue denotes the start of the next line, creating an overlap. Two groups of text side-by-side are to be spoken simultaneously. In cases where each piece of text is the same length, try to start and end them at roughly the same time. In cases where one line starts later or ends earlier, try to be as precise as possible with that timing.

On basketball
These characters are proficient basketball players. Your actors don't need to be. The premiere production of this play didn't have a single basketball onstage, and everything was suggested by precise choreography and rhythmic soundscape. It worked gorgeously, and meant that there were no basketballs bouncing around to get in the way of the intricacies of the text.

On pace
The play was written with a very specific pace, rhythm, and music in mind. Keep it moving. Keep it active.

On casting
The members of this team can and should reflect the diverse makeup of a contemporary Canadian high school. Please do the work to cast accordingly.

On blackouts
No blackouts except for the very end, for the love of god.

One more thing
Empathy first. Empathy always. Despite the intense circumstances, there's tons of love between these young women. Embrace it every chance you get.

It starts in the high school gym at White Oak Secondary School. There's a game play energy to this whole play. Even when they're not actually playing basketball.

Preshow, ALICIA, MIRANDA, JENNA, and JESS, four core players of the White Oak Senior Girls Basketball Team, are warming up, stretching, practising fundamentals. A whistle blows.

ALICIA: Welcome back ladies!
I hope we all enjoyed the break
Unexpected as it was.
But we've got some extra practices to play catch-up so
Let's get back in it
And kill the rest of this season.
We'll get started when everyone's here.
Warm up
Stretch
Whatever you need to do.

MIRANDA: Guys tell me I dreamed that
Tell me Coach actually chose Amy Schneider
AKA the best and most qualified player at those tryouts
For our
You know
Biggest and most important season ever?
Tell me Bobbie Brantwood is not about to walk in that door.

JENNA: Miranda don't be like
Mean

MIRANDA: I'm not
I'm sure she's a lovely human
But let's be real
I mean just because her brother was great
Like
You can't tell me this wasn't a pity pick.

ALICIA: Bobbie earned it too
            She deserves it.

JESS: Becky can suck my dick for leaving.
            Midway through season?
            Fucking Becky
            Dead to me

JENNA: Blame her dad

JESS: Fucking Becky's dad
            Dead to me

ALICIA: Oh how dare he get a job!
            Monster!

JESS: A job in Pickering though?

MIRANDA: Whatever
            Can't change it now
            We just have to make it work.
            With
            Bobbie Brantwood.

ALICIA: She was focused
            She was present
            I saw it
            Coach saw it
            She'll be great
            Coach wouldn't blow the season on someone who sucks.

MIRANDA: Like she disappears from school for like ever
            And the first day she comes back
            She's like
            Hmm maybe I should join the ball team?
            She's never even played before.

ALICIA: So?

MIRANDA: So some of us worked hard to get here
            Some of us still work our asses off
            And someone walks in
            Who's never trained
            Who's never played for real before
            Who looks like a boy band dropout
            And oh here you go
            Here's a spot

JESS: Boy band dropout
            Oh my / god I'm gonna pee

ALICIA: I think it's the right choice

MIRANDA: We'll see.

JENNA: Hey what do we say to her about Ben do / we say

JESS: Nothing are you crazy?

JENNA: Well like I don't want it to be weird so
And besides the gym?
Ben Brantwood Memorial Gym?
We can't really avoid it so

ALICIA: She'll be here any minute
And when she gets here
We're not gonna be weird
We're not gonna treat her weird
We're gonna welcome her
We're gonna be like
Welcome to our team
Because we're a team
And she earned it
Just like we did when we joined
Let's warm up

> *They break off and get ready. BOBBIE rushes in.*

BOBBIE: Yo sorry sorry
Anderson wanted to talk to me after math
And it uh went long
Am I late?

ALICIA: No no no you're fine
We're just all early

BOBBIE: Anyway I'm uh
I'm here I'm ready let's uh
I've never done anything like this before
I've never played like legit before
Whatever it's
I'm Bobbie by the way
I don't / think we

MIRANDA: Miranda
Nice to meet you
Congrats on making the best team in the district.

BOBBIE: I think this'll be cool
I mean I'm excited to / uh

MIRANDA: It will be
My advice though?
Just be ready to work
You have a lot of catching / up to

ALICIA: I think you're gonna do great
Welcome to the team
How have I never seen you play before now?

BOBBIE: I've been around and uh
I mean my brother and I
We used to play together
One on one
So I just kinda learned by doing it

ALICIA: Well consider me impressed
Anyway get settled
I've gotta go check in with Coach before we start

> *ALICIA walks away. MIRANDA flings a basketball at*
> *BOBBIE, who misses it completely.*

MIRANDA: Catch

BOBBIE: Shit

MIRANDA: Rule one
Always be ready
Always be present

BOBBIE: I wasn't uh

MIRANDA: Ready
That's what I'm saying
If you're on this team
You're present
You're here
No matter what

BOBBIE: I'll keep that in mind

MIRANDA: We've been playing together for a long time
So make sure you work extra hard
Because it's a big year
There's a lot for all of us if we make it to the top
Scholarships
Scouts
This is real
But you obviously know that.

BOBBIE: Absolutely

MIRANDA: Hey can you do a figure eight?
        Just for fun
        Show me a figure eight

BOBBIE: Aren't we about to do like drills / and stuff?

MIRANDA: But we don't usually do figure eights

BOBBIE: I mean I haven't
        Okay I think I uh

> BOBBIE *tries it and fails. JESS, watching from afar,*
> *giggles and runs off.*

BOBBIE: Shit
        Had it for a sec

> BOBBIE *chases the ball.*

        I'll have to work on that

MIRANDA: Sure
        Hey
        This is new
        I get it
        We were all new once.
        Oh also
        And please don't take offence to this
        We all got the same speech from Coach but
        It helps to like you know
        Hit the gym a bit
        Work on your like
        You know

BOBBIE: My

MIRANDA: Like we all need muscle tone
        Like I mean you're really tall
        Which is obviously great
        I just don't want you to get hurt

BOBBIE: Noted
        I'll eat a lot of steak I guess

MIRANDA: Su / re?

> JENNA *enters, sees* BOBBIE, *and runs up excitedly to*
> *hug her from behind.*

JENNA: Baaaaaaaabe what are you doing here you
            Oh my god / shit sorry

MIRANDA: Jesus / Jenna

JENNA: I just touched you from behind like a creeper
            You looked just like my boyfriend from behind
            James
            Clearly you're not.

BOBBIE: Sorry to disappoint

JENNA: You're the new recruit

MIRANDA: The new Becky

JENNA: I'm Jenna

BOBBIE: Bobbie

JENNA: So uh
            How are you holding up?

BOBBIE: Fine?

JENNA: I just wanna say like
            If you ever need a
            Like people say I'm good to talk to
            I mean I know I don't know you yet / but like

BOBBIE: Yeah yeah it's cool thanks uh

MIRANDA: I just noticed your nose ring

BOBBIE: Oh uh

MIRANDA: Coach is probably gonna make you get rid of that

BOBBIE: Really?
            I mean I've had it for forever
            It's kinda part of who I am / so

MIRANDA: And someone could hook you wrong
            And grab it and pull

                    ALICIA returns.

ALICIA: Right!
            You could totally bleed out
            And die

BOBBIE: I uh / don't

ALICIA: Kidding I'm kidding
            Is she bugging you?

BOBBIE: Nah nah it's fine
            Uh
            Thanks

MIRANDA: We're all friends here
            Like that's what a good team is
            And it's so easy to get hurt here
            And I'd hate
            To see you get hurt

BOBBIE: Me too

MIRANDA: I'm gonna stretch
            You all probably should too

            MIRANDA leaves.

ALICIA: She's just stressed out
            She can be an asshole
            Don't take it personally

BOBBIE: Wait isn't her dad / a

ALICIA: A ball legend?

JENNA: Yep

BOBBIE: His picture's / up on the wall outside

ALICIA: Up on the wall outside yeah.
            He was legit and he went pro

BOBBIE: Right!

JENNA: He's a DILF

ALICIA: She wants to do it too
            Play pro be like dad
            He's breathing down her neck so
            So is everyone actually
            I mean it's not totally fair
            She shouldn't have to be as good as her dad
            But naturally everyone compares
            And that probably gets to you.

BOBBIE: Is she always like that?

JENNA: Like what?

BOBBIE: It just feels like she doesn't uh
            Like me

ALICIA: Oh no no she's just sizing you up

JENNA: She's a control freak

ALICIA: But don't worry
           You earned your place

JENNA: We all had to
           For me it was my ex

ALICIA: Here we / go

JENNA: Shhh Leesh / just let me

ALICIA: She tells this story like / every day

JENNA: Anyway my ex
           This fuckboi Chad
           You've probably seen him he's like
           The fuckboi
           And so he played on the boys' team
           And he was like
           "Hey baby hey maybe you should try out for cheer squad"
           And I was like not a chance that sounds awful
           And he's like "come on baby come on you'll get to cheer me
           on"

JENNA/ALICIA: "Don't you wanna cheer me on?"

JENNA: And then I realized like
           Oh my god
           There's nothing I'd rather do less
           So I tried out.
           For this team.
           And I just thought of his fucking face the whole time.
           And I got in.
           And it pissed him off so much that he broke up with me
           And I can play circles around him now.

JENNA/ALICIA: Fuck you Chad

                 JENNA and ALICIA high-five.

BOBBIE: Uh cool

JENNA: What made you join?

BOBBIE: I guess I just wanted to uh
           Carry the torch?
           For my uh

JENNA: Right wow uh yeah
           That's cool that's
           I mean he was a killer player

BOBBIE: Th/anks

JENNA: Like we all thought so

BOBBIE: Thanks

ALICIA: And here comes Miranda 2.0

JESS runs in.

JESS: I want to meet the rookie

BOBBIE: My friends call me Bobbie

JESS: Jess

BOBBIE: Didn't we have Bio
together last year?

JENNA: I should go stretch too

JESS: I don't know
maybe?

I pulled a hammy last
time and yeah

Nice flannel

JENNA goes to stretch.

BOBBIE: Thanks

JESS: Where's your jersey?

BOBBIE: I uh
Don't have one yet?

JESS: I saw you talking to Miranda

BOBBIE: Yep she's uh
Pretty direct

JESS: She can be kinda harsh for sure
But she's totally right

BOBBIE: About what?

JESS: Like this is not a losing team so
If you suck at layups
Get good at layups
If you suck at passing
Get good at passing
Because we don't lose

ALICIA: How many Red Bulls did you have this morning?

JESS: Just one why do
you care?

JENNA: Leesh can you come do
that lower back thing?

ALICIA: Coming Jenn

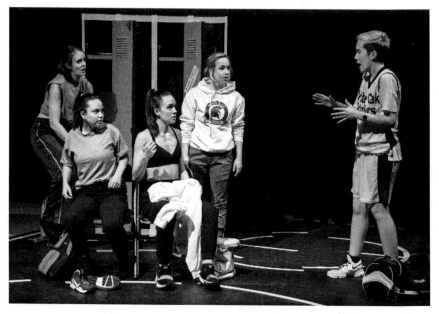

In the locker room, Jenna (Laura Welch), Jess (Kaylyn Valdez-Scott), and Alicia (Kaitlin Race) look on at an awkward moment between Miranda (Emily Lukasik) and Bobbie (Lennon Braford). (L–R) Laura Welch, Kaylyn Valdez-Scott, Emily Lukasik, Kaitlin Race, Lennon Bradford.
Photo by Lauren Garbutt.

> *ALICIA walks to JENNA and does an assisted stretch.*
> *JESS stretches.*

JESS: Well don't just stand there

> *BOBBIE kinda awkwardly follows her lead.*

BOBBIE: I have a hoop on my driveway
I'll practise
And uh
Get better at my weak spots

JESS: My advice?
Just stay out of Miranda's way and you're good.

BOBBIE: Yeah I got that feeling

JESS: She wants this to be her career for real so
There's a lot on the line.

BOBBIE: So I guess you want that too

JESS: What?

BOBBIE: Like a career?
In this?

JESS: Uh no why?

BOBBIE: I mean it's just
You've got that same driving like
Intensity about you

JESS: Uh

BOBBIE: Sorry that came out weird I uh
That was supposed to be a a a compliment / and

JESS: Well I'm not trying to like
Like I mean obviously if something happened I wouldn't turn it down

BOBBIE: Of course

JESS: But like
This is important either way no matter what we wanna do.
Everyone wants to be friends with the winners.
But anyway I have my own thing I'm gonna do my own thing so.

BOBBIE: What's your thing?

JESS: Don't know yet.
But that's obviously okay

BOBBIE: Yeah / yeah

JESS: There's obviously time / so

BOBBIE: Yeah yeah
            So much time.

ALICIA: Okay ladies
            Welcome back

MIRANDA: Wait where's Coach?

ALICIA: She's in her office for a sec
            She said start and she'll join us.
            Anyway you've all met Bobbie
            Our newest Warrior
            Make her feel welcome
            She's one of us now.
            Coach says the usual
            Wind sprints
            Dribbling
            Passing
            Then shooting
            Go go go!

                        A whistle blows. Drills. All except BOBBIE dribble and
                        perform with rhythm, synchronicity, precision. Like a
                        percussive ballet. BOBBIE performs well enough but is
                        often the discord. Another whistle.

            Good work ladies
            Clean up!

BOBBIE: Hoooooooly

ALICIA: You'll get used to it

BOBBIE: I haven't
            Run like that in
            Actually I've never run like that

ALICIA: Be conservative
            That's the most important thing
            This takes a lot of energy
            And if you give it all up at the top you bust
            Happened to me one of my first games
            I actually passed out from exhaustion
            Middle of the court

BOBBIE: Get out

ALICIA: I was fine
          I just didn't learn how to breathe

BOBBIE: Uhhh

ALICIA: There was actually this study at McGill
          It showed that women are more shallow breathers than men
          Because our respiratory muscles are more active
          The trick is to breathe deeply and fully
          Like you're trying to fill your whole body like a balloon
          It opens you
          Try it
          Try breathing in like you're a balloon
          Let the air just fall in

BOBBIE: Uh
          I'll try

                    BOBBIE inhales.

ALICIA: Then out slowly.
          Different right?

BOBBIE: How do you know all this stuff?

ALICIA: It's kinda my jam
          I wanna study kinesiology at McGill actually

BOBBIE: That's awesome

ALICIA: I mean my application is in so
          Fingers crossed
          And if our team makes it to provincials this year
          That could mean scholarships and stuff
          Which I mean would help a lot.

BOBBIE: Yeah?

ALICIA: Well like
          School's expensive obviously.
          So help is always great.

BOBBIE: Yeah yeah of course I mean
          Duh.

ALICIA: What do you wanna do?

BOBBIE: Like?

ALICIA: Like after this

BOBBIE: Ha what?
            No idea
            None
            Thanks for this by the way
            Teaching me how to uh
            Breathe
            Ever forget how?
            Like sometimes you notice you're breathing
            And then it feels like this thing you have to do like
            Manually
            And you're like
            Shit
            How does this go again?
            Or maybe that's just weird

ALICIA: Let's get cleaned up

                        The locker room. They're changing.

JENNA: And so I was like
            Now or fucking never
            Is this real or not?
            Like what are we even doing?
            And he was like
            You know I love you baby you know I do
            And I was like prove it
            Like let's stop messing around
            And he was like
            Okay okay no more games I promise
            And he was like
            Just don't say things like break-up
            I hate hearing that unless you mean it
            Don't just throw it around
            And I was like
            Oh my god
            I've never been more turned on in my life
            And then like
            Best sex we've ever had
            He actually teased me
            He never teases me
            He just gets his part and then done
            And I'm always like really?
            Like seriously?
            But this
            So maybe I should pull that card more often

JESS:	Like yeah Then you've got the power
JENNA:	What do you think Bobbie?
BOBBIE:	Huh? Uh I / dunno
JESS:	Yo I fucking reek Smell that
JENNA:	No get / away
JESS:	Smell it
JENNA:	I'll puke on you / stop
ALICIA:	Hey good job today Bobbie You're / really
JESS:	Hey what about us?
ALICIA:	All of / you
JESS:	Gee thanks Cap'n Cap'n / Crunch
JENNA:	Jess does literally everything have to be about / you or like what
JESS:	No no no I'm just saying I'm saying that it / was all of all of
JENNA:	Well yeah but like she's talking / about
MIRANDA:	Can I help you?
BOBBIE:	Uh what?
MIRANDA:	Never mind sorry just I saw you that's all
BOBBIE:	Did I uh miss something or Sorry I zoned out / for a
JENNA:	What's / going on?
ALICIA:	Miranda what's your problem She didn't do anything
MIRANDA:	She was staring at my uh
BOBBIE:	Whoa no I'm uh what hey I didn't uh realize or I I wasn't uh.

> *Silence. MIRANDA throws on a hoodie and leaves.*
> *Everyone else gets dressed more awkwardly. Shift to*
> *the next day. It's lunch. The girls sit. Except BOBBIE,*
> *who practises alone in the gym.*

JENNA: Is this yesterday's pizza?
           I think it's yesterday's / pizza

MIRANDA: I wouldn't eat any day's pizza here

JENNA: You and your quinn-wa

JESS: Her what?

JENNA: Quinn-wa

MIRANDA: It's pronounced quinoa

JENNA: Whatever I don't care stop ganging up on me

ALICIA: Yeah guys
           Just eat your quinn-wa and stop ganging up on Jenna

JENNA: I'm quitting this team.

JESS: Hear back from Mohawk yet?

JENNA: No and it's killing me
           If I don't get into any schools I'll have to stay home
           And my mom says I'll have to pay rent now
           Which means I'll have to work
           Probably at McDonalds
           And I'll just gorge myself on nuggets

JESS: Yo that's like the dream

JENNA: Not for me

ALICIA: I'm sure it'll be okay

JESS: And it's fine to take some time off
           That's what I'm doing

JENNA: Do you guys think I'm dumb?

ALICIA: No not at   MIRANDA: Oh my   JESS: Jenna no
           all   god this   you're not
                                   again

JENNA: It's just like I feel like
           Dumb all the time
           I feel like I'm gonna leave here with nothing

JESS: Jenna don't do that you're
           You're great.

JENNA: Great is not the opposite of dumb

ALICIA: Where's Bobbie?

JESS: Probably too embarrassed
           Right Miranda?

ALICIA: Seriously guys
           This is not what this team is / about

MIRANDA: Well if yesterday is any indication
           She's got a lot
           A lot
           Of work to do.

JESS: I hope Becky's having a miserable time

JENNA: She lives in Pickering now that's punishment enough

MIRANDA: I don't know Bobbie's also weird
           Like we're a team
           She doesn't feel like
           You know

JESS: Part of the team

MIRANDA: Part of the team

> *JESS goes to high-five MIRANDA. MIRANDA ignores it.*

ALICIA: She literally just started
           She'll adapt
           It feels like you're threatened

MIRANDA: She can do what she wants I don't care
           Just don't like whatever
           Like she's so in your face about it
           Like she wants you to know
           Like ohhh I'm different I'm different
           She rubs it in

JESS: Yeah like don't get me wrong
           I'm a very liberal minded / person but

ALICIA: I wanted to make her feel welcome
           And we did like the exact opposite.
           None of us know what it's like to go through that so
           Maybe take it down a notch?

MIRANDA: Obviously she's had a terrible time I know that
But we all have problems
We take them off with our jeans on the way in
We leave them out the door
She needs tough love Leesh
A good captain uses tough love
That's how you get good
How you win a season
That's how my dad does it
That's what happened to him
Tough love
And look at what / he's

JENNA: Ooh I'm Miranda
I'm bitter that I didn't get captain / ooh

MIRANDA: Shut up that's not it at all

JESS: Yeah Jenna shut up

ALICIA: Okay see you guys later

JESS: Where are / you

ALICIA: I'm not gonna be around you when you're being shitty
Get a better attitude.

ALICIA leaves.

JESS: So what do we do / about

MIRANDA: We just have to make it work
Don't we?

ALICIA joins BOBBIE in the gym.

ALICIA: Feels weird, right?

BOBBIE: Ho
Holy

ALICIA: Sorry
I'm light on my feet

BOBBIE: I was just uh
Practising
What feels weird?

ALICIA: Being in the gym by yourself
I mean like I know for me
I feel kinda like
Selfish?
Like all this space
Just me

BOBBIE: I don't mind
            No one can see me like
            Fuck up

ALICIA: Oh I can go / if

BOBBIE: Nah nah that's okay
            I've just got a lot of work to do
            Coming in mid-season isn't exactly easy so

ALICIA: I mean Coach picked you for a reason

BOBBIE: I guess

ALICIA: Plus I think it's your fire

BOBBIE: My what?

ALICIA: Your fire
            There's like something burning
            And everyone around you feels it
            And they're scared of it
            Some of them
            But it's there
            Ready to burst.
            You know we have new balls
            You don't have to use the old beat-up / pieces of

BOBBIE: This one was my brother's actually

ALICIA: Oh uh

BOBBIE: He used to say it had magic

ALICIA: Everyone thought he was gonna be really great.

BOBBIE: Yeah I uh
            I know.

ALICIA: Wanna play some one on one?

BOBBIE: Wait 'til I'm a little better first
            So it's you know
            Fair

ALICIA: Deal
            Wanna come eat lunch?

BOBBIE: I don't really uh
            Do that

ALICIA: Eat?

BOBBIE: I just like being alone at lunch usually so

ALICIA: Me too actually

BOBBIE: But I always see you around people

ALICIA: See everyone's always like
           Like literally everyone talks to me
           Which is cool like that's okay
           But then there are days you wish no one would talk to you
           So I get away when I can
           I come here actually
           So I mean it's / okay if

BOBBIE: No no like
           Usually but
           This is okay

ALICIA: Want some of my nuts?

BOBBIE: I love that sentence and yes I do

ALICIA: I just have like a mix

BOBBIE: Is that the one with the cashews?

ALICIA: Duh

BOBBIE: It's just I'm jonesing for a cashew

                    They eat.

           My mom used to buy these like
           Tins of these
           And they were supposed to last like a week
           And I'd see it in the grocery bag and be like
           Oh shit
           And I'd steal it
           Eat the whole tin in a night
           Like one after the other
           Handfuls
           Like I'm like
           There's no such thing as too many cashews
           But like
           Yes there is
           And I'd be sick and my mom would be like
           See Bev?
           You're nuts!
           She thinks she's funny

ALICIA: Bev?

BOBBIE: Oh uh that's uh
           My real name is Beverley
           But I hate it because
           Beverley
           It's just too like
           Dainty
           So I call myself Bobbie
           And everyone calls me Bobbie
           Except her
           She's like
           That's not your name

ALICIA: Parents are weird with names
           My mom always does the middle name too
           Like Alicia May
           Alicia May
           I mean I know that's not the same
           Does your dad call / you

BOBBIE: He doesn't call me anything because he uh
           Because he left.
           Couldn't take it after Ben
           So you know
           He's kinda dead to me.

ALICIA: That sucks uh

BOBBIE: Yeah so it's just me and my mom
           And she's fine
           She just thinks I'm someone else
           Like she buys me pink shit
           I'm like really?
           When do I ever?
           She hates that I wear stuff like this
           She wants me to be more girly or whatever
           Probably because after Ben
           I mean like he wore makeup and stuff and he
           So she's scared that I'll like
           That the same thing will uh

ALICIA: What?

BOBBIE: Never mind uh.
            Anyway a lot of it is like
            These were my brother's
            And she hates seeing them because it reminds her
            But like I feel at home in them
            Like this watch was his
            I always loved it because it's huge and heavy
            My mom's like
            That watch looks stupid on you

ALICIA: It's beautiful

BOBBIE: Ben loved his bling
            Yo I'm talking a lot
            Sorry I'm / weird

ALICIA: No I talk a lot too I get it

BOBBIE: I guess when you don't talk for a while
            There's a lot to say waiting to come out
            So I mean I guess there's my life story

ALICIA: Are you okay?
            You're moving around a lot

BOBBIE: I feel like I can never get comfortable
            Do you feel like that?
            Like you can't get comfortable?

ALICIA: Sometimes I guess

BOBBIE: For me it's always.
            Okay take these cashews away before I hurt myself

ALICIA: Take the rest if you want
            I kinda hate nuts actually
            They're really dry

BOBBIE: Then why do / you

ALICIA: My mom's a health nut
            And like she always wants to make sure I'm
            But I crave those mini powdered donuts all the time

BOBBIE: Holy shit don't get me started

ALICIA: And chocolate-covered almonds

BOBBIE: Stop oh god now I'm craving everything
            I'm gonna get so fat now

ALICIA: Well Miranda did tell you to bulk up

BOBBIE: Shut up
Hey uh
You can eat whatever you want
Don't let people
Yeah.

ALICIA: Anyway lunch is almost over we should
And you can finish practising if you want

BOBBIE: Hey uh
Alicia?
What made you join this team?

ALICIA: Good question

BOBBIE: Like I know it's been a while but

ALICIA: Well I mean
Life's a lot sometimes
The pressure right?
And this is something to just
Throw yourself into
Blow it all off
Get it out
And like not take it too seriously
Or else you become a Miranda
And I'm okay at it so
I just run
I go hard
And I feel clean after
What about you?

BOBBIE: I guess I'm here for the people who can't be

> *ALICIA leaves. BOBBIE shoots her ball. When it lands,*
> *so do multiple others. Everyone runs in and warms up.*

JESS: Hey
Rookie
You here?

BOBBIE: Uh
Yeah?

JESS: You're zoning out don't do that

> *JENNA enters late, clearly upset.*

JENNA: Sorry I'm late I uh / I'm

BOBBIE: Jesus Jenn
           Are you okay?

JENNA: I broke up with James

BOBBIE: Wow / I'm sorry

JESS: What happened?

JENNA: So like
           Last night he was like
           Let's have sex
           Right now
           On my mom's couch
           And I was like no I'm not in the mood
           And he was like come on
           And I was like I'm not in the mood
           And he was like come on it's been a long day
           And I was like I'm not just not in the mood I'm also on my
           period
           Okay?
           My period?
           Is that okay with you?
           And he's like what I don't care that's fine
           And I said no and that I'm not comfortable and he should
           know that by now
           And then we were quiet all night
           And then he was saying like
           The team is more important than he is
           Because we're here practising so much
           And I was like no way no way that's not
           But he was like I feel second I feel second
           And I was like is this because I didn't wanna fuck?
           And he was like no it's soooooo many other things
           And I said you know what we're fucking done
           If you can't deal with my life if you're gonna get jealous or
           whatever
           I'm not doing this.

JESS: Good for you
           What a piece of shit.
           Hey
           Use it today
           Pretend the ball is his shitty face

JENNA: I'm gonna rip it to fucking pieces / just watch

ALICIA: Good stuff ladies
            You heard Coach
            Keep working
            You know things are tight
            Quarterfinals are two weeks away
            And I don't need to tell you what a big year this is
            It's all about now right?
            It's all about us
            And who are we?

ALL: White Oak Warriors!
            White Oak Warriors!

                    They scream a ferocious and ecstatic war cry.

ALICIA: Let's run Loyola next
            Ready Bobbie?

BOBBIE: I mean I uh
            I guess

ALICIA: You'll get it soon
            I know it.
            Let's go!

                    *A whistle. Practice begins. Time slows. Hearing
                    the dribbles, BOBBIE goes into her head, working
                    through a spoken word poem.*

BOBBIE: I remember coming home
            The air was like
            Broken
            That doesn't make sense
            But it was broken
            And he'd already been taken away
            So it was like
            That's it
            So I fell and I kept falling and I still am
            And now I'm here
            And the dribbles go through the floor
            And into my feet
            And up to my chest
            And for the first time
            In a while
            I feel something.

BOBBIE's ball flies into MIRANDA.

MIRANDA: Hey watch it

BOBBIE: Whoa whoa sorry I guess I zoned out / or

MIRANDA: Uh well maybe don't zone out
            On a play you're featured in
            Come on.

ALICIA: Hey enough
            It was clearly an / accident

BOBBIE: I'm really sorry   MIRANDA: That hurt

ALICIA: Do you need to go to the nurse's office or / something?

MIRANDA: Uh obviously not

ALICIA: Then cool it and keep
            Actually
            We're done
            That's time ladies!
            Great work!
            You okay Jenna?

JENNA: I'm working on it.

ALICIA, JENNA, and JESS leave.

BOBBIE: Hey Miranda hey uh
            Hey can we talk for a sec?

MIRANDA: I'm getting water / so

BOBBIE: Just for a sec
            So uh
            I feel like we got off on the uh
            And I don't know if I did something to piss you off
            Or what but
            I just wanted to make sure we're cool
            Like I'd love to like
            Be your friend like be on the team
            But I dunno if this started off the best way and yeah.
            I just wanna make sure we're cool
            Are we cool?

MIRANDA: Can I be honest with you?

BOBBIE: Uh
           Sure of course

MIRANDA: My dad has done a lot obviously
         And he expects a lot of me
         Of us
         And like what's important is that we're all happy
         Like we should all be happy right?

BOBBIE: I agree

MIRANDA: And I mean
         Okay I'm just gonna say it
         This isn't therapy.
         Like I know things are so tough
         Like I can't imagine what / you're

BOBBIE: No I mean
           That's okay I just
           Sorry if I seem like
           But I wanna do well too
           And that's important to me

MIRANDA: Oh of course I totally get it
         But this is not the time to zone out
         Quarterfinals are a blink away
         And if we lose
         We're out.
         We lose everything.
         No scholarships
         No scouts
         And like we all wanna go to good schools right?
         We all wanna have futures

BOBBIE: No totally I uh
           I get that
           And I'm doing my best.

MIRANDA: Just remember that this is big
         For a lot of us.

BOBBIE: Gotcha
           Hey Miranda?

MIRANDA: Yeah?

BOBBIE: Maybe try not being an asshole?
            It's ugly on you.

                    Two weeks later. Quarterfinals. They stretch.

JESS: Quarterfinals bitches let's do this
            The Saints are gonna eat shit

JENNA: Didn't we lose to them last time?

MIRANDA: Definitely not
            It's the Saints.

JENNA: Did you guys see there's a scout?
            From the States?

MIRANDA: Oh my god don't tell me that

JENNA: I thought you knew
            I mean your dad brought him

MIRANDA: No.
            I didn't.
            But thanks for that.
            Jesus.

JESS: Hey can we watch our words thanks.

JENNA: What?

MIRANDA: Jesus?

JESS: Yeah

MIRANDA: You're religious now?

JESS: Yeah

MIRANDA: No you're not

JESS: Yes I am I have been for a long time

JENNA: She does this Miranda

JESS: Uh what / do I

JENNA: She tries a new thing each week
            And acts like
            "What? I've always done this."

JESS: Fuck you

ALICIA: You okay Bobbie?

BOBBIE: Yeah yeah just

Yeah

ALICIA: You sure?

You're really pale right now

BOBBIE: Nah it's

I mean

It's a lot to uh

JENNA: You swear more than all of us combined

You're going to Hell

JESS: Fuck you

JENNA: Did you know that religious

Rhymes with self-righteous?

JESS: No it doesn't

Whatever drop it let's get in the zone

ALICIA: You're so ready.
You rock these plays.
Breathe remember?
Find my eyes if you have to.
Okay ladies bring it in.
Forget who's out there
Now we know the Saints
We know these girls are forceful on Offence
So I wanna see some strong D out there
We're gonna play 54 to start
Miranda be assertive
Bobbie be ready for those rebounds
Jenna hang back be ready
Play safe
Play strong
Make Coach proud
Who are we?

ALL: White Oak Warriors!

ALICIA: Who are we?

ALL: White Oak Warriors!

> *A whistle. The game. The team moves through space. They're losing.*

MIRANDA: Bobbie!

> *MIRANDA passes to BOBBIE, who shoots and misses.*

BOBBIE: Shit shit

MIRANDA: Get it together come on!

> *Play continues. MIRANDA falls. A whistle.*

Foul my ass!

> *The team is still losing. ALICIA calls a time-out. A whistle. The team huddles.*

We're so blowing it and / this is

ALICIA: It's okay guys
There's still time
We're gonna play Loyola

MIRANDA: Seriously?

BOBBIE: Loyola oh uh / I

ALICIA: Bobbie you know this you can do this
We've drilled it tons
Just be patient with it

BOBBIE: That's a lot of uh

ALICIA: I believe in you
We all do
Come on guys
Let's turn this around
Break!

> *A whistle. MIRANDA leans into BOBBIE.*

MIRANDA: If only you were as good as your brother.

> *Game continues. Suddenly BOBBIE jumps into gear. Laser focused.*

JESS: Bobbie!

JENNA: Shot!

> *BOBBIE scores.*

ALICIA: Yes yes amazing   JENNA: She shoots she scores
amazing!   you whores!

MIRANDA: Shit / shit shit

ALICIA: Come on guys we got this
Stronger on D Jenn stay low

MIRANDA: Corner!

ALICIA: Watch the cutter!

> *Play continues. BOBBIE scores again. Silence. Then, a whistle blows. The game ends. They scream and celebrate and howl. MIRANDA sulks.*

ALICIA: Bobbie you were   JESS: SEMIFINALS HERE WE
          incredible!   COME FUCK YEAH!

BOBBIE: Whatever it was / just yeah

JESS: THEY FUCKING ATE SHIT WE CLEANED UP BITCHES
          I AM SO FUCKING AMPED WOO

ALICIA: You came alive

BOBBIE: That felt really / good I uh

JENNA: Hey Miranda you good?

MIRANDA: Yeah?

ALICIA: We won.

MIRANDA: I know
          Good for us.
          I just blew it that's all
          I was in my head and I fucking / blew it

ALICIA: No no you were great / we all were

JESS: Don't be hard on yourself you did / awesome

MIRANDA: Don't talk down to me.

JESS: Uh / sorry I

ALICIA: Seriously amazing guys.
          And Bobbie you were so grounded
          You played like you've been with us since the start

BOBBIE: It's nothing I
          Practice works I guess
          Your breathing thing
          Anyway that guy over there said he uh
          Wants to talk to me?
          So uh good job guys

> *BOBBIE leaves. JENNA and JESS go to get cleaned up.*

MIRANDA: Well let's not get too excited
          We're not done / yet so

ALICIA: Come here okay?
          Before you head out

MIRANDA: What's the

ALICIA: Anything you wanna talk about?

MIRANDA: I'm good thanks

MIRANDA turns to leave.

ALICIA: Hey wait wait wait
           Stay here for a second
           You know if you ever need to talk I

MIRANDA: I'm good thanks

ALICIA: It seems like you're under stress
           And I don't want you to break yourself

MIRANDA: I'm fine

ALICIA: Suit yourself
           But the negativity has got to go.

MIRANDA: Negativity

ALICIA: Seriously.
           And the way you're treating Bobbie is not cool.
           She's on this team too.
           Why can't you let her have this?

MIRANDA: I'm not doing anything
           She has it

ALICIA: You wanted her to be in it
           To play well
           And she was and she did.
           So what's the problem?

MIRANDA: I don't have a problem whatever
           Anyway it's not just me who's
           You're stressed too Leesh we all are
           So don't come down on me.

ALICIA: But you're being selfish out there
           Coach is noticing too
           You're better than that.

MIRANDA: You applied to McGill right?
           You're applying to scholarships and stuff right?

ALICIA: Yeah what / does that

The White Oak Warriors run drills with Bobbie (Lennon Bradford) on her first day with the team. (L–R) Lennon Bradford, Emily Lukasik, Kaylyn Valdez-Scott, Laura Welch, Kaitlin Race.
Photo by Lauren Garbutt.

MIRANDA: Well I want a future too
You know how that happens?
Scouts
Recruiters
Like the one who saw me shit the bed just now.
From the States?
That my dad arranged to come see me?
And I saw him watching Bobbie
And my dad watched him watch Bobbie.
And now she's over there
So you know
I can't wait to hear what my dad says.

ALICIA: It'll be okay.

MIRANDA: You don't get it Leesh.
You have stuff
You have tons of shit you do
You have options
This is all I do
This is one hundred percent it.

ALICIA: You played fine you / always

MIRANDA: I don't want to play "fine"
"Fine" doesn't get you anywhere.
I've tried giving her a chance.
We were balanced with Becky and now it's
She's throwing me off she doesn't know what / she's doing

ALICIA: Well you'd better adapt
And if you keep acting like this
I'm taking it up I'm going to Coach.
Okay?

MIRANDA: We're not in the clear yet Leesh.
We're just getting started.

> *The next day. Training. MIRANDA is shooting a ball as everyone else warms up. BOBBIE is missing.*

JENNA: God weren't we just here?
I feel like I literally never leave this gym
I forget what outside looks like

MIRANDA: Well then step outside for a sec or something

JENNA: What's the point
            It's just a big tease
            A big big I I hate this right now I hate / this I

ALICIA: What's up Jenn?

JENNA: I got my last letter
            My last rejection letter
            I'm three for three

ALICIA: Shit I'm sorry

JESS: Was it Mohawk?

JENNA: Yeah

JESS: I know you wanted Mohawk

MIRANDA: You didn't even choose a major

JENNA: I wanted to keep my options open Miranda

ALICIA: It'll be okay
            There's / always

JENNA: Oh my god I've got nothing
            I've got literally nothing now
            What am I gonna
            My mom's gonna kill me
            I promised her I'd keep my average super high this year and
            I
            So I guess now I get to just sit on my couch and rot / away
            and

JESS: Hey don't worry about it
            No rush
            I'm not jumping into anything yet either when I graduate /
            so

JENNA: Not all of us wanna sit around doing nothing
            I'm gonna feel like a loser.

JESS: Uh hey
            I'm not a loser.

JENNA: Oh no no / no that's

JESS: Just because I'm still figuring stuff out doesn't / mean I'm a

JENNA: That's not / what I

JESS: Oh my god you sound like my mom

JENNA: Your mom calls you a loser?

JESS: No.
            No no no that's not what
            You know what forget it forget I tried to to
            I don't care about your school thing okay?
            Don't come to me for stuff ever okay?

JENNA: That came out really wrong
            I wasn't trying to uh.

ALICIA: Let's all just breathe
            Guys I know it's a weird time
            I know we're all stressed as shit
            That's okay
            Be stressed
            But use it
            Let's just be here right now.

JENNA: It's a really hard day for that

MIRANDA: Just pick yourself up

ALICIA: Can we just get to warm / up please?

JENNA: I've had a tough week

MIRANDA: We all have them
            I'm just saying it's not worth dwelling on

JENNA: Just let me be sad for a bit okay?

MIRANDA: Where's Coach?

ALICIA: She said she'd be right back
            So let's warm up / while we're waiting

JENNA: She always does / this

JESS: I heard she gets high out the back of the gym

JENNA: Shut / up

ALICIA: Warm up / guys listen

JESS: With / Anderson

ALICIA: Guys

JENNA: Are they fucking?
            They're totally / fucking

JESS: Wait isn't he married / too?

ALICIA: Guys!
             Now!
             Warm up!
             Shut up!
             Don't make me ask you again!

A small pause. Whoa.

JENNA: Yikes sorry

ALICIA: No I'm sorry I'm just
             That was unnecessary I uh
             I'm not sleeping a lot so

JESS: Well sleep is important

ALICIA: It's scholarship   JENNA: Hey someone's missing.
        season   Hey where's Bobbie?

        And between this   MIRANDA: Late I guess?
        and class I have
        like   JENNA: That's weird she's never
                                       / late
        No time so uh.
                                MIRANDA: Well we're starting
        Let's just get ready   when Coach is back

JESS: What's on for   She'd better hurry
        today?

ALICIA: Coach just
             said drilling
             fundamentals so

BOBBIE: Hey hey hey sorry sorry I'm late but I uh
             I can't find my ball has anyone seen my ball?

ALICIA: Bobbie are you / okay?

BOBBIE: Yeah yeah yeah I just I really need my ball it's it's
             I'm kinda freaking out so uh please / did anyone uh

JESS: Holy shit chill / breathe or something

BOBBIE: It was it was in the locker room by my locker
             And I can't find it and it's super / important and

JENNA: What's happening / right now

BOBBIE: Miranda?
             Miranda hey / hey that's

MIRANDA: What?

BOBBIE: Hey that's mine why did / you did you

MIRANDA: What I found this in the / locker room

BOBBIE: That's mine please give it back

MIRANDA: Can you calm down first?
You're freaking / me out

BOBBIE: Please

MIRANDA: Don't come near me
You're freaking / me out

ALICIA: Miranda stop

MIRANDA: What?

JENNA: Just give her the ball

MIRANDA: Well here let's play for it come on

> *MIRANDA starts dribbling and jumps into competitive mode.*

BOBBIE: Stop stop stop doing / that please

ALICIA: Miranda

MIRANDA: This is your warm / up

BOBBIE: Please / please just

MIRANDA: Come on Bobbie you can do it
Work / for it

BOBBIE: Miranda please!

MIRANDA: What you won't   JESS: Go on Bobbie what's the
even try?   hold up?

She won't even try!

Come on you can /
take me

BOBBIE: Stop!

ALICIA: Miranda I'm serious / cut it out

MIRANDA: Come and get it what's / the hold up?

BOBBIE: Give me back my fucking / ball you

MIRANDA: Whoooaaa easy   JENNA: I'm super
there   uncomfortable

BOBBIE: It's my brother's ball okay it's my brother's ball
Take your hands off it!

MIRANDA: Fine fine holy shit
Calm down
It's not a big deal.

MIRANDA hands the ball to BOBBIE, who immediately smashes the ball in MIRANDA's face. She screams.

JENNA: Holy / shit Bobbie

BOBBIE: What did you say   MIRANDA: Oh my fucking god fuck
to me what did you   fuck fuck my fucking
just   nose

Oh no no no what   Oh my god oh my god
did I what did I
                                   Fuck fuck
I'm so sorry I just I
                                   You stupid stupid I'm

ALICIA holds MIRANDA back.

ALICIA: Whoa hey Miranda   JENNA: Oh my god shit's about
                                       to go down
Hey hey hey / let's
all   Holy shit

BOBBIE: Shit / shit shit

JESS: You fucking psycho
Why / would you

BOBBIE: I'm so sorry I'm so sorry

MIRANDA: What did   JENNA: Oh god   ALICIA: Miranda
you do   there's blood   hey
what did   on the ball
                                            Let me look
Oh my god   Oh god it's   let me see let
                     on my hand   me
I'm   eww
bleeding
I'm   Eww ewww
bleeding   eewww

BOBBIE: Oh my god oh my god I'm sorry I lost my
Oh my god shit shit

BOBBIE runs out. ALICIA chases after.

ALICIA: Bobbie hey hey wait!

JESS: Is it broken can I get you / ice or

MIRANDA: Don't touch me no one touch me!

> *MIRANDA leaves. JENNA and JESS stand in silence.*

JENNA: So are we cancelling practice or

> *Fifteen or so minutes later. A stairwell.*

BOBBIE: Double dash flick flick bounce
            And a few to the side
            The back
            The pulse
            Boom
            The pulse and / uh

ALICIA: Wanna hear something gross?

BOBBIE: Whoa shit
            You uh
            How did you know I was here?

ALICIA: Because I come here sometimes
            It's like the only private spot in the whole school
            She's okay by the way
            Nothing's broken
            She's just dramatic

BOBBIE: I don't know what that was I
            I haven't been that fucking mad since the uh
            Since the day
            It's uh
            It's still really raw I guess
            Eight months later

ALICIA: That's okay
            I can't imagine how you
            Yeah
            I don't really know what to uh

BOBBIE: I thought getting back into everything
            That it would help
            And this is all just
            It reminds me that no one understands and
            Fuck I fucked it all up
            I let him down I let Ben down / and

ALICIA: Dude if someone did that to me
          Like I don't even know what I'd

BOBBIE: Miranda totally knew what she was doing
          And she has no idea what this is like

ALICIA: I'll be talking to her

BOBBIE: Don't bother.

ALICIA: It's unacceptable.

BOBBIE: Whatever
          I'm gonna get suspended now anyway right?
          What did Coach say?

ALICIA: I don't know actually I uh
          She wasn't back and I came to find you right away so
          So I don't know.
          Sorry did I interrupt

BOBBIE: Nah I mean I'm kinda glad you're here
          I was feeling
          Sorry I mean uh
          I'm a little high right now sorry I had to get
          Get high
          It just it calms me down and then I can just
          Anyway it's nice to see a face that doesn't think I'm shit

ALICIA: No one thinks you're shit

BOBBIE: Maybe I joined for the wrong reasons
          Maybe Ben would be like
          "Yo don't join the team are you an idiot kiddo?"
          "That's not you."
          I'm not me
          I never even got high before and now I just
          Do.
          I'm just fucked.
          And after what happened today?

ALICIA: I'm sure they all understand

BOBBIE: That's the thing is that no one does.
            Like not even me I don't understand
            Like Ben that happened because
            Well a lot of things but
            But because he was
            Like me
            And people hate different people
            And he dealt with that too
            You can be the best player in the world but if people
            Keep throwing shit at you
            And you get to a point where it's like
            That's it.
            Like our parents didn't understand us
            Like they love us and whatever
            But they're always like
            Why?
            Like two gay kids is impossible or something
            So it's all fucked
            So I uh
            Sit and write a lot now

ALICIA: What do you write?
            Whatever you were saying before sounded cool

BOBBIE: Oh uh nothing just like stupid uh
            Uh poems?
            Spoken
            Spoken word poems?

ALICIA: You do spoken word?
            That's really cool

BOBBIE: I don't really do it
            I just kinda do it for myself
            I took it up when everything happened
            I like it because there are no rules

ALICIA: I used to go to this great spoken word thing downtown
            I'm not creative like that so I'd just watch
            Maybe you should try it
            It could / be cool

BOBBIE: No nooooo way

ALICIA: Well is it really spoken word unless you speak it?

BOBBIE: I do speak it
Just to myself
In the mirror
And I've been trying to write something
For him
Nothing feels right yet
Wow I just told you a lot
Maybe I'm more high than I uh

ALICIA: I had them by the way

BOBBIE: What?

ALICIA: The mini donuts
My mom saw them and was like
What are those?
And I said it doesn't matter
You don't have to eat them
But I'm going to
And I'm going to love every second

BOBBIE: And?

ALICIA: Oh my god like deadly
And I mean kinda comforting?
I don't know if that

BOBBIE: No totally
Kale doesn't do it for me either

ALICIA: We'll split a box next time so I don't feel so guilty

BOBBIE: Use our fat bellies for rebounds!

ALICIA: Opponents will fear us!

BOBBIE: Yeah
Except uh
I don't know if I'm gonna uh.

ALICIA: What?

BOBBIE: Would you hate me if I left?
The team I mean.

ALICIA: No not at / all

BOBBIE: It's just I don't want everyone to like
           Wanna kill me
           But I've been thinking and uh
           I mean I'm not fully sure yet but
           Like I really don't wanna let this go
           Because it's for Ben obviously
           But yeah.

ALICIA: It's up to you
           I mean we could make it work
           It'd really really suck to lose you though.

BOBBIE: So the gross thing?

ALICIA: Huh?

BOBBIE: You asked me if I wanted to hear something gross
           And I totally do.

ALICIA: Oh uh
           They can't get the blood off Miranda's jersey
           They've been scrubbing and using bleach
           But there's still this big stain
           It's kinda hilarious

BOBBIE: I mean not gonna lie
           It felt pretty good

ALICIA: Well anyway
           Whatever happens I mean
           Whatever you decide
           I hope we can still hang out

BOBBIE: I'd like that.

> *ALICIA leaves. BOBBIE begins gathering her stuff.*
> *MIRANDA runs in, icing her face.*

MIRANDA: Hey Bobbie wait!

BOBBIE: Oh uh maybe not now / can we

MIRANDA: I heard you were gonna go talk to Coach
           And I / wanted to

BOBBIE: Look Miranda I'm really sorry
           I lost it and that wasn't cool
           But I really don't know if I should do this anymore / so

MIRANDA: I wanted to apologize actually.
I shouldn't have done that back there
That was messed up and I took it too far.
And I'm sorry.
For a lot actually.

BOBBIE: Really?

MIRANDA: Look things are tense right now
We all feel it
And we all do stupid shit sometimes.
And I was stupid
And I'm sorry.
Can we maybe start again with this?
I know things have been so rough for you so
Like I can't imagine

BOBBIE: They have.
I'm sorry I uh
Broke your face.

MIRANDA: Honestly I'd probably react the same way you did
I mean like don't do it again / obviously

BOBBIE: Yeah for sure.
But what did Coach say / about

MIRANDA: Nothing.
I'm not gonna tell her.
And I told the others not to either.

BOBBIE: For real?
Why?

MIRANDA: Because
Because we need you.
We're screwed if we lose you now.
We don't have to be like best friends
I know I haven't been in the best place lately
But it's just because I care like
About you guys about us
And like you were really good the other day
And we can't lose you.
I mean I know this is important to you too right?

BOBBIE: Yeah it uh
Yeah.

MIRANDA: We need to work together on this.
We need to if this is gonna go well.
I'll tell Coach I fell or whatever.
Let's put it past us and be a team
Start fresh
Work together
Crush this season.
Will you stay?

BOBBIE: Okay.
Yes I'll uh
I'll stay.

MIRANDA: Great.
That's great that's
I'm so happy we did this.

BOBBIE: Yeah me too

MIRANDA: Oh yeah by the way
I don't know if Alicia told you but
We usually have this party after we win
For the team to like
Blow off steam
It's my place tomorrow night if you wanna

BOBBIE: Yeah maybe
I'll see if I'm uh free
Check my sched.
Is Alicia gonna be there?

MIRANDA: Definitely
Well see you there maybe
And hey
Keep up the good work.

> *MIRANDA smiles. Shift. Dance music. MIRANDA's house. The team is partying, drinking beer. JESS is dressed weirdly similar to MIRANDA. JENNA is a mess.*

JENNA: This carpet is so soft I / love this carpet

ALICIA: Anyone want another while I'm in / the kitchen?

JESS:		JENNA:	
Moi s'il vous plait!		It's like a fluffy fluffy little kitten	
Tout le monde			
Bonjour		Little pussy cat	

MIRANDA: Jenna are / you

JENNA: Shh I'm petting the kitty carpet

              A knock.

JESS: *Entrez mon amie*

BOBBIE: Uh hey guys

JESS: Yo dude   ALICIA: Bobbie   MIRANDA: Come on in
             wassup   you   get comfy
                                    made it!

JENNA: You smell extra lesbiany today

ALICIA: Jenna

JENNA: Like Old Spice
             And leather

BOBBIE: I actually use Old Spice so

JESS: The night just started and you're already plastered

JENNA: I'm fine leave / me alone

JESS: You're literally in a ball on / the floor

JENNA: I said I'm / fine

BOBBIE: Whoa did you guys plan that?

MIRANDA: Nooooo we absolutely / did not.

JESS: Yeah like I just came in and it was like holy fucksicle we're
             twins

JENNA: Twinsssiii/eeessssss

JESS: Super weird right?
             Miranda isn't that weird?

MIRANDA: So weird.

JESS: Well get comfy
             Stop standing / like a creep

MIRANDA: Someone get her a drink

ALICIA: Hey Bobbie want a drink?
             We have beer and beer and also beer

BOBBIE: Uh sure
             One of each

ALICIA: I'm drinking to celebrate tonight

BOBBIE: The game?

ALICIA: No I uh

Okay I was gonna
wait so

Shh they don't
know yet but

I got into McGill!

BOBBIE: No way amazing
amazing that's /
incredible

ALICIA: Shhh they don't
know yet

But I've been
screaming all day

My voice hurts

JESS: I feel like we should
invite some others

And get fuckin' turnt
am I / right

MIRANDA: No way we are not
destroying this house

We are leaving it
spotless

JESS: Man that's such a such a
stupid

We could fit another 78
people in here easy

JENNA: Shh Jenna don't
complain.

Wait I'm Jenna oh my
god did you just hear
me?

What is wrong with me
what is

Oh my god why is
today so / so

BOBBIE: Whoa what's up with Jenna?

ALICIA: James already has a new girlfriend
And she is not taking it well

JENNA: Fucking Janet Griffin!
She doesn't even have a nice name!

MIRANDA: If your snot nose stains my dad's carpet he'll kill you
Then he'll / kill me

JESS: I hate this music

MIRANDA: Whatever / it's just music

BOBBIE: I'm fine / with it

MIRANDA: Did you already finish that whole beer?

JESS: Chug chug / chug chug!

MIRANDA: Have another one
Have as many as / you like

JESS: Paid for with Daddy's NBA dollazzzzz

BOBBIE: Your house is insane
Like I feel like I shouldn't even be here

MIRANDA: Have a look around
Go exploring

BOBBIE: Maybe in / a bit

ALICIA: You're drinking that beer like it's water

BOBBIE: Am I?
I overdo it when I'm / uh

MIRANDA: Here have another

BOBBIE: But I'm not even done this one

MIRANDA: Saves you a trip

BOBBIE: Oh uh
/ Thanks

JESS: So Bobbie uh
How are you feeling how's it going?

BOBBIE: Fine I guess?

JESS: I just wanna make sure you're doing okay

BOBBIE: Yeah fine
Do I not / look fine?

JENNA: Okay bitches I wanna play a game let's play a game

ALICIA: What game?

JENNA: I don't know like Simon fucking Says
Or I Spy
Or Never Have I Ever
/ Or

MIRANDA: Hey yeah
Let's do that
Never Have I Ever

BOBBIE: Never Have what?

JESS: You've never heard of Never Have I Ever?

BOBBIE: I mean I'm not much of a partyer so

JENNA: Kay so here
            We all pour a shot
            And we have our shot in front of us
            And one of us says
            Never have I ever
            And something you've never done
            Like

MIRANDA: Never have I ever not been a slop show at a party

JENNA: If you've done the thing the person says

MIRANDA: Like you've really never been a slop slow at a party

JENNA: Then you do a shot
            And nothing is off limits
            That's important

BOBBIE: Okay / cool

JENNA: Jess get something to drink

JESS: Where?

MIRANDA: My dad's liquor cabinet

JESS: Oooh how about the Lagavulin?

MIRANDA: No way that's / like $150

JESS: Please / please please come on

MIRANDA: My dad will shit no no
            Just grab like the Grey Goose / or whatever

JENNA: Oooh Grey Goose

MIRANDA: Sit in a circle
            Shot glass for you /
            For you
            For you

JESS: Grey Goose it is

ALICIA: Who's gonna start?
            Bobbie?

BOBBIE: Nah I'll watch first

JENNA: I'll go I'll go

JESS: Of course

JENNA: Okay uh
            Never have I ever
            Failed a class

ALICIA and JESS drink.

JESS: Oh suck my dick
            You have like a 3.8

ALICIA: I failed grade nine math
            Like I could have avoided it
            I just never did my homework

JESS: I can't believe what I'm hearing

JENNA: Alicia you go next

ALICIA: Okay uh
            Never have I ever
            Stolen my parents' money

Everyone drinks. BOBBIE sputters.

BOBBIE: Blech

ALICIA: Wow a bunch of kleptos here I see / how it is

JESS: Oh what you're telling me you haven't?

ALICIA: I'm a good girl Jessie

JESS: Who failed grade nine math

JENNA: Okay Leesh you pick who's next

ALICIA: Bobbie you go

BOBBIE: In a bit / I'm

ALICIA: Come on
            You've watched you get it now
            It's fun come on
            Bobbie!
            Bobbie!

ALL EXCEPT BOBBIE: Bobbie!
            Bobbie!
            Bobbie!
            Bo / bbie!

BOBBIE: Okay okay!
            That was intense / wow uh

MIRANDA: Here Bobbie	JENNA: Hey are there any
Have another shot here	snacks or Oh wait there's chips

BOBBIE: Yo are you trying to like kill me
            That's so you're / so uh

JENNA: Oh my god she's already tipsy

BOBBIE: Shut up / no

JENNA: You light / weight

BOBBIE: No I'm no I am not
           Okay okay listen okay
           Okay never have I ever uh
           Never have I ever played never have I ever

All except BOBBIE drink.

MIRANDA: Okay but that one   JENNA: Come on we want
         sucked   something good make it
                                              good

BOBBIE: Okay next time I guess

JENNA: Okay now you have to pick

BOBBIE: Jess hasn't gone

JESS: Oh my god I've got a good one
           You are not ready for how good this is
           Ready?

JENNA: Fucking ready set go

JESS: Never
           Have
           I
           Ever
           Had sex at school

JENNA and MIRANDA drink.

           Of fucking course Jenna

JENNA: Don't judge me

JESS: Well where you have to say where

JENNA: Staff washroom

JESS: Bull / shit

JENNA: Mr. Anderson almost caught us swear / to god

ALICIA: Hey Miranda you drank too

MIRANDA: Yeah?

ALICIA: You've had sex at school?

MIRANDA: That would be why I drank

JENNA: You're a virgin
           There's / no way

MIRANDA: No I'm not
　　　　　And yes there is because I've done it

BOBBIE:　Where

MIRANDA: Places whatever a bunch / of places

JESS:　　Guys leave her / alone

JENNA:　With who?

MIRANDA: None of your / business?

JENNA:　Liar

MIRANDA: No

JENNA:　Liar liar / lalala liyaaaaaa

MIRANDA: Whatever okay
　　　　　Shut up hey / shut up

ALICIA:　Hey Miranda it's　　JENNA:　Whoaaaa okay there
　　　　　fine she's just

BOBBIE:　We're just messing around

JESS:　　Yeah well stop it's not funny

MIRANDA: Jess you stop

BOBBIE:　Let's just let's just keep playing
　　　　　Alicia back to / you

JESS:　　Jenna control / yourself

JENNA:　I'm just pouring the / shots

JESS:　　You're spilling everywhere
　　　　　Jenna's off pouring duty
　　　　　Here / gimme

JENNA:　Hey

JESS:　　Alicia go

ALICIA:　Sure
　　　　　Uh
　　　　　Never have I ever
　　　　　Gotten a tattoo

　　　　　　　　BOBBIE drinks.

JESS:　　What for real?

BOBBIE:　Yeah yes sure absolutely

JESS:　　Where where is it show / it to us

BOBBIE:　Nah / I

JENNA: No no no show it you have to show it
How have we never / seen this?

ALICIA: I never knew you had / a tattoo

BOBBIE: Okay okay here
Hold on
It's riiiiiight here
On my ribcage

JESS: B?
Like B for Bobbie?

BOBBIE: Uh
B for
For Ben

JESS: Oh

MIRANDA: Did you get that before or after he...?

ALICIA: Miranda Jesus   JENNA: Whoaaaaaaaa that was
Christ

MIRANDA: What no I'm legitimately asking

JESS: It's a legit question

BOBBIE: Uh
After okay / whatever let's

JENNA: Uh oh

JESS: What?

JENNA: I'm gonna be
Oh no

MIRANDA: Oh shit bathroom's down the hall run
Now now / now seriously

JENNA: Guys I'm dizzy
Your bathroom is so far away
Aaaaahhhh okay oh shit

Everyone freaks out. JENNA runs.

MIRANDA: Go!

ALICIA: Someone should go with her

JESS: Not me I'll puke if I   MIRANDA: She's fine she does this
see her puke   every time

ALICIA: Fine I'll go

ALICIA chases after JENNA.

BOBBIE: I'll uh I'll come / too

MIRANDA: No no stay
She doesn't need two people stay

Retching sounds.

ALICIA: She made it!

MIRANDA: Thank god.
Hey Bobbie I have to ask
How did your chat go?

BOBBIE: My what?

MIRANDA: With the scout?
I'm dying to know
I mean that's a big deal.

BOBBIE: Okay I guess?

MIRANDA: Details details

BOBBIE: I mean uh
He just said I played strong I guess?
That I could do well?

MIRANDA: Wow that is so so great that's amazing

BOBBIE: But I don't think I'd / ever uh

MIRANDA: So good things on the way for you maybe?
Well here
Do a shot with me

BOBBIE: I'm good
I'm already feeling like uh
And we'll keep playing in / a sec

MIRANDA: Whatever do a shot with me
One for you
One for me

JESS: What about me?

MIRANDA: This is me and Bobbie

BOBBIE: Okay uh
Here's to
Here's to what?

MIRANDA: To the future

BOBBIE: To the future

> *They drink.*

MIRANDA: Another one

BOBBIE: No thanks

MIRANDA: Come on don't be so / like

BOBBIE: I don't wanna become Jenna
Speaking of which

> *JENNA comes back with ALICIA.*

MIRANDA: Hey sweetie you okay?

JENNA: Better waaaaay / better

MIRANDA: Did you make a mess?
Did she make a mess?

ALICIA: Nope
Not at all

JENNA: A slam dunk

JESS: Take it easy / Jenn

ALICIA: Here you're drinking water

JENNA: But I wanna keep playing

ALICIA: Well you're playing with water

JENNA: Unfair that's no fun

JESS: Neither is alcohol poisoning

JENNA: Wow look at me here with my water shot mmmmm

JESS: You go now Miranda

MIRANDA: Here's a good one
Never have I ever kissed a girl

> *BOBBIE and ALICIA drink.*

JENNA: Alicia!

ALICIA: So?

JESS: You've kissed a girl?

ALICIA: So what?

JESS: This is blowing my   JENNA: Ooooh look at
mind   yooooouuuuuuu

ALICIA: It's not a big deal at all
            It was one time
            At a party like this
            Just for fun don't make / it a

MIRANDA: Hey why don't you two kiss right now?

ALICIA: Uhhh how about no?

> *BOBBIE has kinda zoned out and is late on the uptake.*

BOBBIE: Wait what?

MIRANDA: You were the only ones who drank

BOBBIE/ALICIA: No way

MIRANDA: I dare you to kiss

BOBBIE: Well ha we're not playing Truth or Dare / so

JENNA: Just a quick one a quick peck
            Do it
            Do it

ALL EXCEPT ALICIA AND BOBBIE: Do it
            Do it
            Do / it

BOBBIE: You guys chant a lot

MIRANDA: Come on Leesh
            You're so tightly wound as usual

ALICIA: I am not / tightly

MIRANDA: Whatever she's not gonna do it why are / we even

ALICIA: Okay fine fine
            Sure why not

BOBBIE: What really?

ALICIA: I mean if you want to
            If you're okay
            It's just for fun

JESS: It's just for fun!

JENNA: Oh my god you're blushing Bobbie's / blushing

BOBBIE: No I'm / not

JENNA: You're flustered   JESS: Your face is so red
                                                you're like a potato uh
            You totally have a
            lady boner   A tomato

BOBBIE: Shut up I / don't I

MIRANDA: Oh my god just do it already

BOBBIE: Alright alright fine just quick

> *JENNA and JESS scream. BOBBIE and ALICIA move into the circle.*

Is this uh
Okay / just uh

ALICIA: Yeah let's just uh

> *BOBBIE and ALICIA kiss.*

ALL EXCEPT BOBBIE AND ALICIA: Woooooooooo!

> *MIRANDA has pulled out her phone and is recording the two of them. ALICIA notices.*

ALICIA: Bobbie stop stop stop get off get off!

> *ALICIA pushes BOBBIE back.*

BOBBIE: Whoa sorry was / that

ALICIA: No no no Miranda was filming

BOBBIE: Hey what the / hell

MIRANDA: No I wasn't   JESS: She wasn't I was
                                                    watching

ALICIA: I saw / you!

BOBBIE: Show me your phone / then

ALICIA: Delete it / right now if

MIRANDA: Why would I film that?
            I'm just holding my phone

JESS: She's just holding her phone
            She wasn't filming / I saw

ALICIA: Really?

MIRANDA: You're overreacting

BOBBIE: Then why are you giggling?
            Like a
            Hey never mind let's keep playing then

JESS: Good / idea

BOBBIE: Never have I ever filmed someone without permission.

MIRANDA: Oh my god / I didn't

BOBBIE: Okay no no / bullshit

JENNA: Guys please
          Let's just
          Never / have I

BOBBIE: Show me your / phone if

ALICIA: Hey / guys

JENNA: Never have I ever
          Eaten cotton candy!

BOBBIE: Is this why you had me over?
          So you could / mess with me?

MIRANDA: You have no idea what you're / talking

JENNA: Guys stop!
          I hate this!
          This used to be fun
          My last year of high school is supposed to be fun!
          It's ruined.
          I have accomplished literally nothing
          And if we don't win?
          That's it
          I'll leave as the the
          Stupid like
          Who couldn't even get into Mohawk fucking College!
          My parents are gonna think I'm so so
          You all have something
          You all have futures
          And I
          I'm too I'm too drunk for this

> *JENNA retreats to a corner, devastated. BOBBIE grabs MIRANDA's phone.*

MIRANDA: Hey don't touch / my

BOBBIE: Let's see let's see

          You did film   MIRANDA: You don't just grab my
                                          phone
          Look she did film

          You are / trying to

ALICIA: Hey what the hell Miranda

MIRANDA: Guys it was just for fun we're / just having fun

BOBBIE: I'm deleting it right now
          Before you you you ruin my life I'm deleting it

> *BOBBIE deletes the video. JENNA pulls out her phone.*

JENNA: Miranda why'd you text me?
          I'm right here.

> *ALICIA looks at MIRANDA. Then she grabs JENNA's phone.*

ALICIA: You did a group text?

BOBBIE: Wait / what?

ALICIA: To like a ton of people.

MIRANDA: What are you talking about?
          No I just sent it to us just us.

ALICIA: No look

> *ALICIA shows MIRANDA the phone.*

MIRANDA: Whoa wait no no that wasn't
          That was an accident I swear

BOBBIE: Oh / wow sure

MIRANDA: Seriously it was just supposed to be a a joke
          For us
          I was just messing / around

BOBBIE: That doesn't make it better at all
          That was a private thing and you / you

JENNA: Yeah Miranda that's actually kinda / messed up

MIRANDA: I seriously didn't mean to I must have hit something weird
          / or

JENNA: Oh my god it looks so bad Miranda / why would you

BOBBIE: Do you know what people are gonna / say about

MIRANDA: Don't worry it's just like three seconds and it's
          Everyone's gonna forget like instantly
          These things are like stupid
          It's not that big a deal

JESS: Right it's / not a

MIRANDA: Stay away from me Jessica.

BOBBIE: To you maybe
To me it's a pretty freaking big deal.
I thought we were cool.
I thought we were gonna be cool.
Wow.
Whatever
It's done.
Do what you want.
I'm done.

BOBBIE hands back MIRANDA's phone, then runs out.

ALICIA: Bobbie wait!
Miranda what the hell?

MIRANDA: Okay look
I made a mistake
I'm sorry
I was just trying to
I don't know
Get her back for like
But it wasn't supposed to be like that really / I just

ALICIA: Get her back?
Get her
Okay you know what?
This is toxic.
This was never about us
This was about you

MIRANDA: No / no that's not

ALICIA: We have our own shit right now okay
This is a big time for us all okay
I can't keep doing this!
I can't keep fucking taking care of everyone else!
I have my own shit and / I need to

MIRANDA: Stop yelling / holy

ALICIA: No fuck you!
This is / this is

JENNA: Wh/oa

ALICIA: Ugh no no no you know what?
            Okay.
            It's okay.
            I mean we're done anyway.

> *ALICIA grabs some chips and ravenously, cathartically shoves them in her mouth.*

            I got into McGill today!
            So I'm leaving
            I'll be far away from you
            And you'll be stuck
            This team is screwed.
            Because of you.
            You ruined it for all of us.

MIRANDA: It doesn't matter no one's even gonna care / it's

ALICIA: I care.
            Bobbie cares.
            That matters.

MIRANDA: It's okay I can uh
            I'm gonna text everyone again and
            And tell them that it's just stupid and to ignore / it and

ALICIA: You think this isn't going to spread?
            You think we're gonna be able to play after this?
            You think we're still a a a team?
            Teams don't do stuff like this.

MIRANDA: Well don't you need this for like scholarships or / or

ALICIA: I guess I'll have to find another way won't I?
            We're done.
            So good job.
            Goodbye.
            Good luck.

> *ALICIA comes down a bit, wipes her face and brushes the crumbs off her clothes.*

            Come on Jenna let's get you home.

JENNA: Okay.

> *ALICIA and JENNA leave.*

JESS: What is she talking about?
            Miranda?
            What's gonna / happen?

MIRANDA: Just go

JESS: Is that it?
         What's happening?

MIRANDA: You can go

JESS: But I wanna stay / and

MIRANDA: Why do you think we're friends?
         We're not friends.
         We're nothing.
         Leave me alone.

A moment.

JESS: Okay.
         Fine.

JESS turns to leave and then...

I don't wanna be friends with someone shitty anyway so.
Have a nice life.

JESS leaves. MIRANDA drinks. Shift. Monday. The gym. It's empty, except for MIRANDA, who's practising alone. Then BOBBIE comes in.

BOBBIE: I had a feeling you'd be here.

MIRANDA: Why are you here?
         You quit.
         I mean not that we're not fucked anyway.

BOBBIE: I'm just getting my stuff out of my locker
         When I was walking here just now I uh
         Everyone's looking at me weird
         Like even weirder than before.
         Or laughing
         And I think someone called me a pervy dyke?
         I mean I figured that was gonna
         I'm guessing basically everyone's seen it now.

MIRANDA: I guess you came to give me shit right?

BOBBIE thinks about this for a moment.

BOBBIE: Hey you knew Ben didn't you?

MIRANDA: Uh.
         We talked kinda.
         Not much.

BOBBIE: There was this uh
           This one day when he came home
           After this big game with Ashdale
           He crushed it as usual of course
           And the fam zoomed home first ready to celebrate
           Mom bought champagne and shit and we're waiting
           And he comes home
           And storms into his room
           Shuts the door
           I knock
           And like he wouldn't let my parents in
           But he let me in
           And he was a mess
           Like blood
           Like seriously seriously hurt
           I never saw him cry much before but
           And I was like
           What is this what happened?
           And he didn't want to talk
           He said he just wanted to sit with me
           So we sat
           And we didn't talk
           And I had to find out later from someone else
           That after the win
           He left in the dark he left to come home
           And he got jumped
           The other team
           Calling him fag screaming it
           Saying
           You think you're better than us fag?
           And Ben didn't fight back ever like he just didn't
           So he just tried to like
           Block
           He got kicked in the face
           They spit
           On him
           It was three of them over top so
           And like they fucking stopped thank god
           But even when he won
           He didn't win.
           He never could.

MIRANDA: Why are you telling me this?

BOBBIE: Because it's hard to win sometimes.
            And you're not alone in that.
            I just uh
            Thought you should
            Because I saw you and your dad
            I saw the way he talked to you after the Sherwood game

MIRANDA: Uh that's / not

BOBBIE: Does he make you feel like you aren't good enough?
            Like you'll never be good enough?
            I want you to know that's not true
            You're good enough
            You're actually a really good player
            And if your dad can't see that
            That's his / issue

MIRANDA: Well until you've been told you're a waste of a jersey
            Until you win but you should've won better
            You cannot talk.
            You don't know
            Anything
            About me.

BOBBIE: No I don't
            And that's why I wanna ask you
            Why do you hate me so much?

            MIRANDA doesn't respond.

            I know a lot about being hated
            Because people don't agree with who I am
            I'm no stranger to that.
            But why?

            Again, no response from MIRANDA.

            Okay
            Then I only have one more thing to say
            And I really hope you hear this
            You're standing in the Ben Brantwood Memorial Gym
            That shouldn't be the name
            But it is
            And you know why?
            My brother is gone
            Because of people
            Like you.

> *BOBBIE bounces a basketball to MIRANDA, who catches it. Shift. A stage at a poetry slam. Just BOBBIE and ALICIA.*

ALICIA: You're gonna be great
Remember to breathe
Find my eyes if you have to

> *ALICIA leaves. BOBBIE walks up to a microphone in a pool of light. She freezes, and doesn't speak for a very, very long time.*

BOBBIE: Um.
So.
Okay.
Come on.
Yeah I
I can't.
Sorry I.

> *BOBBIE almost walks away, but…*

Okay so uh
This is my first time doing this
I mean for people
So uh
Go easy on me I guess?
It's just a friend said maybe it's time people heard
What I have to say
This is for someone
For my uh
And I've been trying to find the way to like
Do something for him
So uh
Okay.

> *A breath. BOBBIE pulls out a sheet of paper.*

A lesson in fear
We teach it
We made it
We can let it make us weak
Or stronger than we ever thought we were
Than we ever thought we could be
Than we were ever told was possible
Whether you're afraid of the dark
Or more afraid of living than dying
Afraid of your own skin
Afraid of the people who tell you no
Afraid you'll never get to say goodbye
Afraid you'll only get to say hello
Afraid of shooting up and crashing down
Afraid of the shots you'll never take
Afraid of the shots you'll never make
There's a lot to be afraid of
And I'm afraid to tell you
It's you against it
It against you
And you go.
And you go.
And you go.

> *BOBBIE crumples the sheet of paper into a ball, then shoots it into the air like a basketball. And before it lands...*

THE END

Notes on *The Team*
by Michael Kras

In a lot of ways, *The Team* was a weird play for me to write.

I'm not female-identifying, so I don't have a personal inroad to that experience. I don't play or watch basketball, or any sports for that matter. So why the heck did this play about teenage women and high school basketball beg to be brought from my brain to the page?

Theatrically, the framework of this play felt like a potentially powerful way to explore topics that matter personally to me: the extreme pressures of a hyper-competitive realm, the fearful transition from youth to adulthood, the mental health struggles of young Canadians, and what it means to be growing up at this cultural moment in time in our changing world. I wanted to write about these things because I wanted to give young audiences and young actors a play that authentically and complexly captures their realities.

Plus, artistically, I like a good challenge: finding my writerly way respectfully and empathetically into the lives of five complicated, vulnerable, fallible, and powerful young women was one of the most humbling learning experiences of my life, and the open-hearted actors involved at each stage of development taught me so much about these characters every step of the way.

I'll never forget sitting in on early rehearsals for the Essential Collective Theatre world premiere production of *The Team*, in a room with the most thoughtful artists a playwright could want. It was during the first days of table work as I listened to the acting company speak about the play through the lens of their lived experiences that I began to realize something: even though I wrote the play, I hadn't fully internalized the total weight and intensity of what these five characters go through.

As a cisgender male playwright writing much of this story from the outside, some of the deepest and most tragic implications of what happens to the young women in this play sort of eluded me. The actors blew my mind as they excavated depths I didn't even know were there, and gave me goosebumps every time I watched them in performance. In that way, this play doesn't really belong to me; it belongs to every actor who knows these stories in their bones, and it comes alive in the ways those actors bring pieces of themselves into it.

The Team is about so many things, and everyone who performs, reads, studies, or sees this play will probably find totally different entry points to it. It's a play about the ways we manage our grief and our trauma. About the toxicity of being pushed to become the best. About the crushing expectations on young people as they try desperately to figure themselves out. About being a team. About growing up. About wanting to want something, and needing to belong.

Oh, and it's a little bit about basketball, too.

Out in the Open

Dave Deveau

Dave Deveau

Dave Deveau is an award-winning writer whose work has been produced across North America and in Europe. He is the Playwright in Residence for Vancouver's Zee Zee Theatre who have premiered six of his plays including *My Funny Valentine* and *Elbow Room Café: The Musical* (with Anton Lipovetsky). His first three plays for young audiences were commissioned and premiered by Green Thumb Theatre and continue touring: *Out in the Open, tagged,* and *Celestial Being* (Jessie nomination), followed by the Dora Award nominated *Ladies and Gentlemen, Boys and Girls* for Roseneath Theatre. He is devoted to developing intelligent, theatrical plays for young people that foster conversation and is currently working on a new musical for teens for Nashville Children's Theatre. He is represented by Marquis Literary. He lives in Vancouver with his husband and their son Dexter.

Photo by Brandon Gaukel.

Acknowledgments

Out in the Open was commissioned by Green Thumb Theatre under the leadership of Artistic Director Patrick McDonald and General Manager Ivan Habel, who were the play's biggest champions throughout the process.

It continued on to have additional years of life with To Be Determined Theatre.

Production History

Premiere Production (Touring 2011–2012):

Produced by Green Thumb Theatre

Directed by Patrick McDonald

Raes Calvert as Adam

Gaelan Beatty as Stephen

Stage Management by Robyn Lamb

Set & Props Design by Marshall McMahen

Costume Design by Connie Hosie

Sound Design by Kevin Coles

Scenic Painting by Omanie Elias

Carpentry by Al Frisk

Production Management by Rachael King

Tour Management by Michele Frazer

Green Thumb General Manager Nadine Carew

Green Thumb Artistic Director Patrick McDonald

Subsequent Green Thumb tour in 2012–2013 with the following cast:

Joel Ballard as ADAM

Alex Rose as STEPHEN

Out in the Open received four Jessie Richardson Award Nominations including Outstanding Production, Direction, Set & Props Design and Performance (Raes Calvert).

Cast

ADAM, 16, rough and tough and rugged,
outdoorsy, questionable hygiene,
STEPHEN's best friend

STEPHEN, 16, clean-cut and preppy,
a metrosexual, ADAM's best friend

Scene 1 – School

ADAM and STEPHEN stand at their school lockers.

ADAM: So we'll pick you up at seven, Stevie.

STEPHEN: Huh?

ADAM: In the morning. And dress warm.

STEPHEN: What are you talking about?

ADAM: Camping. Long weekend.

STEPHEN: Camping?

ADAM: You're kidding me, right?

STEPHEN: Camping?

ADAM: Yes, camping. Is there an echo?

STEPHEN: Adam, what part of me looks like I want to go camping?

ADAM: Oh, shut up, you said you'd go.

STEPHEN: When?

ADAM: Like two weeks ago.

STEPHEN: No, I didn't.

ADAM: So I'm lying?

STEPHEN: I barely like going outside to catch the bus. Why would I tell you I'm going camping?

ADAM: Because I invited you. It beats spending all weekend with your mom raking leaves in exchange for hot chocolate.

STEPHEN: I like hot chocolate. I hate the outdoors.

ADAM: Come on, raking versus weekend with your best friend.

STEPHEN: You're missing the point, I'm not crapping in a bush all weekend.

ADAM:	Why would you crap all weekend? What do you eat, man? Just be ready at seven.
STEPHEN:	I didn't agree to that.
ADAM:	Bring a good sweater, it's gonna be cold.
STEPHEN:	What are you, my mom?
ADAM:	Fine, be cold. Freeze your butt off, just be ready.
STEPHEN:	Adam, picture me in the woods. Are you picturing it? Do I look happy?
ADAM:	You're hopeless.
STEPHEN:	Camping? Me.
ADAM:	Yes. Long weekend.
STEPHEN:	What's so fun about sleeping outside? In the rain?
ADAM:	What, have you got a better offer?
STEPHEN:	Don't get all pouty about it. I'll have to ask my parents.
ADAM:	Too late, already did.
STEPHEN:	You called my mom?
ADAM:	She finds me very charming.
STEPHEN:	How?
ADAM:	Just say you'll be ready, Stevie.
STEPHEN:	What if we want to stay inside where there aren't any mosquitoes? And there's electricity.
ADAM:	You don't quite get the concept of camping, do you? It's fun.
STEPHEN:	So is indoor plumbing!
ADAM:	What, you've never peed in the woods?
STEPHEN:	What kind of a question is that?
ADAM:	Really?! Never?
STEPHEN:	Adam, there's this amazing thing, you may have heard of it, it's called a toilet.
ADAM:	Funny. I've gotta get home to help pack the car.
STEPHEN:	You're so excited it's pretty much gross.
ADAM:	Seven o'clock.

STEPHEN:	That's a disgusting time.
ADAM:	You're a disgusting time.
STEPHEN:	Your mom's a disgusting time.
ADAM:	And your mom thinks I'm charming.
STEPHEN:	Gross.
ADAM:	See you at seven, dickwad.
STEPHEN:	I can't believe I'm agreeing to this.
ADAM:	What's the worst that can happen?
STEPHEN:	With any luck you'll get mauled by a bear.

Scene 2 – The Woods

ADAM enters the woods wearing a massive backpack. He calls behind him to STEPHEN.

ADAM: No, I'm totally serious. Where did those things come from? Did she just sprout them overnight? Like is there something in the water? I just think that if she's going to be sitting right there in the front row, she needs to wear a baggier sweater or something to let the rest of us focus. I was so distracted I couldn't even see she had a face. How can they expect me to do a decent oral presentation in front of the whole class when her milkshake's bringing all the boys to the yard? No wonder I'm on the verge of failing! Stevie?

He notices STEPHEN has really fallen behind.

STEPH (*Off.*):   You never cease to amaze me.

ADAM: No, come on. I think it's a sound argument. If I didn't have to face such huge obstacles my grades would be soaring.

STEPH (*Off.*):   I somehow doubt that.

ADAM: What is taking you?

STEPH (*Off.*):   There are about a thousand trees, Adam, I don't exactly want to get swatted in the face with a branch.

ADAM: We sure wouldn't want to scuff up that Ken doll face of yours, would we?

> *STEPHEN enters. He's dressed ridiculously for the woods: far-too-preppy, far-too-clean, think country club rather than camping trip. He carries the tiniest and most improbable of bags.*
>
> *ADAM turns to look at him.*

Wow. You know, I've said it once but it's worth repeating. You look ridiculous. I keep staring. What, did you think we were going on a boat cruise? Why would you wear that into the woods?

STEPHEN: You gotta look good to feel good, Adam.

ADAM: Oh phew. And here I just I thought you had to look gay to feel gay. Wow. It's just… mesmerizing. Every time I look at you it's like the tiniest bit of my dignity dies.

STEPHEN: What dignity?

ADAM: At least you won't accidentally get shot by a hunter.

STEPHEN: Hunter?!

ADAM: How about you just focus on moving a bit quicker.

STEPHEN: Where are we going? You said two kilometres, it must have been like twenty by now.

ADAM: We've only been walking for ten minutes.

STEPHEN: .   Ten minutes? More like ten hours. My back hurts.

ADAM: Why? Purse too heavy?

STEPHEN: At least I don't look like a bag lady. Now which way?

> *ADAM searches in all directions. He clearly has no idea.*

ADAM: Well…

STEPHEN: What, you're not gonna tell me this is it. I thought you said there was a campsite. Like with washrooms.

ADAM: I did say that.

STEPHEN: Adam, what are you telling me?

ADAM: There is a campsite. Somewhere.

STEPHEN: Did you seriously get us lost?

ADAM: I wouldn't say "lost."

STEPHEN:	I guess I should have asked before we left whether you were failing Geography as well as everything else.
ADAM:	I'm not failing. I got a D+ on the midterm.
STEPHEN:	The plus doesn't make it positive. It's still a horrible grade.
ADAM:	Again, not my fault, remember? Big chest? Distraction?
STEPHEN:	Oh yeah, you should lodge a complaint with the principal about that one.
ADAM:	Hers are just as distracting! I don't want to be in a room alone with her.
STEPHEN:	Mrs. Reilly? You are disgusting.
ADAM:	What happened to Stevie the womanizer?
STEPHEN:	I think you have me confused with you. The way you look at girls in homeroom, you're like a seagull at the dump. I worry for some of the bushes around here, if you look at them in the right light you might mistake them for some unsuspecting girl and…
ADAM:	It's a wonder she can move at all. You'd think she'd be too top-heavy.
STEPHEN:	Are you even listening to me?
ADAM:	The physics of it alone.
STEPHEN:	Adam! Focus!
ADAM:	Maybe I should have signed up for Biology after all. Maybe that would offer some kind of an explanation.
STEPHEN:	Earth to Adam. Which way do we need to go? My iPhone won't work.
ADAM:	No service out here.
STEPHEN:	Can't you, I don't know, read the moss or lick your finger and figure out where the wind's blowing? Something like that?
ADAM:	You're totally clueless.
STEPHEN:	So what, we're going to stay here?
ADAM:	Why not? Life's an adventure, Stevie.
STEPHEN:	Yeah, grab it by the balls. I just don't want to freeze mine off.

ADAM: Then we'll make a fire.

STEPHEN: Good, I brought matches.

ADAM: And you said you didn't like the outdoors.

STEPHEN: It's not nature I object to. I watched a few episodes of that *Planet Earth* show, it's nice, don't get me wrong. Save the planet, all that. Recycle. Absolutely, yeah. Don't use hairspray, bring your own cup to Starbucks. Great, gotcha. But that doesn't mean I need to be *in* it, you know?

ADAM: That's sad, man.

STEPHEN: Says the one who begged me to come.

ADAM: Hey, I thought we'd have a good time, just the boys. Get out of suburban hell for a bit.

STEPHEN: We could have gone into the city.

ADAM: Too expensive, and besides, what would we do?

STEPHEN: Really, you can't think of one thing?

ADAM: We'd need IDs.

STEPHEN: I thought your cousin was making them.

ADAM: He got busted. Too many kids at our school with Hawaiian licences. Besides, the city's for homos. The woods are where real men go to escape.

STEPHEN: I forgot how much of a real man you are. What, do you drive a Hummer now?

ADAM: So how was Tanya's party?

STEPHEN: I didn't go.

ADAM: Why not?

STEPHEN: I was busy.

ADAM: On a Friday night?

STEPHEN: I've got a life, Adam. Just because I'm not doing something with you it doesn't mean I'm not doing something.

ADAM: Or someone.

STEPHEN: You wish I told you all the details.

ADAM: So you skipped Tanya's party to get together with a girl and…

STEPHEN: Stop.

ADAM: I'm just asking if you…

STEPHEN: My lips are sealed.

ADAM: Ha! Who is it?

STEPHEN: I'm not talking about it.

ADAM: Oh, so you actually like this one.

STEPHEN: You think we're safe out here?

ADAM: Changing the subject and everything. But yes, we are, unless we stumble on a bear, but if you keep those sneakers pristine maybe you can reflect light into his eyes and distract him.

STEPHEN: Very, very funny. You don't think girls are into nice shoes?

ADAM: Yes. But usually on themselves.

STEPHEN: I bet Erica would disagree.

ADAM: Wait, Erica? Like Erica with the…

>   *He gestures breasts.*

You and Erica? Really?

STEPHEN: Shut up.

ADAM: There's no way.

STEPHEN: Fine, don't believe me. Doesn't mean it's not true.

ADAM: Erica.

STEPHEN: Yup.

ADAM: Erica who sits in the front row in Social.

STEPHEN: Yes.

ADAM: Erica who made me fail my presentation?

STEPHEN: Adam, yes, we both know which Erica I'm talking about.

ADAM: Okay.

STEPHEN: I'm just saying….

ADAM: You be careful.

STEPHEN: Careful?

ADAM: Next thing you know you'll be failing too. Those torpedoes are locked and loaded.

STEPHEN: You and your precious theories.

ADAM: This one is perfectly logical.

STEPHEN: Why do you care about whether I went to Tanya's party?

ADAM: I don't. But you got invited.

STEPHEN: So?

ADAM: So that must be nice.

STEPHEN: Who cares?

ADAM: I don't know. I wouldn't have gone, but...

STEPHEN: But you would have liked to be invited.

ADAM: Maybe. So what?

STEPHEN: Since when do you care? I'm sure it was a lame party.

ADAM: Yeah, probably.

STEPHEN: And you wouldn't have liked the people there.

ADAM: Obviously.

STEPHEN: And we would have just sat in the corner making fun of everyone.

ADAM: You're probably right... It's just when you're the one person who doesn't get invited to a party...

STEPHEN: A lame party.

ADAM: Let's just drop it.

STEPHEN: Fine. Yes. It's just delectable out here.

ADAM: Delectable? You've got to be kidding me.

STEPHEN: It's a word, Adam. Look it up.

ADAM: How many hair products do you own?

STEPHEN: Why?

ADAM: How many?

STEPHEN: Seven, why?

ADAM: Wow.

STEPHEN: Fine, look like a homeless dude. That seems to be working out really well for you.

ADAM: I've got lots of love in my life, don't you worry about me.

STEPHEN: Oh, I'm more worried for them.

ADAM: Shut up, I'm a catch.

STEPHEN: Well, yeah, they probably could catch something from you.

Gaelan Beatty as Stephen and Raes Calvert as Adam in *Out in the Open*.
Photo by Dennis de la Haye, courtesy of Green Thumb Theatre.

Gaelan Beatty as Stephen.
Photo by Dennis de la Haye, courtesy of Green Thumb Theatre.

ADAM tackles STEPHEN. They wrestle.

ADAM: Who's catching what now?

STEPHEN: Watch my pants!

ADAM: No, not the pants.

STEPHEN: Get off, I have to take a leak.

ADAM: Come on, Stevie, don't let a little rumble make you go all girly on me.

STEPHEN: If you want me to piss all over you, keep it up, otherwise I'd get off me.

ADAM hops off.

ADAM: Alright! Nasty! Mercy!

STEPHEN stands and looks around nervously.

Well? I thought you had to take a leak.

STEPHEN: You said there would be bathrooms.

ADAM: Oh god, Stevie, the world is our toilet.

STEPHEN: Eww.

ADAM: Come on, the great outdoors are man's best friend.

STEPHEN: Officially dogs are supposed to be man's best friend.

ADAM: Does that make you a dog?

STEPHEN: If I'm peeing on a tree, I'll certainly feel like one, won't I?

ADAM: I'll keep you company if you're scared to go off by yourself.

STEPHEN: Right, because nothing will relax me more than having you peering over my shoulder.

ADAM: Yeah right, Stevie. You know you want me.

STEPHEN: Eww.

ADAM fishes a Ziploc bag of toilet paper out of his bag and throws it to STEPHEN.

Thanks.

STEPHEN steps offstage, into the woods.

ADAM: You okay, Stevie-boy? You don't need me to shoo away spiders or test out my ninja moves on a bear?

STEPHEN: You said there wouldn't be any bears.

ADAM: I said there likely aren't any.

STEPHEN: I love the idea of you against a bear. What would you do, shove its face in your armpit and knock it out with your B.O.?

ADAM: No, but that's a tempting move for you later when you fall asleep.

STEPHEN: Gross.

STEPHEN steps back in the camp area.

You're right. There's something wonderfully earthy about peeing in the woods.

ADAM: Earthy?

STEPHEN: Yes, like connected to the planet. I'm having some kind of *Avatar* moment here.

ADAM: You just stepped in poison oak.

STEPHEN: I did?!

ADAM: No, but I like how easy it is to freak you out.

STEPHEN: It's not awful out here.

ADAM: There's one for the movie poster: Critics agree, camping "isn't awful." It's not really a rave review.

STEPHEN: What do you want, the night is young. It hasn't exactly been love at first sight.

ADAM: You just stepped on a bear turd.

STEPHEN: Really funny this time.

ADAM: So not kidding.

STEPHEN looks down. Sure enough, he has.

STEPHEN: Ewww. Are you for real?

ADAM: Maybe it's not bear, do I look like a park ranger?

STEPHEN: You look more like one of the animals.

ADAM: And you look like one of the prissiest people I've ever met. Okay, so, look, how about we just pitch the tent.

STEPHEN: I really don't want to pitch a tent with you, thanks for the offer, though.

ADAM: I'm saving my tent for Erica. Why her, anyway?

STEPHEN: Why Erica what?

ADAM: Why Erica and not Stephanie?

STEPHEN: Her name.

ADAM: Her name?

STEPHEN: Stevie and Stephanie. It's too much.

ADAM: You look at Stephanie and all you can think about is her name? You need to get your brain scanned.

STEPHEN: Not everyone just sees boobs.

ADAM: Everyone I know does.

STEPHEN: And yet you're one hundred percent single.

ADAM: Am I? You think you know everything there is to know about me?

STEPHEN: I'd say so. Yup.

ADAM: So what if I told you that… Forget it. What could you and Erica possibly have in common?

STEPHEN: She reads.

ADAM: Okay, but you don't read.

STEPHEN: I read all the time. Just because I don't do it with you doesn't mean it doesn't happen.

ADAM: When do you read? On the toilet?

STEPHEN: I read when I'm not around you. I wouldn't want to confuse you with all those multisyllabic words.

ADAM: So you read. What else?

STEPHEN: I've got style.

ADAM: You've got something.

STEPHEN: She told me she liked my cardigan.

ADAM: Oh, I bet she did. She probably wanted to try it on.

STEPHEN: Which would mean she'd want me to take it off.

ADAM: Yeah, Stevie, she's just begging for a strip show.

STEPHEN: I've got moves you couldn't even dream of.

        STEPHEN starts dancing. He's truly terrible.

ADAM: That's sad, man. Just straight up sad.

STEPHEN: You ever been to the gym?

ADAM:	Uhh, what? Yeah, we have gym together. Fourth period. You having a brain fart?
STEPHEN:	I mean like a gym, like bodybuilding stuff.
ADAM:	I don't need to bodybuild.
STEPHEN:	Right, I forgot how ripped you are. Buff.
ADAM:	Buff?
STEPHEN:	Yeah, buff.
ADAM:	Who says buff?
STEPHEN:	Buff, like fit.
ADAM:	Why didn't you just say fit?
STEPHEN:	Because I said buff. What's the big deal?
ADAM:	Buff?
STEPHEN:	Yeah, buff.
ADAM:	Just a weird word to use.
STEPHEN:	I use the words I use.
ADAM:	So you want to go to the gym so you can bodybuild and be all "buff." And look at all the buff guys in the locker rooms? Be all buff with them in the showers?
STEPHEN:	It would beat the heck out of looking at your hairy butt.
ADAM:	You've been checking out my butt?
STEPHEN:	You wish.
ADAM:	So what, you're going to join a gym?
STEPHEN:	I'm thinking about it.
ADAM:	For Erica?
STEPHEN:	Forget I said it.
ADAM:	Does Erica like buff guys?
STEPHEN:	She likes them more than dickwads.
ADAM:	Help me with the tent.
STEPHEN:	What, you need help pitching?
ADAM:	Shut up.

Having unsheathed it, the tent is self-activating and pitches itself. It catches STEPHEN by surprise.

STEPHEN:	Woah! That's it?
ADAM:	My mom bought this cop-out cheater's tent.
STEPHEN:	I like her style.
ADAM:	My dad didn't like her spending the extra money.
STEPHEN:	Your mom's awesome.
ADAM:	Oh god, trade away. Take her. She's all yours. I'll take hot chocolate over ballistic screaming any day.
STEPHEN:	How are your raking skills?
ADAM:	Good enough.
STEPHEN:	You got a deal.

> *They shake on it.*
>
> *STEPHEN pantses him.*

	Prissy, but scrappy.
ADAM:	Oh, now you're gonna get it.

> *He chases STEPHEN around the tent, this way and then that. STEPHEN's quicker on his feet than you'd think.*
>
> *ADAM catches him and tackles him to the ground.*

STEPHEN:	Get off me!
ADAM:	Not until you say "Erica wants Adam more than me."
STEPHEN:	I'm not saying that.
ADAM:	Then it's gonna be an uncomfortable night for you.
STEPHEN:	Get off!
ADAM:	I have no problem doing that, just after you say one little sentence.
STEPHEN:	Ow, my shoulder.
ADAM:	Just say it.
STEPHEN:	Erica… wants….

> *STEPHEN flips ADAM over – the roles have reversed. He sits on ADAM, victorious.*

	… Me like you can't even handle.
ADAM:	All right. Point for Stevie.

STEPHEN:	Oh sure, Adam, you don't need bodybuilding at all. You're definitely all pumped up if you're getting pinned down by prissy old me.
ADAM:	Can I get up now?
STEPHEN:	I don't know, this is actually pretty comfortable. What's in it for me?
ADAM:	What do you want?
STEPHEN:	Oh, I don't know. Your boots?
ADAM:	My boots?!
STEPHEN:	I'm not wrecking my shoes because you decided to get us lost.
ADAM:	We're not lost.
STEPHEN:	We're also not where we should be. It's the same thing. Boots.
ADAM:	And what am I going to wear?
STEPHEN:	I don't know, play caveman and go barefoot. If you're so in tune with the outdoors.
ADAM:	You want me to go barefoot so you don't scuff up your shoes?
STEPHEN:	I could stay like this all night.
ADAM:	Fine. Fine, take 'em.

STEPHEN takes off ADAM's boots.

STEPHEN:	A pleasure doing business with you.

He gets off ADAM.

STEPHEN puts the boots on.

Oh that's much better.

ADAM:	Your shiny sneakers aren't warm enough?
STEPHEN:	Let me tell you about those sneakers – they're limited edition, like really limited.
ADAM:	So probably best to keep them behind glass.
STEPHEN:	I spent $300 on them.
ADAM:	I don't know if I'm supposed to be impressed or tell you you're an idiot.

STEPHEN: They only made 400 pairs.

ADAM: Do you know how many jars of Cheez Whiz you could buy with $300?

STEPHEN: Right. Cancer in a jar is a way better way to spend it. Sometimes I really do wonder about you.

ADAM: What? It's good in eggs.

STEPHEN: Your mom lets you eat Cheez Whiz in eggs?

ADAM: She taught me the recipe. Add banana peppers and you've got a morning.

STEPHEN: That's vile.

ADAM: So are your pimpin' shoes. Why would you wear them this weekend? Brain malfunction?

A rustling sound comes from the bushes.

STEPHEN: What was that?

ADAM: Shh…

STEPHEN: What is it?

ADAM: Nothing.

STEPHEN: There was a sound.

ADAM: You think? We're in the woods.

Another rustling sound.

STEPHEN: There it is again.

ADAM: Relax, Stevie, we're not in some low-budget horror flick. There isn't a twelve-headed bear that's about to pop out from behind a pine tree and devour you whole.

STEPHEN: Why me? Why wouldn't it devour you?

ADAM: It smells fear.

STEPHEN: Shame it doesn't smell stupid.

ADAM: You still hearing it?

He listens attentively.

STEPHEN: No.

ADAM: Exactly.

STEPHEN: There was something.

ADAM: Yeah, the voices in your head "Stevie... we're coming to get you... we've been tracing your every move through the tracking device planted in your expensive sneakers..."

STEPHEN: I sincerely hope you find yourself funny because no one else does.

ADAM: Except your mom.

STEPHEN: Who's your mom since we traded, so joke's on you.

ADAM: You're paranoid. I get that. Not easy to be outside your comfort zone. Out in the woods, by yourself, where anything could happen... You just never know out here in the wild.

STEPHEN: At least if we run out of food I have someone I can roast.

ADAM: All muscle, baby. I'd probably taste tough.

STEPHEN: Right. Cuz "tough" is a flavour. You gonna start that fire?

ADAM: I don't know, you wanna have a singalong and paint my toenails and roast marshmallows?

STEPHEN: Did you bring any?

ADAM: Cuddle up for warmth?

STEPHEN: No. Not happening. If it were life and death, maybe. But not if you farted on me. Deal breaker. I'll settle for a campfire.

ADAM: I'll get twigs.

STEPHEN: I'll guard the fort.

ADAM: Sure...

> *ADAM exits. STEPHEN removes his sneakers from his bag along with his water bottle. He empties it all over the shoes, trying to clean them. ADAM returns to discover this scene.*

What are you doing?

STEPHEN: Saving $300.

ADAM: You bring any other water?

STEPHEN: No, you said the campsite had...

ADAM: Newsflash: we're not at the campsite.

STEPHEN: Well, I didn't know we were...

ADAM: I rest my case. Clueless.

STEPHEN: Not when it counts.

ADAM: It's fine. I've got some. Some. We'll just have to ration it.

STEPHEN: What is this, *Survivor*?

ADAM: I don't think they have tents and hand sanitizer on *Survivor*.

STEPHEN: Sure they do.

ADAM: You actually watch *Survivor*?

STEPHEN: You don't?

ADAM: Umm… no!

STEPHEN: You don't like *Survivor*? Everyone likes it. It gets like 10 million viewers.

ADAM: It's the same thing every year. Eating slugs and throwing balls in baskets to win a BBQ and phone call from their moms. What's there to like? It's dumb. *Survivor*? Honestly?

STEPHEN: Shut up, girls in bikinis.

ADAM: Yeah, and dudes in loincloths.

STEPHEN: They're not loincloths. They're called buffs.

ADAM: I'm sorry, what?

STEPHEN: Buffs. That's what they're called. Buffs.

ADAM: Buffs? No, they're not. Come on. Buffs? Really? Buffs?!

           ADAM bursts out laughing.

STEPHEN: I didn't mean… That's not what…

ADAM: BUFFS?! Next time on *Survivor*: Buff bods in buffs!

           He dances around singing the Survivor *theme tune.*

STEPHEN: Adam, *Survivor* is an anthropological cross-examination of human nature.

ADAM: You memorize too many textbooks.

STEPHEN: Least it gets me A's.

ADAM: Yup, cuz there's nothing more important than getting an A. Except maybe getting buff in your buff.

STEPHEN: At least it's getting me something.

ADAM: Shut up.

STEPHEN: A's and Erica. What have you got to show?

ADAM: I've got stuff.

STEPHEN: Yeah, you keep hinting at it.

ADAM: Leave it alone, Stevie. I've got stuff, okay?

STEPHEN: Sorry, A-Bomb. Or should I say D-Plus Bomb?

ADAM: I've got tons going on. Like I've got someone, too.

STEPHEN: Oh, really? Who is she?

ADAM: Nobody you know.

STEPHEN: Well, that makes it all easy, doesn't it?

ADAM: In the city.

STEPHEN: The city? You hate the city. When were you in town?

ADAM: Two weeks ago.

STEPHEN: Really?

ADAM: Just because I don't tell you something doesn't mean it doesn't happen.

STEPHEN: So what happened "in the city"?

ADAM: The bus is brutal. It's never on time and people smell like deep-fried vomit.

STEPHEN: Vivid. Skip to the part where you meet this city girl.

ADAM: We met online. It's… new.

STEPHEN: Come on, Adam. Cyber girlfriends don't count.

ADAM: It counts. And I didn't say… And it's not like that.

STEPHEN: Why isn't it like that? Because she's "the one"? Love at first type? Have you even seen a picture?

ADAM: Obviously.

STEPHEN: I hope for your sake it's actually her.

ADAM: I never said… Yes, the picture's real, okay?

STEPHEN: I wanna meet her.

ADAM: Good. Fine. You will.

STEPHEN: Fine.

ADAM: Good.

STEPHEN:	Great.
ADAM:	I'd call right now, but…
STEPHEN:	Yeah, yeah, no reception. Of course. Good thing, too. Fake phone conversations are so embarrassing. How's that fire going?
ADAM:	Slowly, I'm trying.
STEPHEN:	Am I still being a dick?
ADAM:	Pretty much.
STEPHEN:	Sorry.

Another sound from the bushes.

Shhh….

ADAM:	What?
STEPHEN:	Sh….

More rustling.

ADAM:	What, again?
STEPHEN:	It sounds closer.
ADAM:	Really, Stevie?

STEPHEN remains distracted by the noises.

STEPHEN:	Are you sure we're okay?
ADAM:	Just trust me.
STEPHEN:	Because it's getting closer and closer.
ADAM:	Stevie, I have some news… You're not gonna meet her. The city girl. My city…
STEPHEN:	Don't you hear it?
ADAM:	Stevie, listen to me. You're not going to meet her because…
STEPHEN:	Shh. Listen.
ADAM:	She doesn't exist. She's not…
STEPHEN:	It sounds big. And awful.
ADAM:	What I'm trying to say is…
STEPHEN:	She doesn't exist.
ADAM:	She's a dude, Stevie.
STEPHEN:	Sure, Adam.

ADAM:	You're not listening.
STEPHEN:	Yeah, yeah. Big scary noises in woods. Focus.
ADAM:	I'm not kidding.
STEPHEN:	Neither am I.
ADAM:	Did you hear me?
STEPHEN:	Yup.
ADAM:	And you really don't believe me?
STEPHEN:	I don't believe most of what comes out of your mouth, don't take it personally. Now shut up, there's something out there…
ADAM:	I can't believe you'd actually think I'd make this up.
STEPHEN:	Aren't you supposed to be all outdoorsy? You don't have any brilliant ideas for how to get out of this one?
ADAM:	Can you just listen to me for a second? I'm gay!

He sees a different ADAM for the first time.

STEPHEN:	You're…
ADAM:	Yes.
STEPHEN:	Shit.
ADAM:	Yes.
STEPHEN:	You mean…
ADAM:	Yes.
STEPHEN:	Oh. Wow. Oh. Well that's…
ADAM:	Uh…
STEPHEN:	You want a graham cracker?
ADAM:	No, um, I don't think I do actually.
STEPHEN:	Suit yourself.

He starts nervously eating graham crackers right out of the bag.

ADAM:	You probably shouldn't bring food out if there's something wandering in the woods.
STEPHEN:	Shit, uh…

STEPHEN scrambles to put it away.

An awkward silence ensues.

ADAM: So, now what?

          Pause.

          Okay. That's that then.

STEPHEN: What do you want, Adam? You want me to console you? Hold your hand and sing "Kumbaya"?

ADAM: What are you talking about? And what the hell is "Kumbaya"?!

          More rumbling in the woods, from behind ADAM.

STEPHEN: Please tell me this isn't happening.

ADAM: It's because of the food. The bear's back. Get in the tent, Stevie.

STEPHEN: I'm not getting into anything with you.

ADAM: I'm not kidding, get in the tent.

STEPHEN: And then what, hop in the sleeping bag with you?

ADAM: Just shut up and get in.

STEPHEN: You trying to get me in a vulnerable position?

ADAM: Shut up, Stevie, and move.

STEPHEN: Do you think it's really a bear or are you being a dick?

          ADAM physically pushes STEPHEN into the tent.

ADAM: Looks like the real deal.

STEPHEN: So there's a bear out there.

ADAM: Probably lots of them, there just happens to be one nearby.

STEPHEN: What do we do?

ADAM: We stay still and we stop talking. Move over, I'm coming in.

STEPHEN: I don't want you in here.

ADAM: It's not about what you want, Stevie, it's about what the bear wants, okay? And if the bear wants to claw my face off, I'd much rather at least be in the tent so there's some kind of obstacle between us. So move over now!

          STEPHEN won't let him in.

          Fine, you're not going to let me in, I'm finding a tree to climb.

He heads into the woods.

STEPHEN: Adam?

ADAM (*Off.*): Shut up, Stevie.

STEPHEN: Adam?

Rustling in the woods.

Does you being gay make the bear more or less likely to eat you first? ADAM!!!!

Growling and roaring. Struggling sounds, and then all of a sudden absolute silence.

Adam?!

Slowly a small corner of the tent unzips. STEPHEN peers out, nervously.

Adam? Adam? Are you… Is it gone?

ADAM enters and kicks the tent, STEPHEN screams.

ADAM: Relax, it's just me.

STEPHEN: You scared me. Really macho.

ADAM: You wouldn't let me in. I had to do something. So I punched the bear.

STEPHEN: You what?

ADAM: My fist really hurts.

STEPHEN: You punched the… What an asshole thing to do.

ADAM: Umm, you're welcome?

STEPHEN: I'm supposed to be grateful for that?

ADAM: Kind of, yeah. I saved your life.

STEPHEN: Sure you did.

ADAM: Oh, sorry, I forgot how useful screaming "HELP! ADAM! WE'RE GOING TO DIE!" is.

STEPHEN: Screw you.

ADAM: Screw me? If I wasn't here you probably would have been mauled to death by now.

STEPHEN: That's it. I'm done.

ADAM: Why, because I punched a bear?

STEPHEN: Because of what you said. Because you're…

ADAM: So, what, you didn't suspect?

STEPHEN: Suspect what? That the worst dressed, most girl-hungry person I know is a f –

ADAM: Is a what, Stevie?

STEPHEN: Okay. So you're gay. Wow. Great. Glad you've figured your stuff out. Really happy for you. Hope it all works out great. Is that what you want me to say? Is that how the conversation's supposed to go? Do I pat you on the back, hug you?

ADAM: How am I supposed to know? You think I do this every day? It just sort of came out. I said it. That's as far as I got.

STEPHEN: Great planning… You're gay.

ADAM: Yes.

STEPHEN: Like gay gay?

ADAM: What's with you?

STEPHEN: I don't…. No, this isn't happening, right? I'm not actually in the woods with you, my shoes aren't actually ruined. This is just some sick joke. What is this, a hidden camera show? Some twisted *Big Brother* episode?

             ADAM bursts out laughing.

             This is not funny.

ADAM: I'm sorry…

STEPHEN: Stop laughing.

ADAM: It just blows my mind that you can make this about you. How does that brain of yours work?

STEPHEN: What do you want from me?

ADAM: Nothing. I want you to be my friend. I want you to shrug and not care.

STEPHEN: Well, what if that's not going to happen, huh? What if I do care?

             Pause.

             I don't know what to think about what you say to me. "You know you want me, Stevie." Are you trying to make a big move?

ADAM: You're not my type.

STEPHEN:	You have a type?!
ADAM:	I don't know.
STEPHEN:	You don't think this is hard enough?
ADAM:	What do you mean?
STEPHEN:	How long have we been friends?
ADAM:	Since grade five, what?
STEPHEN:	Since grade five and now you're telling me this?
ADAM:	Yeah, Stevie, I am.
STEPHEN:	Well, perfect. Stuck in the woods with…
ADAM:	With your best friend.
STEPHEN:	I don't like camping. Or gym class. I have fancy, overpriced shoes. I care about what my hair looks like. You think I need any more reason for people to think I'm gay?
ADAM:	Are you?
STEPHEN:	No, Adam. Not at all, you're missing the point.
ADAM:	And you're making this huge deal out of something that's really not.
STEPHEN:	Really? If it isn't such a big deal then why announce it, huh? Why tell me at all? We don't tell each other everything. If it's not a big deal, why say it?

ADAM checks on the fire.

ADAM:	The fire won't start. The wood's too wet.
STEPHEN:	I don't care about the wood.
ADAM:	Not for now, but you will.
STEPHEN:	Why, I'm not staying here.
ADAM:	So, what, you're going to find your way out of here yourself?
STEPHEN:	If that's what I need to do.
ADAM:	Um, remember the bear?
STEPHEN:	The bear sounds a lot less risky than you.

That hurts.

Look, I'm gonna go.

Gaelan Beatty as Stephen and Raes Calvert as Adam.
Photo by Dennis de la Haye, courtesy of Green Thumb Theatre.

Raes Calvert as Adam.
Photo by Dennis de la Haye, courtesy of Green Thumb Theatre.

ADAM:	Fine, go.
STEPHEN:	Fine.
ADAM:	Fine.
STEPHEN:	I'm going.
ADAM:	Good.
STEPHEN:	Yes, it is good.
ADAM:	Don't get lost.
STEPHEN:	I'll be fine.

STEPHEN starts to leave.

ADAM:	Cuz I'd hate to have to save you again tonight. You wanna know what's gay? Having seven hair products. And hating the woods. And pansying out when the bear arrives.
STEPHEN:	Oh, so I'm the gay one now because I didn't want to come here?
ADAM:	No, you're just a jerk.
STEPHEN:	Just stop talking.
ADAM:	Why? I thought you were leaving anyway. What, you scared now?
STEPHEN:	Shut up, Adam.
ADAM:	I may be gay, but at least I'm not a chickenshit.
STEPHEN:	Yes, you are. Because it took you this long to tell me. What were you so scared of?
ADAM:	This exact conversation, Stevie. And that look in your eye.
STEPHEN:	What look?
ADAM:	The "everything is different now" look. I tried to tell you before.
STEPHEN:	When?
ADAM:	A thousand times, but it's not easy, okay? You're my best friend, I couldn't just spit it out. I need to… I needed to tell you. I'm sorry if you don't like it.
STEPHEN:	And do you feel better now?
ADAM:	I don't know. It feels different.
STEPHEN:	But the timing's pretty awful, isn't it?

ADAM:	What do you mean?
STEPHEN:	You couldn't have told me in the summer when there was nothing else to worry about. Oh no. You decided to wait until I'm days away from really making Erica happen. And we have three projects due this month alone. That's sensible timing, Adam. Easy transition into that one.
ADAM:	I'm so sorry that my life doesn't fit perfectly in your agenda.
STEPHEN:	Apology not accepted.
ADAM:	You sound like a child. Why do I hang out with you?
STEPHEN:	You don't, okay? Not anymore.

Beat.

ADAM:	What are you saying?
STEPHEN:	I'm saying that you... I'm saying that I'm getting out of here.
ADAM:	Are you? You seem to still be here.

STEPHEN goes to leave again.

You're the only one that knows. Who else can I talk to?

STEPHEN:	Find someone.
ADAM:	And that's it?
STEPHEN:	Looks like.
ADAM:	You have no idea what this is like!
STEPHEN:	And you've never had someone spring this on you. So there we go. We're both screwed.
ADAM:	But...
STEPHEN:	No. Stop. It's bad enough that you told me. I came on your little coming-out trip, now it's my turn to...
ADAM:	Stop. Forget it. Never mind.
STEPHEN:	Never mind? No. Sorry. Never mind stopped being an option when you decided we were going to spend the weekend in a tent together.
ADAM:	Is that what this is about? You think I'm going to hit on you?
STEPHEN:	I don't know what I think.
ADAM:	I didn't peg you for a homophobe.

STEPHEN:	I'm not a homophobe.
ADAM:	Then what?
STEPHEN:	There are gay kids at school, aren't there? Like Roger. He's obviously gay. He's really gay. A hell of a lot gayer than you, and I'm not exactly the person who gives him a hard time, am I? I was his lab partner for an entire semester and that was fine, okay? We dissected a fish together. So don't tell me I'm a homophobe.
ADAM:	But you don't want me near you now?
STEPHEN:	It's different when it's your best friend. That's all I'm saying.
ADAM:	Fix your hair, Stevie, I wouldn't want anyone to catch you without everything all perfect.
STEPHEN:	Two guys camp in the woods together all alone and then one of them's gay and people aren't going to talk?
ADAM:	But no one knows. And no one's going to.
STEPHEN:	So just stop.
ADAM:	Stop talking?
STEPHEN:	Stop being gay, Adam.
ADAM:	That's not how it works.

> *ADAM starts tending to the fire in earnest. They play a delicate game of avoiding one another. If one gets closer, the other one steps away, as they avoid eye contact at all costs.*

STEPHEN:	So, you've been with a guy?
ADAM:	Have you been with a girl?
STEPHEN:	That's not the same.
ADAM:	Why?

> *Beat.*

Do you really want to know?

STEPHEN:	You have?!

> *ADAM remains silent.*

We can't talk about this.

ADAM:	You asked.
STEPHEN:	You can't talk about this. Ever. Okay?

ADAM: You think it was easy to tell you? You think you're the one who this is hard for?

> *Beat. ADAM dives on STEPHEN and starts messing up his hair.*

STEPHEN: STOP!

ADAM: What are you gonna do about it?

STEPHEN: Get off.

ADAM: There. Much better. Less prissy.

STEPHEN: Don't touch me. Ever again.

ADAM: Don't touch you? Don't touch you. Why? Because my gay germs are going to creep into your pores and infect you?

STEPHEN: It's different now.

ADAM: Different why?

STEPHEN: Because everything I know about you is a lie. Everything. Your city girl, your…

ADAM: I didn't say it was a girl.

STEPHEN: So, what, your online girlfriend is actually…. Oh god.

ADAM: I only saw him once.

STEPHEN: Shut up.

ADAM: It's not what you think.

STEPHEN: I said shut up.

ADAM: Can I just tell you the truth or do you just want to make up horrible details in your mind?

STEPHEN: No, I don't wanna know.

ADAM: He was nice.

STEPHEN: Stop talking.

ADAM: I didn't know him. He sent me a message. I said I'd meet him and…

STEPHEN: Stop. Gross.

ADAM: Why? Because he didn't have tits?

STEPHEN: You're the tit man, not me.

ADAM: But I'm not.

STEPHEN:	You're... I don't get it. What's even real in all this? Adam who's always talking about boobs and who makes fun of me for dressing gay? Where's that guy? I liked that guy. He was fun.
ADAM:	I'm still here.
STEPHEN:	Where?
ADAM:	Have you ever told a lie, Stevie?
STEPHEN:	Everyone tells lies.
ADAM:	Not like this. Because one leads to another and another and soon there's too many to take back. You've dug yourself too deep one leading to another and so the only choice you have is to lie down in the hole and bury yourself. That's what it feels like. It's smothering.
STEPHEN:	Lovely and melodramatic.
ADAM:	Are you listening? I'm trying to explain why I told you, don't you care at all? I can't sleep, Stevie. Like at all. I need to tell you so I could...
STEPHEN:	Is that why you invited me out here? Honestly?
ADAM:	What if it is? What if I needed to tell you and I needed us to be away from school and everything else? Okay, Stevie?
STEPHEN:	Stephen.
ADAM:	What?
STEPHEN:	Call me Stephen.
ADAM:	But you're Stevie. You've always been Stevie.
STEPHEN:	Things change.
ADAM:	Fine, Stephen... you're making this harder than it needs to be, I think.
STEPHEN:	I am? What, you don't think locker rooms get really complicated now?
ADAM:	Why? Because you think I'm going to jump you all of a sudden?
STEPHEN:	No. Maybe. I don't know.
ADAM:	Just because you would be a molester if you got to be in the girls' locker room? It's not the same.

STEPHEN: It's exactly the same. I wear nice clothes and do my hair and watch crappy reality TV. But you know everything there is to know about me. Always have.

They're silent a while.

ADAM: It's exhausting. Not talking about something takes all the energy I have. So it's really great for you, that you have amazing grades, great shoes and great grades. But if you need me, I'll be over in the corner half asleep because... I just want a good night's sleep. That's why I told you. Is that awful? Is that such a horrible selfish mistake?

STEPHEN gets up to leave.

STEPHEN: I'm going.

ADAM: Are you? Or you just want to keep saying that?

STEPHEN: I'm actually going.

ADAM: Are you coming back? What about the bear?

STEPHEN: I don't give a shit.

STEPHEN exits. Long beat. ADAM looks around trying to find a way to busy himself. He starts gathering wood, then drops it.

STEPHEN really is gone.

ADAM: STEVIE? STEPHEN? You wonder why my life blows chunks?

He notices STEPHEN has forgotten his sneakers.

You forgot your...

He puts them on.

Scene 3 – School

School hallway, at lockers.

ADAM sits in front of his locker for a time. STEPHEN arrives and starts clearing his locker out. They don't speak for some time.

ADAM: So pop by at seven?

STEPHEN: Huh?

ADAM: Tonight. It's Tuesday.

STEPHEN:	What are you talking about?
ADAM:	Cheap movie night.
STEPHEN:	Don't.

STEPHEN keeps packing.

ADAM:	I could bring…
STEPHEN:	Don't look at me.
ADAM:	Why not?
STEPHEN:	Just don't.
ADAM:	Uhh… okay. I called you all weekend.
STEPHEN:	I've been busy.
ADAM:	Clearly. So are you…
STEPHEN:	We can't do this. I'm sorry, Adam. But you can't talk to me here.
ADAM:	I can't talk to you?
STEPHEN:	Not like this, no.
ADAM:	Why?
STEPHEN:	I'm sorry, Adam, but I can't be your friend here. Not for now. I need to forget about it. For a while.
ADAM:	How is it that you get to call all the shots?
STEPHEN:	Because you… Because you're…
ADAM:	You really are a jerk.
STEPHEN:	I'm a jerk?
ADAM:	Listen to you. Why would I want to be friends with you if you won't even look me in the eye?
STEPHEN:	Things are different now.
ADAM:	Yeah. They sure are. Why did I bother with you at all?
STEPHEN:	I'm switching lockers.

ADAM looks at him.

You needed to do what you needed, and so do I.

ADAM:	Good. Go. See if I care.
STEPHEN:	Adam, I'm not saying we're never going to talk again.
ADAM:	Then maybe I am. Okay? I'm not a different person. So take it or leave it. You're in or you're out.

STEPHEN: It's weird now.

ADAM: Something sure is.

> *STEPHEN goes to punch his locker.*

That's probably about as hard as a bear's skull. It's going to hurt like hell if you do it. You just wait.

STEPHEN: What else am I gonna hit?

ADAM: What, you want to hit me? Have twin bruises?

STEPHEN: I want to feel better.

ADAM: You're still making it about you. Wow. Forget it. I'm clearly wasting my time.

> *ADAM goes to leave.*

STEPHEN: Wait.

ADAM: What?

STEPHEN: ...

> *STEPHEN can't find the words.*

ADAM: I'll see you around.

> *ADAM exits. Stephen tries to say something but it's too late. ADAM's gone.*

THE END

Discussion Questions for *Out in the Open*

1. Why do you think Adam chose to tell Stephen? Would you have made the same choice?

2. Why do you think Stephen reacted the way he did? What would you do in that situation?

3. What do you think homophobia is? Is Stephen homophobic? Can you identify any moments of homophobia in the play?

4. What do you think was the most important moment in the play? Why?

5. If the play had continued, what do you think would have happened next?

6. Do you think your school is safe for LGBTQ+ students? Why or why not?

7. Could you relate to either of the characters? Why or why not?

Writing Prompts for *Out in the Open*

• Write a scene between Adam and Stephen that provides an alternate ending to the play.

• Write about a time when you witnessed or experienced homophobic bullying. What did you do?

• Write about a relationship that is really important to you.

• Think about the end of the play. Write a journal entry from either Adam's or Stephen's point of view about what happened.

• Imagine a safe school. What does it look like?

These questions and activities were excerpted from the study guide for Out in the Open *created by Green Thumb Theatre.*

A Bear Awake in Winter

Ali Joy Richardson

Ali Joy Richardson

Ali Joy Richardson is a playwright, director, and producer. Originally from Dartmouth, Nova Scotia, she has been Artistic Producer of Toronto's Paprika Festival for young artists, was a director-in-residence with Canadian Stage's RBC Emerging Artists Program, and a playwright in Nightwood Theatre's Write From The Hip unit. She is a book writer and director with Education Arts Canada (creating touring musicals about mental health for preteens) and directed *In Real Life* (by Nick Green & Kevin Wong) for Sheridan College's Canadian Music Theatre Project. Ali has created multiple hit fringe shows including her solo show *Roxy* about an unorthodox motivational speaker / self-defence coach. She lives, bikes, and works in Toronto with her partner Neil. For more about her and her work, visit www.alijoyrichardson.com.

Photo by Neil Silcox.

This play is for my sister, Andrea.

It's also for the boys who are brave.
We need you in the fight.

Production History

A Bear Awake in Winter was first workshopped through Canadian Stage's RBC Emerging Artist Program: Director Development Residency in February/March 2018. It received a reading as a finalist in the Safe Words Festival on June 1st, 2018.

The play was first produced by Binocular Theatre in the Toronto Fringe's Next Stage Theatre Festival. It ran on the mainstage of Factory Theatre from January 10th to 20th, 2019 with the following creative team:

KEYS.. Hershel Blatt

FLUTE/THERESA .... Michaela Di Cesare

TROMBONE/MATT .... Andrew Di Rosa

BARI ....Bria McLaughlin

TRUMPET.. Danny Pagett

PERCUSSION .... Natasha Ramondino

MR. HILL ....Andy Trithardt

Director: Ali Joy Richardson

Assistant Director: Bryn Kennedy

Stage Manager: Lucy McPhee

Lighting Designer: Steph Raposo

Sound Designer and Fight Choreographer: Neil Silcox

Thank you to Hailey Gillis, Katie Ryerson, and Courtenay Stevens for their creativity and generous support in developing the play through its early workshopping and readings.

Setting

Fall, 2007. A public high school in Dartmouth, Nova Scotia.

A note on scene 4:

Please feel free to change the actor Hill references to any early-2000's actor who resembles the person playing Hill.

A note on bullying:

The bullies in this story know how to make something spiky enough to hurt you, while being subtle enough to make you question whether they ever meant to.

A word, a breath, a silence – anything can be a weapon.

Characters

The Kids

TRUMPET
18, athletic, charming goof, he genuinely likes
Kelly Clarkson (probably wouldn't admit it
though), hides a giant heart

PERCUSSION
17, she knows good music, has never been kissed,
can be both sharp and silly, posts a lot of fan art
on DeviantArt

KEYS
17, Arts Rep on student council, has never been
told he's talented, only child, driven

BARITONE SAXOPHONE (BARI)
17, sees things from the outside, only person at
school who has watched all of *Seinfeld*, she'll find
her people in college, deep down she'd trade
everything some days to be gorgeous

FLUTE
18, new at school, can dazzle or disappear,
a guarded heart, she's growing armour

TROMBONE
18, new at school, reads thick non-fiction,
a coiled spring, he's at war inside

The Adults

HILL
Late 30s, a teacher

MATT
30s, HILL's husband

THERESA
Early 40s, TROMBONE's mother

The actor who plays TROMBONE
doubles as MATT.

The actors who plays FLUTE
doubles as THERESA.

Pictured (L–R): Michaela Di Cesare, Andrew Di Rosa, Hershel Blatt, Andy Trithardt, Natasha Ramondino, Danny Pagett, Bria McLaughlin.
Photo by Neil Silcox.

Pictured (L–R): Natasha Ramondino, Danny Pagett, Bria McLaughlin.
Photo by Neil Silcox.

Prologue

Four students and their instruments.

TRUMPET: I joined band to meet girls.

PERCUSSION: I joined band to meet girls.

KEYS: I joined band because our school doesn't have a drama program.
Or a choir.
Or a dance team.

TROMBONE: I didn't join band.
They asked me to join because they didn't have any low brass and I already played for the Cadet Tri-Service Band, so I –

KEYS/BARI/
PERCUSSION: We know.

BARI: I asked to play trumpet but they said they already had one and I look "strong enough" so I should play baritone sax.
Now, I drag this to school using like a luggage cart and a bunch of bungee cords.
Guess who didn't get asked to the dance?

ALL EXCEPT
TROMBONE: Me.

A school bell rings.

1. Waiting

A high school band classroom.

Four students wait, holding their instruments.

TROMBONE: I'm taking this girl from Halifax who goes to a different –

KEYS/BARI/
PERCUSSION: We know.

KEYS: Where is he?

TRUMPET: Maybe he bailed.

PERCUSSION: Maybe he's fallen into one of the parking lot potholes.

BARI: They'll never find him.

> *TROMBONE empties his spit valve by noisily blowing it out onto some paper towel on the floor.*

> *PERCUSSION pretends to throw up.*

TRUMPET: Where's everybody else?

BARI: (*Sucking on her reed.*) Oh, this is one hundred percent it.

TRUMPET: Shit, eh.

> *TROMBONE plays a wha-whaaa slide.*

> *It sounds like disappointment.*

> *PERCUSSION tries to spin a drumstick.*

PERCUSSION: If he's not here in five, we can go, right? And not get docked for it?

KEYS: Where're you trynna be?

PERCUSSION: Anywhere he isn't fucking spraying.

> *TROMBONE empties more spit.*

BARI: Were we supposed to prepare anything?

TRUMPET: No. This school's so fucking relieved to have some actual artsy stuff going on, we can't go wrong. We're doing them a favour. I can't even play the trumpet.

> *Beat.*

PERCUSSION: Actually?

KEYS: C'mon.

BARI: (*Still sucking her reed.*) Are you being serious?

TRUMPET: It's three buttons. How hard can it be?

> *Everyone stares at him.*

               Oh my GOD I'm kidding. I play.

> *TRUMPET plays a few notes. It isn't good.*

               So.

KEYS: This was a terrible idea.

2. Late

The school parking lot.

HILL is in his car, on his phone, flipping through sheet music.

HILL: Just. Terrible.
They're not even gonna know what *Gilligan's Island* is.
I know!
But I feel like it's better to be overtly campy than trying to be cool.
No one wants the teacher who's like "Hey kids, I'm all up on the hippity hop."
I don't know. Probably.
Or maybe not. I don't *have* to tell them.
Because, Matthew, we're in Dartmouth now.
Maybe I should just find my footing first.
Yeah, well, you're *from* here.
No, I don't mean that makes it easier, I'm just…
Nine a.m. Yeah.
Unless – *fuck.*
(*He digs for his schedule in the sheet music.*)
Just-wait-I'm-digging-for-the-thing –
I definitely looked, and it definitely said –
It said –
Fuckfuckfuckfuckfuck –
(*He finds his schedule.*)
Eight-forty?!
That's not a real time!
I'm late. I'm going.
I love you.

3. New

The band classroom.

The students are warming up their instruments.

It sounds like an angry swarm.

KEYS: He's not coming.
This school sucks.

KEYS starts to leave and nearly collides with HILL, who rushes in, arms full, limping a little.

HILL: Hi!
                I'm so embarrassed, I fucked up the –
                (*Ooohs from the students.*)
                Ah! I totally messed up the –
                I thought we started at nine.
                And then I tripped in a pothole out in the –
                But you're all here.
                You're all ready.
                That's great.

                > *HILL looks at KEYS who's standing beside him, staring at him.*

                Hi.

KEYS: Hi.
                Sorry.
                (*He steps back to the keyboard.*)
                I play keys.

                > *KEYS leans on the keyboard and accidentally hits the demo button.*

                > *Romantic music suddenly plays from the keyboard.*

                I don't know what I did!

HILL: (*Reaches over to turn off the demo function.*) Here.

TRUMPET: Oh boy.

PERCUSSION: What's your name?

HILL: Joel.
                Hill.
                Mr. –
                Mr. Hill.

TRUMPET: Are you okay?

HILL: Yeah.

KEYS: I can take some of that.

HILL: Oh yeah, thanks.

                > *KEYS helps unload HILL's arms.*

TRUMPET: (*In a cough.*) Suckup.

KEYS: Take a shower.

TRUMPET: Sorry. Allergies.

> *TRUMPET pretends to sneeze and sprays his valve oil on BARI beside him.*
>
> *She shrieks.*

BARI: AUUUGH.

> *PERCUSSION plays a 'ba-dum-ching.'*
>
> *TRUMPET douchebag-finger-slap-snaps.*

TRUMPET: OH!

BARI: You're the actual worst.

HILL: Sorry guys – just getting sorted –

BARI: (*To HILL.*) Are you from here?

HILL: No, actually, but my –
I –
Just moved here. From Toronto.

TROMBONE: (*Under his breath.*) Torawnaw.

KEYS: (*To TROMBONE.*) What?

TRUMPET/
TROMBONE: Ooooh!

HILL: Yeah.
I'm new. What about you?
Do you all know each other already?

KEYS/PERCUSSION/
TROMBONE/BARI: Yeah.

TROMBONE: I just moved here from Tantallon.

KEYS/
PERCUSSION: We know.

TROMBONE: Did you teach in Toronto?

HILL: Yeah, I taught music. But like – for little kids.
I want to teach band though.

TROMBONE: Is that why you moved here? To teach band?

BARI: (*To HILL.*) What do you play?

KEYS: He probably has to play like everything.

> *TROMBONE makes kissing noises.*

And not in a cadet band.

HILL: I play piano and guitar but my band instrument was
                 trumpet.

TRUMPET: Yeh yeh!

HILL: Only three buttons.

TRUMPET: *Thank* you!

HILL: You're *wel*come!
                 So, shall we dive in?

TROMBONE: How old are you?

BARI: Rude.

HILL: 37. How old are you?

TROMBONE: I'm in my last year.
                 Where'd you study?

PERCUSSION: (*To KEYS, re: TROMBONE.*) Like he'll even know it.

HILL: York.

TROMBONE: Right.

                 HILL takes out a conductor's baton.

                 The kids are impressed, but secret about it.

                 HILL leads them well.

HILL: Let's start with concert B flat.
                 Everyone sitting up straight, edge of your chair.
                 Breath in – !

                 Downbeat.

                 Disaster.

                 HILL cuts them off.

                 …Great.
                 Let's…tune.
                 (*To KEYS.*) Can you give us a B flat, please.

                 KEYS plays an eighth interval, B flat.

                 Trumpet first, please.

                 TRUMPET holds a high, clear note.

                 Suddenly, another student enters.

                 It's FLUTE.

                 She's carrying a flute case.

She is beautiful.

TRUMPET: (*Stops playing.*) Hi.

FLUTE: Hi. Sorry.

HILL: It's okay, come on in.
We're just getting started.

FLUTE approaches an empty chair beside TROMBONE.

FLUTE: Can I…?

TROMBONE: No.
You're supposed to be at that end.

FLUTE: …Okay.

HILL: It's fine, just grab a seat.
Glad you're here.

FLUTE sits beside TROMBONE.

He pulls the music stand towards him.

(*To TRUMPET.*) Let's have that again.

TRUMPET plays his tuning note.

Great.
(*To BARI.*)
Now you.

BARI plays her tuning note.

Little sharp.
Pull out a bit.

TRUMPET snorts.

BARI adjusts her mouthpiece and tries again.

Close enough for jazz.

FLUTE: Is there another stand?

TROMBONE slides the stand back towards her.

TROMBONE: We can just share this one, you know.

FLUTE: Sorry. Thanks.

HILL: All right, together now.
Breathe –!

Their tuning notes waver. Not quite right.

TROMBONE plays his note loudly.

4. We'll See

After school. The school parking lot.

HILL is in his car, on his phone.

HILL: Hi.

Um…it was okay.

I forgot how…self-possessed teenagers are.

There's only five of them in the senior group.

No, six.

One girl came late.

The instrumentation's weird but maybe it doesn't matter?

Yeah, they're super, super green.

There's a guy on piano who I think is actually pretty good.

Our percussion girl could go either way.

Another girl on sax who I didn't hear much today…she might not have actually been playing all the time.

And then two guys on brass.

Our trumpet player's okay.

And the guy on trombone is way more experienced than the others.

Yeah, I think he's trying to impress me.

No, I *don't* think it's that.

He's very young-military-Maritimer-guy.

She plays flute.

I don't know if she's gonna stay, though.

I just get a vibe.

Well, that's very nice. I'm sure they'll be very inspired.

Can Neil Patrick Harris play me in the movie?

Excellent.

So.

We'll see, I guess.

5. Heeey

After school.

KEYS and PERCUSSION are at home in separate spaces.

KEYS calls PERCUSSION.

KEYS: Heeey.

PERCUSSION: Heeey.

KEYS: Are you coming over?

PERCUSSION: I can't. I'm babysitting.
My mom's at a church thing.

KEYS: I hate being at my dad's.

PERCUSSION: Is he home?

KEYS: No. He's working.
But just his place depresses me.
Everything's corduroy and smells like smoke.
And like, nothing in his fridge actually came from the ground.

PERCUSSION: I made Jeremy microwave s'mores for supper.
I'm a bad sister.

KEYS: *Yer sooo bad.*

PERCUSSION: *I knowww.*
(*Calls off.*)
Jeremy?
(*No answer.*)
Yeah, he's dead.

KEYS: Sooo.
What did you think?

PERCUSSION: Oh, she's a snob.

KEYS: Don't hold back.

PERCUSSION: She just like strolls in halfway through class, "*Sorry.*"
Like "Oops, I was busy being pretty somewhere – did you need me?"
Also, I'm sorry, but how long does she spend on her hair? I have other shit to do in the morning.

KEYS: Aw, you should really tell her if you like her that much.

PERCUSSION: She's hot but like I don't trust her.
She clearly knows she can get away with stuff.
Hill seems nice.

KEYS: Yeah. And gay.

PERCUSSION: He might just be like…Toronto.

KEYS: No, he's gay.
             Finally.
             A grown-up gay who isn't Father Don.

PERCUSSION: Why would anyone *move* to Dartmouth.

KEYS: To teach *baaand*.
             Or maybe his partner got a job.

PERCUSSION: How do you know he has a partner?

KEYS: He's wearing a ring.

PERCUSSION: On his right hand.

KEYS: Exactly. 'Cause he doesn't want dickheads like cadet boy
             knowing.

PERCUSSION: Fuckin' Tantallon.

KEYS: He kind of gives me the creeps.

PERCUSSION: Oh, he's harmless.
             He's just working hard to make up for the fact that he
             plays trombone in a cadet band.

KEYS: He seems pretty proud to me.

PERCUSSION: Too many pockets.
             Looks like a crossing guard.

KEYS: He was probably a rattail kid.
             You can see it in his eyes.

PERCUSSION: That stain never leaves you.
             God, I have to get out of here.

KEYS: One more year.

PERCUSSION: No, I'll probably die here alone, arm flab flapping in the
             wind, complaining how you can never get a ring tone
             that just sounds like a phone anymore.

KEYS: You are not your mother.
             Come with me.
             I plan to die with the jawline of a god in Vancouver.

PERCUSSION: I wish.

KEYS: Shit. I think my dad's home.
             He'll want the line free.

PERCUSSION: I should probably make sure Jeremy's still breathing.

KEYS: Love you.

PERCUSSION: Love you more.

BOTH: Byeee.

6. Break

> *Later that evening, behind a fast-food restaurant.*
>
> *BARI and FLUTE are on break at work together.*
>
> *FLUTE is drinking an energy drink from a can.*

FLUTE: I think if I could just be like *"byeee"* we'd have a better world.

BARI: What about "the customer's always right"?

FLUTE: That's the problem. We're rewarding bad behaviour.
It turns people into dicks.
The next time some old guy's like, "Lookit miss, this is right cold and tastes like shit, I paid for this ya know," I can be like, "Thanks, bye, we don't need you. No, really, your money's no good here. Exit's on your left."
Then maybe people would learn.
You can't treat people like garbage and expect them to remake your burger.

BARI: Wouldn't that be bad for business?

FLUTE: Probably, yeah.

BARI: Or it'd give us cachet.
"No soup for you!"
Can I try some?

> *FLUTE passes her the energy drink.*
>
> *BARI takes a sip.*

How do you drink that?!
It's like a poison freezie.

FLUTE: I don't even really taste them anymore.
It's the only way I'll stay awake and not fall to my death in the deep fryer.

BARI: (*As the old guy from before.*)
"Lookit miss, there's a girl's face in my fries!"

FLUTE: Ohmygodew.

BARI:	We should definitely go back in.
FLUTE:	Nooo.
BARI:	Were you out late?
FLUTE:	No, I just like don't really sleep. Like ever.
BARI:	I had to stop watching TV at bedtime. Have you seen *Planet Earth?* That shit's intense.
FLUTE:	You're so weird.
BARI:	I'm not kidding. Animals are crazy.
FLUTE:	What do you do now, a sudoku?
BARI:	Oh, wow, thanks.
FLUTE:	You are KIND of an old man.

FLUTE drains her energy drink can.

BARI:	How late are you on tonight?
FLUTE:	Probably close.
BARI:	Same. Is Chris coming to get you?
FLUTE:	Yeah. We can drive you home.
BARI:	I don't wanna crash a date.
FLUTE:	It's not a date. He just doesn't like me bussing.
BARI:	That's sweet.
FLUTE:	I guess.
BARI:	I hate taking the bus late. It just doesn't feel safe.
FLUTE:	Nothing's safe. Safety's a dream we made up to rip off women.
BARI:	Is that like, from something?
FLUTE:	No. It's just true.
BARI:	It's weird seeing you at school now.
FLUTE:	Thank you?
BARI:	It is! It's like my work and school lives are colliding. Do you like it here?
FLUTE:	I didn't move. I just, changed schools.
BARI:	Yeah, yeah, I mean, do you like it at our school?
FLUTE:	We'll see.

> *FLUTE puts her empty can on the ground.*

BARI: Why'd you have to switch?

> *Beat.*

FLUTE: Cause people are dicks.

> *FLUTE stomps on the empty can.*

7. Dad

> *That evening. TRUMPET is at home, on the phone with this dad.*

TRUMPET: Hey Dad, it's me, I uh was just callin' to say happy birthday.
Yeah. Yeah.
Uh, it's good. Yeah. I uh started band today.
Band.
Yeah, with like instruments and…music?
Hah, no, I'm not. Don't worry.
There's a new guy from Tantallon in the class, he's pretty good actually.
Yeah, military family, I think.
Oh yeah, you probably worked with –
Yeah, that's him.
Really?
Holy shit. Yeah, I remember that.
That was fucked up.
Sorry, that was super messed up.
That was his dad?

> *TROMBONE appears, apart.*

> *He's playing a slow, beautiful piece on TROMBONE.*

Whoa.
I guess that's why they moved, eh?
Yeah, I won't say anything…
That'd really suck to have to –
Oh, okay.
Yeah, no, yeah, no, no worries.
Kay Dad, well you have a good birthday and I'll talk to you –
(*His dad has hung up.*)

8. Smoke

The next morning before first bell. Outside the school.

FLUTE is smoking. TROMBONE arrives.

TROMBONE: Yikes.
Those can kill you, you know.

FLUTE: Got it, thanks.

TROMBONE: I used to smoke.

FLUTE: I'm sure you did.

TROMBONE: Too expensive.
I wanted to put my money towards something useful.

FLUTE: Look at you and your goals.

TROMBONE: How long have you smoked?

FLUTE: A while.

TROMBONE: Did you buy those yourself?
Fake ID?

FLUTE: My boyfriend bought them for me.

TROMBONE: Great.
What's your boyfriend's name?

FLUTE ignores him.

Ooookay.
Is that like a touchy subject for you?

FLUTE continues to ignore him.

Lemme guess.
He doesn't go here.
He's older.
You wish it was more serious.
Right?

FLUTE: Why are you talking to me?

TROMBONE: Is that…not a thing?
Can't have a conversation?

FLUTE: Maybe you're not very good at conversation.

TROMBONE: Wow.

FLUTE: I think you like putting people on the spot.

TROMBONE: Maybe *you're* not very good at conversation.

> *FLUTE goes back to ignoring him.*

All right, all right.

> *TROMBONE backs away.*

> *He stands farther from FLUTE.*

Is this good? Is this okay now?

> *FLUTE scoffs.*

Oh good, I got a laugh.
Was that a laugh?

> *FLUTE ignores him.*

…still deciding?

FLUTE: Do you need something?!

TROMBONE: Yes, actually.
I'm really lonely and I need a friend.

> *Beat.*

Fuck, I'm just shootin' the shit, sorry.

FLUTE: It just feels like you're digging for something.

> *TROMBONE laughs.*

TROMBONE: I can promise you, *no* one's paying that much attention to you.
Jesus.

> *FLUTE walks past TROMBONE into the school.*

9. Class

> *Before class, in the band room.*

> *TRUMPET and KEYS are alone.*

TRUMPET: Okay, you can't say anything, but remember that navy guy who hung himself on the ship?

KEYS: Yeah.

TRUMPET: Like on the deck, and a bunch of people saw him in the morning?

KEYS: Yes, I remember.

TRUMPET: Yeah. So.

> *PERCUSSION and BARI enter midway through his next line.*

The guy who hung himself –
You can't say anything to anybody –

> (*Gesturing to TROMBONE's chair.*)

That was *his* dad!

PERCUSSION: WHOA.

BARI: I knew that. You guys didn't know that?
I'm sure that's why he and his mom had to move.

PERCUSSION: That's so sad.

TRUMPET: Shit, guys, you can't tell anyone.

KEYS: Who's left to tell?

TRUMPET: Really, don't make it weird.

> *FLUTE walks in. They all freeze.*

FLUTE: What.

BARI: We thought – we were just –

TRUMPET: Okay, you can't repeat this, but I just found out his dad was the guy who hung himself on the ship.

FLUTE: That's so sad.

TRUMPET: But really guys, we shouldn't tell people.

KEYS: And again, he asks…who's left to tell?

> *TROMBONE walks in.*

TROMBONE: Tell what?

TRUMPET: (*To KEYS.*) Yeah, tell what?

TROMBONE: We're all friends here.

TRUMPET: Yeah.

KEYS: (*To TROMBONE.*) Nothing.

TROMBONE: Nah, what were you talking about.

KEYS: Nothing important.

TROMBONE: So why don't you just tell me?

> *Beat.*

PERCUSSION: We were just talking about Mr. Hill being gay.

HILL walks in.

HILL: Pardon?

> *The students immediately start playing their instruments.*
>
> *HILL watches them, then gets settled at his music stand.*

Good morning. Let's tune.
(*To FLUTE.*) Let's start with you.

> *KEYS plays a B flat, FLUTE plays her note softly.*

TROMBONE: (*To TRUMPET.*) You smell that?

TRUMPET: Wasn't me this time.

TROMBONE: Smells like cigarettes.

HILL: (*To FLUTE.*) Oh, I wanted to tell you, I think I saw you in a commercial!
For the SportsPlex? You're dancing?

FLUTE: Oh. Yeah.

PERCUSSION: (*To KEYS.*) Called it! It's totally her.

TROMBONE: So you're an actor?

FLUTE: No. They were just filming people who did stuff at the SportsPlex.

TROMBONE: So you're a dancer?

FLUTE: I used to dance, yeah.

TROMBONE: What kind of dance?

HILL: Didn't mean to put you in the hot seat.

FLUTE: I was on a dance team.

TROMBONE: And what kind of dance did the dance team do?

KEYS: (*To TROMBONE.*) You hoping to join?

FLUTE: A bunch of different kinds.

TROMBONE: Wow. A bunch of kinds.

TRUMPET: Did you do the dance with the swords?
Like –
(*He makes bagpipe sounds while imitating the footwork.*)

FLUTE: No, that's highland dance.

BARI: Can you do pointe, or whatever that's called? 'Cause that's crazy.

FLUTE: I did, yeah. I mostly did ballet.

TRUMPET: Can you tap-dance?

FLUTE: Yeah, actually, it was funny, when they were shooting the commercial, we tried to –

TROMBONE: (*To HILL.*) Are we still tuning?

        Beat.

FLUTE: Sorry.

HILL: It's my fault. I got us off topic.
Let's take a look at this.

        HILL passes around sheet music.

        KEYS plays the first two bars of the piece:

        Beethoven's 9th ("Ode to Joy").

TRUMPET: Drink Milk Love Life!

PERCUSSION: Beethoven's 5th.

KEYS: 9th.

PERCUSSION: Whatever.

        TROMBONE plays the first four notes of Beethoven's 5th.

TROMBONE: That's the 5th.

TRUMPET: NERDS!

HILL: Let's give this a shot from the beginning.
Sitting up straight.
Three, four – !

        They play.

Okay. That's…something!
I think I'll request that at the dance tonight.

        Some obliging laughs.

Or, is the dance not a thing?

ALL: It's a thing.

HILL: It's a thing you…hate?

PERCUSSION: It's gonna be good, guys. We got a good DJ!

TRUMPET: If you mean your cousin, he's not a "good DJ."
                 He just plays your weird music.

PERCUSSION: He's bringing lights.

TRUMPET: *Lights?!*

KEYS: (*To HILL.*) Are you gonna go?

HILL: Do teachers go?

PERCUSSION: Yeah, but they don't dance.

BARI: You're allowed to dance.

KEYS: And you can, like, bring someone so you're not stuck with us.

TROMBONE: (*To HILL.*) Are you gonna bring your wife?

                         Beat.

PERCUSSION: That's pretty personal.

TROMBONE: I'm just making conversation.

                 (*To HILL.*) Are you married?

HILL: I…don't have a wife.

KEYS: That's cool, you can totally just come alone.

TROMBONE: Or bring a girlfriend.

FLUTE: Stop it.

TRUMPET: Whoa!

TROMBONE: (*Re: FLUTE.*) Oh, I forgot. I'm not allowed to talk to people.

FLUTE: He's the teacher.

HILL: It's okay.

TROMBONE: (*To FLUTE.*) Are you going with anybody?

FLUTE: No.

TROMBONE: Wanna go with me?

TRUMPET: Bold.

HILL: Okay –

FLUTE: No thank you.

TRUMPET: (*To TROMBONE.*) Aren't you bringing someone?

TROMBONE: She can't go now.

                 (*To FLUTE.*) So you'd rather go alone?

BARI: That's allowed, you know.

TROMBONE: Was I talking to you?

HILL: All right, guys –

PERCUSSION: Guys, relax.

TROMBONE: (*To PERCUSSION re: BARI.*) She interrupted me.

BARI: Sorry. Jeez.

TROMBONE: (*To BARI.*) That's okay.

HILL: Let's try this again, gang.

> *They prepare to play. In the second before they do –*

FLUTE: (*To BARI.*) Thank you.

> *TROMBONE catches this and joins BARI in answering.*

BARI/TROMBONE: (*To FLUTE.*) You're welcome.

FLUTE: Oh my god.

HILL: Three, four – !

> *They play.*

10. Better

> *After school, outside the school.*
>
> *HILL is talking on his phone.*

HILL: They totally know.
I know it doesn't matter.
But no, it does, actually, it does matter.
I was like "I…I don't have a wife."
I felt like I was seventeen again and asking my friend to take a prom photo with me so I'd have something to show my grandparents.
I forgot how kids are.
Like tiny, mean adults.
Suddenly there's like a spark in the grass that you have to put out.
I feel like I woke up and I have to live adolescence again.
I wanna be like "No! I did this already!"
I hate this feeling.
Thank you.
No, I really think I should be there.
I promise I won't take fancy photos with anyone but you.
Oh god, what do I wear?

KEYS approaches HILL.

Sorry, one of my students is –
No, I haven't left yet. I'm sorry.
I'll see you soon.
Kay. Bye.

KEYS: Hey.

HILL: Hey! Everything good?
You're doing great, by the way.
I promise I'll bring in something soon that gives you a real part.

KEYS: It's cool.
I just wanted to apologize for starting that conversation about the dance.

HILL: It's okay.
I'm pretty sure I did.

KEYS: I mean, I said you could bring someone.
That's personal. I shouldn't have…I wasn't trying to like, challenge you.

HILL: It didn't seem like you were, I promise.

KEYS: I hate that. When people show off by talking to teachers like they're friends or something.

HILL: It's really okay.

KEYS: Anyway, I'm sorry it got weird.

HILL: I've lived through weirder.
And hey – I knew there'd be these moments.

KEYS: Yeah?

HILL: Yeah. My…my husband thinks I should just tell people.

KEYS: Does he work in a school?

HILL: No. He works construction. Restoration.

KEYS: And he tells people?

HILL: He kind of makes a point to.

KEYS: Wow.

HILL: But privacy's healthy, too.
Everybody should do it in their own way.

KEYS: I just wanna graduate and get out of here.

HILL:	Where do you want to go?
KEYS:	UBC, Vancouver campus, for Anthropology or Environmental Design.
HILL:	Wow.
KEYS:	My mom wants me to stay here for law school.
HILL:	They always do. It does get better after high school. Not perfect. Obviously.
KEYS:	But better than this.

> *Beat.*

I should let you go.

HILL:	See you at the dance tonight?
KEYS:	Yeah! Yeah.
HILL:	Thanks for checking in.
KEYS:	Sure.
HILL:	Okay.

> *HILL gives a wave.*
>
> *He instantly regrets the wave.*

11. Hate

> *Later that evening, behind a fast-food restaurant.*
>
> *BARI and FLUTE are on break at work together again.*
>
> *BARI's eating Crispers from a bag.*

BARI:	Are you okay?
FLUTE:	I hate him.
BARI:	He *was* being a dink.
FLUTE:	Exactly. So I hate him.
BARI:	My mom used to say that saying you hate someone means you want them to die.

> *Beat.*

(*Offering the Crispers bag.*) Crisper?

FLUTE:	No thanks. He was doing it to Mr. Hill too!
BARI:	He probably likes you.
FLUTE:	Don't say that.
BARI:	It's true. He's probably got a big ol' crush on –
FLUTE:	*Stop.*
BARI:	…Sorry.
FLUTE:	I hate that. He's a dick 'cause he likes you. The guys at my old school used to snap my bra straps and my mom was like "take it as a compliment." That they were paying attention to me.
BARI:	It's a little bit true…?
FLUTE:	Compliments don't make you cry.

Beat.

BARI:	Is that why you changed schools? The guys snapping your bra straps?
FLUTE:	No.
BARI:	Was it something about those guys?
FLUTE:	Yeah. Something about those guys.
BARI:	Did one of them do something? You don't have to talk about it.
FLUTE:	I'm just tired.
BARI:	…Right.
FLUTE:	(*Re: the Crispers.*) Can I have some?

BARI gives her the rest of the bag.

BARI:	Are you gonna go tonight?
FLUTE:	I guess. You?
BARI:	Yeah. We'll be done early enough. Do you still dance?
FLUTE:	No.
BARI:	I always wanted to do dance. My mom thought dance girls would bully me so she put me in riding. I got bullied by horses instead.

FLUTE: Fuckin' horses. Always gotta be like that.

           BARI does an offended-horse snort.

BARI: Why'd you quit dance?

FLUTE: I dunno. It just stopped feeling like me.
           Last year, my coach used me as an example for all the
           moms of how to do competition makeup.

BARI: Intense.

FLUTE: Oh, it's all intense. All the dance moms came to class and
           they put me at the front and my coach did my makeup so
           they could see how to do it. She did that thing where you
           run the eyeliner through a lighter so it gets all soft and
           goes on stronger or whatever. And there's this thing for
           competitions where you do black eyeliner but it goes out
           like that and then you put white in the middle.

BARI: Skunk eyes!

FLUTE: Yeah! And then it's all contour and a red lip and she's
           narrating the whole thing and I felt like I was gonna look
           like one of those black and white ballerina photos.

BARI: You can't see their scaggy feet in those photos.

FLUTE: Blugh. And the dance moms were all like, "Mhm, great"
           and taking notes, and then she was done and she let me
           go look in the mirror. And I looked like a Bratz Doll.

           TROMBONE comes around the corner.

BARI: Oh god.

TROMBONE: Hey.

BARI: The entrance is around that side.

TROMBONE: I know.

BARI: Can we help you?

TROMBONE: Just waiting for the bus.
           (*Re: their uniforms.*) You two work here?

BARI: No, we're just fans.

           Silence. FLUTE eats Crispers.

TROMBONE: Okay. See you tonight.

> *He walks past them.*
>
> *As he passes FLUTE, he sticks his hand in her bag of Crispers and takes one.*

Thanks.

> *He leaves.*

BARI: Ice. Cold.

> *BARI puts a hand out for a low-five from FLUTE.*

FLUTE: Why was he here?

BARI: Shortcut?

FLUTE: The bus fully does not come that close to here.

BARI: Oh, he's one hundred percent stalking you then.

FLUTE: I tried to explain to Chris why it makes me so mad.
It's like we don't have the words for it.

BARI: I think he's just super awkward.

FLUTE: But his awkward makes ME awkward and that sucks.
I spend a lot of fucking energy trying NOT to feel awkward.
And then he dumps on the room and we all have to sit in it.
It feels like…

BARI: I saw this thing about how we've forgotten the original word for "bear."
Like, the old, old word.
It was something in like, Scandinavian.
But people were super superstitious and thought that just saying the word would summon the bear…the *thing*.

FLUTE: Very Voldemort.

BARI: Exactly.
So, they just called it "bear" instead.
Bear was code for…it. The monster.
And now the real word is lost forever.

FLUTE: Like just talking about it would make it happen.

BARI: Yeah.

> *A shiver.*

12. Dress

> *That evening. PERCUSSION's bedroom.*
>
> *KEYS and PERCUSSION are getting ready for the dance.*
>
> *KEYS is rubbing at a stain on his pants.*

KEYS: It's gonna look like I jizzed or something.

PERCUSSION: Well, maybe you shouldn't have been drinking Yop in your dance pants.

> *PERCUSSION holds up a dress in the mirror.*

KEYS: Are you even allowed to wear that before the wedding?

PERCUSSION: Fuck it. My cousin's not gonna be at the dance. She'll never know.

KEYS: I still think you should wear a suit to the wedding.

PERCUSSION: Ohmygod my cousin would *never* let me. I'd ruin her bridesmaid photos.
Ohmygod the *fitting*.
Her friend was like, "Tyler hates that I'm spending the day in a store full of wedding dresses – he's terrified!"
And all of us did this like loud, obligatory laugh.
Like, "oh yeah, we're all just so fucking brainwashable and annoying…our poor menfolk! How DO they do it! GAHD."

KEYS: Meanwhile, Tyler actually spent the day jerkin' it to manga.

PERCUSSION: To stave off his terror of the wedding dresses.

KEYS: Hard day for Tyler.

PERCUSSION: It's so stupid. But I laughed. Cause you have to.

KEYS: I'm trying not to laugh these days unless things are actually funny.

PERCUSSION: (*Tossing aside the bridesmaid dress.*) Nope, I hate it.

KEYS: Good call.

PERCUSSION: I don't even think I want a wedding.

KEYS: I do.
          You can wear a suit to mine.
          I want an outdoor dance floor, and we're going to make each other's rings.
          No diamonds. They're really bad for the world.
          And I want like an old Wiccan lesbian to marry us.
          Like an actual witch.

PERCUSSION: Spooky.

>   *PERCUSSION tries on a neck-tie.*

KEYS: Wow, very 2005 Avril.

>   *PERCUSSION picks up the bridesmaid dress and throws it at him.*

          (*Re: the dress.*) Don't tempt me, Frodo.
          You should lay into some eyeliner too.
          Can I borrow some?

PERCUSSION: Ohmygod *yes.*

>   *KEYS and PERCUSSION do their eyeliner together in the mirror.*

          My cousin keeps being like, "Oh, you know guys, I may as well just buy him a suit and tell him when to show up!"
          And then we all do this big laugh and honestly, I don't even get what the joke is.
          Like, are we laughing 'cause guys are stupid?
          Or 'cause we're all such controlling bitches?

>   *KEYS does a big fake laugh.*

>   *PERCUSSION joins him.*

13. Drink

>   *That evening. Behind the school.*

>   *TRUMPET and TROMBONE are alone, waiting for the dance.*

>   *They pass a metal water bottle back and forth. TROMBONE drinks.*

TRUMPET: Easy there.

TROMBONE: I'll be fine.

TRUMPET:	I thought it started at 8. What're you gonna do with this?
TROMBONE:	Stick it in the bushes. Get it later.
TRUMPET:	Sorry your date bailed on you. Girls are flaky.
TROMBONE:	I don't care. I'm not trying to date anyone right now.
TRUMPET:	Sure, sure. Didn't you try to ask out –
TROMBONE:	I was just trying to get her to be real.
TRUMPET:	Right.
TROMBONE:	Girls like her are always so fake.
TRUMPET:	Yeah, I guess.
TROMBONE:	You just gotta shake people up sometimes. Make 'em drop their bullshit.
TRUMPET:	Totally.
TROMBONE:	So, your dad's military?

TRUMPET sputters on a sip.

TRUMPET:	Navy, yeah. You? I mean, your…uh –
TROMBONE:	Yeah, my dad was navy.
TRUMPET:	Right.
TROMBONE:	So, are you gonna…?
TRUMPET:	What?
TROMBONE:	Do the navy thing.
TRUMPET:	Oh. No. I mean. Nothing against it. Just not my thing.
TROMBONE:	What's your thing?
TRUMPET:	I don't know yet. My brother moved to Montreal, so maybe I'll do that.
TROMBONE:	What does he do in Montreal?
TRUMPET:	Music.
TROMBONE:	Really?

TRUMPET: Yeah, right now he's on the road with a band.

TROMBONE: What does he play?

TRUMPET: Well, he doesn't play anything with *that* band.
              He's uh, he's the guy who preps the different guitars and
              brings them out to the band.

TROMBONE: So he's a roadie.

TRUMPET: No, he's like a…technician.
              He knows about the instruments.

TROMBONE: Right.

TRUMPET: He likes it. I think.

TROMBONE: Right.

TRUMPET: I don't mean that that's what I wanna do.
              I might stay here? Go to NSCC? Do their forestry program.
              My cousin did that and now he fights forest fires.

TROMBONE: That'd be cool.
              For all those Montreal forest fires.

TRUMPET: Hah! Right.
              What about you?
              You gonna do the military thing?

TROMBONE: Probably. Good benefits.

TRUMPET: Cool. Yeah.

                    Silence.

                    The muffled beat of music starts from the school gym.

TROMBONE: Ever feel like bad shit's coming?

TRUMPET: What?

TROMBONE: Like it's all been set up for you and you just have to walk
              through it?

TRUMPET: I don't know.

TROMBONE: Like you grow up and you realize, maybe some people
              just have shit lives.

TRUMPET: That's…cheery.

TROMBONE: You haven't realized that yet?

TRUMPET: Didn't…didn't the bad thing already happen to you?

TROMBONE: What are you referring to?

TRUMPET:	Didn't your dad die?
TROMBONE:	Yeah.
TRUMPET:	That really sucks. I'm sorry. For that.

Beat.

TROMBONE:	My dad didn't like your dad.
TRUMPET:	Neither do I, really.
TROMBONE:	He said he was a suck-up. Tried too hard to be liked. Kinda like you.
TRUMPET:	(*Taking the water bottle.*) Alright, gimme that. You're gettin' too truthy.
TROMBONE:	(*Yanking the bottle back.*) Fuck off.
TRUMPET:	Hey man, don't say shit about other people's families.
TROMBONE:	You just asked me about my dad and you knew the whole story. That's fuckin' weird. So maybe don't do that.

FLUTE and BARI arrive.

TRUMPET:	Hey! Come to find the real party?
FLUTE:	Your fly's down.
TRUMPET:	So it is.
BARI:	They're letting people in now. And they're checking water bottles.
TROMBONE:	I'm not taking this in.
FLUTE:	Let's finish it then.
TRUMPET:	(*Finger-slap-snap.*) Yeh!
TROMBONE:	(*Passing the bottle to FLUTE.*) Ladies first.
FLUTE:	Thanks.
BARI:	A bunch of Cole Harbour guys are trying to get in.
TROMBONE:	Any girls?
FLUTE:	'Cause there're none here already?
TROMBONE:	Jeez, relax.

FLUTE:	I'm kidding.

HILL enters and starts to light a cigarette.

BARI:	Oh my god, is that Mr. Hill?
ALL:	(*To HILL.*) Hi.

HILL sees them and quickly takes the cigarette out of his mouth.

HILL:	I can...go somewhere else.
TRUMPET:	No man, you can stay!
FLUTE:	(*Offering HILL the water bottle.*) Want some?
TROMBONE:	(*Grabbing the bottle.*) What the fuck.
HILL:	Can you at least pretend to hide that from me?

HILL tries to pocket his cigarette. BARI sees.

BARI:	Oooh baaad.
HILL:	Don't tell my husband.

Beat.

TROMBONE laughs a weird, short laugh.

FLUTE:	(*To TROMBONE.*) What?
TRUMPET:	(*To HILL.*) Cool, yeah, no, we won't.
FLUTE:	(*To TROMBONE.*) *What?*
TROMBONE:	(*To FLUTE.*) Jesus, relax!
FLUTE:	No, it seems like you have something to say.
BARI:	Can we go in?
TROMBONE:	(*To FLUTE.*) Oh my god, don't get crazy.
FLUTE:	You just laughed.
HILL:	It's okay –
BARI:	I'm cold! Let's go in!
TRUMPET:	Yeah, I'll go with you. (*Like Bowie.*) Let's dance! (*To HILL.*) Don't mean to ditch you, man.

TROMBONE leaves ahead of the others.

BARI:	(*To FLUTE.*) You coming?
FLUTE:	Yeah, I will in a minute.

BARI and TRUMPET leave.

FLUTE and HILL are alone.

FLUTE: I don't care if you smoke.
I used to.

HILL: Thanks.
I probably shouldn't anyway.

FLUTE: How long have you and your husband been together?

HILL: Married for four, together for ten.

FLUTE: Wow.

HILL: He's a keeper.

FLUTE: I love hearing about happy married people.

HILL: What about you, are you seeing anyone?
Is that weird for me to ask?

FLUTE: No.
I was kinda seeing this guy. He's older.
But no, I don't really like guys these days.
They're assholes.
Sorry.

HILL: At your age, some of them, yeah.

FLUTE: I thought this school might be better.

HILL: Not so much?

FLUTE: I don't think I've ever had a real conversation with a guy
my age.
Not since we were like, ten.

HILL: Most of them'll wake up a bit in a year or two.

FLUTE: Is it me?

HILL: Is what you?

FLUTE: I feel like there's a target on me sometimes.
I'm not trying to get attention.

HILL: If anyone's picking on you…
It's not okay if he's giving you a hard time.

FLUTE: Is he?
Or am I making things weird.

HILL: I could talk to him.

FLUTE: Please don't.
           No offence.
           That would definitely make it weird.

HILL: I wouldn't even have to mention you.

FLUTE: I think he'd know, though.

HILL: Would that be such a bad thing?

FLUTE: I think I should just leave it.

HILL: Well, you and I should keep checking in.
           You shouldn't have to deal with this alone.

FLUTE: It's fine.

HILL: I'll keep an eye on him in class now, and if I see anything,
           I'll say something.

FLUTE: Just forget it, I can handle it.

           FLUTE walks away.

14. Dance

           Inside the gym. Lights. Loud music.

           KEYS and PERCUSSION are talking over the music.

KEYS: Remember when we used to just jump at dances?
           Like in a clump?

PERCUSSION: Like a mosh pit?

KEYS: Not as cool.
           More like a bunch of kids jumping.

PERCUSSION: If you start jumping right now, I'm walking away.

           HILL walks up to them.

           Heeey, teach!

KEYS: You're the literal worst.

HILL: Having fun?

PERCUSSION: So much fun. You gonna dance?

HILL: Nope. Not a chance.
           I'm gonna go stand by the wall with the cool kids now.

PERCUSSION: *Booo!*

           HILL walks away as FLUTE walks up.

KEYS: You alone?

FLUTE: Yeah.

PERCUSSION: Wanna get a drink?

FLUTE: I'm good for now.

PERCUSSION: I mean like, from the water fountain. I don't drink.

KEYS: She's very proud of that.

FLUTE: Sure.

> *PERCUSSION and FLUTE exit, leaving KEYS alone.*
>
> *A slow song comes on.*

KEYS: Kay, great, bye.
               I'll just stay here and hope some boy finally gives in to
               his demons.

15. Fountain

> *PERCUSSION and FLUTE are at the water fountain
> in the hall.*

PERCUSSION: My ears are all stuffy.

FLUTE: Can I ask you something?

PERCUSSION: Yeah, what's up?

FLUTE: Am I crazy or is cargo pants weird with me?

PERCUSSION: I think he's just weird.

FLUTE: So it's not specifically me?

PERCUSSION: If you stop giving him any reaction he'll probably get
               bored.

FLUTE: I'm trying.

PERCUSSION: He can probably still tell it bugs you though.

FLUTE: Do I need to yell at him or something?
               Or is that what he wants.

PERCUSSION: I don't know.
               Guys don't do that stuff to me.

FLUTE: So, it *is* me.

PERCUSSION: Well…

FLUTE: What?

PERCUSSION: No offence, but like…you're super…

FLUTE: *What?*

PERCUSSION: You're pretty!

FLUTE: I didn't choose my face.

PERCUSSION: No, but you dress like you're pretty.
Like you *know* that you're pretty.

FLUTE: I think everybody's trying to dress like something.

PERCUSSION: I just mean that, if you look like *you*, people will…

FLUTE: Hate me?

PERCUSSION: Nobody hates you.

FLUTE: Does anybody like me?

PERCUSSION: …Yeah!

FLUTE: Good try.

PERCUSSION: We're just not used to new people.
I'm sure he's gonna get bored soon.

FLUTE: In the meantime, I guess I'll stop washing my hair.
Hope the ugly wards him off.

PERCUSSION: Do you…curl your hair or do you use like a scrunch-spray?

TROMBONE walks up.

TROMBONE: (*To FLUTE.*) I was just looking for you.

PERCUSSION: Jokes.

FLUTE: (*To TROMBONE.*) Why?

TROMBONE: I wanted to apologize.

PERCUSSION: Wow, you smell like somebody dropped a mickey.

FLUTE: (*To TROMBONE.*) Apologize for what?

TROMBONE: (*To PERCUSSION.*) Sorry, were you two having a moment?

PERCUSSION: No, we were just waiting for a guy to roll in so we could make out for him.

TROMBONE: Right.

PERCUSSION: Okaaay, I'll go, you can make your grand gesture now.

PERCUSSION leaves.

TROMBONE: Do you want to go somewhere we can talk?
For real.

FLUTE: Okay.

16. Glue

In the gym. KEYS and HILL are on the edge of the dance floor.

HILL: So, I mentioned my husband.

KEYS: Yeah?

HILL: I mean, I mentioned him in front of your classmates.

KEYS: Whoa. Big step.

HILL: Yeah, they seemed unfazed.

KEYS: Mhm.

HILL: What?

KEYS: No, good for you.

HILL: Why do I feel like I'm having a stupid Torontonian moment?

KEYS: It's just – no one will say it to your face.
But…trust me, it's just easier when people don't know.
I mean, they probably know, but I've never actually *said* it though.

HILL: That's a hard place to stay.

KEYS: One more year.
I tried to be brave and tell the paddling club when I was younger.
Like, get the guys over with.

HILL: Paddling club?

KEYS: Paddling.
Like a boat.
Like, racing?

HILL: Like rowing?

KEYS: No, like paddling.
It's cool here. Just trust me.

HILL: Okay, so you paddle.

KEYS: Paddl*ed*.
           But right before I thought I might tell them, *that* guy…

                    He points out TRUMPET.

           …put superglue on my kayak seat.
           We used to race K2 together.
           It was at a big regatta.
           He got out first, and then when I tried to get out, the kayak flipped.
           I was stuck in the seat, upside down, underwater.

HILL: Holy shit.

KEYS: They flipped me back over, but I was still very much glued to the seat.
           They had to cut me out of my spandex.
           In front of spectators.

HILL: He did that?

KEYS: Yup. I mean, we were 14.
           But, yeah.
           Be careful.

HILL: That's terrible.
           Has he ever apologized?

KEYS: I don't think he even remembers.

HILL: I made fun of a guy in Grade 7 for having holes in his pants.
           Just with my friends, never to his face.
           We didn't think he knew, but then he put paper towel inside, I guess so we couldn't see his underwear.
           But then we could all see the paper towel.

KEYS: Did you ever apologize?

HILL: No. I should have.

KEYS: I'm not holding my breath.

HILL: That sets you free at least.

KEYS: Yeah.

HILL: So, I guess I'll avoid kayaking while I'm here?

KEYS: That's what they all say.

17. Fight

Upstairs, the empty band classroom.

FLUTE and TROMBONE enter.

FLUTE: This good?

TROMBONE: Yeah, I just wanted to be able to talk.

FLUTE: So talk.

TROMBONE: I feel like you hate me.

FLUTE: Why would you care if I did?

TROMBONE: I don't really know what I did wrong.

FLUTE: Wow.

TROMBONE: Okay, so I gave you a hard time about smoking, as a joke. And now you hate me?

FLUTE: I don't hate you. I'm just…exhausted by you.

TROMBONE: Okay, why are you "exhausted by me"?

FLUTE: Don't be condescending, you said you wanted to apologize.

TROMBONE: Can you tell me what I've actually done wrong?

Beat.

FLUTE: You're kind of a dick. You move through the world like an asshole, on purpose, and I think you enjoy it.

TROMBONE: I don't think I'm an asshole. I just don't humour people.

FLUTE: Right, I'm sorry, you're not an asshole.
You're this refreshingly honest, no-bullshit guy who's finally saying what everyone's thinking.
Right?

TROMBONE: You're not very nice.

FLUTE: This is the worst apology I've ever received.

FLUTE starts to leave. TROMBONE steps in her path.

TROMBONE: No wait, I just –

FLUTE: WHOA.

TROMBONE: Sorry, I just –

FLUTE: Do NOT do that to people.

TROMBONE:	Okay, okay.
	I'm sorry I piss you off.
	I don't try to.
	It's just…
FLUTE:	What.
TROMBONE:	Nah, you don't wanna hear it.
FLUTE:	What is it?
TROMBONE:	It's about you.

HILL walks in, holding his phone.

HILL:	What's going on?
TROMBONE/ FLUTE:	Nothing.
HILL:	Is everything okay?
FLUTE/ TROMBONE:	Yeah.
HILL:	I don't think you're supposed to be up here.
TROMBONE:	Probably not.
HILL:	Why don't we all head back to the dance?
FLUTE:	(*To HILL.*) Can you give us a minute?
TROMBONE:	No, we can go.
FLUTE:	(*To TROMBONE.*) No, I want to finish this conversation. (*To HILL.*) Is that okay?
HILL:	I'm sorry, guys, but we should really head downstairs.
FLUTE:	We're working through some stuff.
HILL:	That's good.
	Why don't I just sit over here, but I don't have to say anything –
FLUTE:	Honestly. Just give us five minutes.
	I really need to do this.

HILL considers.

Please. This is helping.

Beat.

HILL:	I'm gonna be right outside that door.
FLUTE:	Thank you.

HILL: And only if you're both sure.

FLUTE: I'm sure.
               (*To TROMBONE.*) You?

TROMBONE: I'm good.

HILL: Okay.
               I'm right outside.
               And in five, we're going downstairs.

               HILL leaves the room.

TROMBONE: I was actually trying to apologize.
               But you obviously don't care.

FLUTE: I just need you to tell me the truth:
               Why are you mean to me?
               No bullshit this time.

TROMBONE: It's gonna make you feel bad.

FLUTE: Is it because your dad killed himself?

TROMBONE: Jesus.

FLUTE: I said no bullshit.

TROMBONE: Does everyone fucking know?

FLUTE: Yeah.
               So what is it?
               Is that your problem?

TROMBONE: Why are you analyzing me?

FLUTE: 'Cause you're not the first guy to treat me like this and
               you won't be the last.
               If I can figure you out, maybe I can fix it.

TROMBONE: Okay. Fine.
               I call you on stuff because you act like you're better than
               everybody.

FLUTE: Really.

TROMBONE: You wanted me to be honest.

FLUTE: What have I ever said –

TROMBONE: It's not like a thing you say.
               It's how you are.
               How you…move. And look at people.
               You're just kind of…above us.

FLUTE: I'm pretty sure that's called confidence.

Pictured (L–R): Hershel Blatt, Natasha Ramondino.
Photo by Neil Silcox.

Pictured (L–R): Michaela Di Cesare, Andrew Di Rosa.
Photo by Neil Silcox.

TROMBONE: You know it's different.

FLUTE: I'm not mean to people.

TROMBONE: No, you just think you're better than them.

FLUTE: I'm good friends with –

TROMBONE: Yeah, and you think you're smarter than her and prettier and she's never gonna get out of here.

FLUTE: No.

TROMBONE: You can tell.

FLUTE: Just 'cause I'm not RUSHING to be your friend or to go to the dance with you doesn't make me a bitch.

TROMBONE: Kay.

FLUTE: And yeah, sometimes, maybe I keep my guard up.
And maybe I'm not nice to everybody.
Can you blame me?

TROMBONE: Right, so you get to pick who you're nice to, but I'm an asshole for making one joke.

FLUTE: Oh my god, it's not about the smoking thing or one joke!

TROMBONE: Then what is it?!

FLUTE: It's a lot of little things.
And you *know* you're doing it.

TROMBONE: I'm really not paying that much attention –

FLUTE: No, I think you are!
I'm not crazy!
I don't think I'm making this up!

TROMBONE: So what do you want me to do?

FLUTE: Just – stop!

TROMBONE: Like, talking to you? Like ever?

FLUTE: Yeah. Maybe.

TROMBONE: Okay. If you really think that'll help. I guess you pick the rules.

FLUTE: It's not like we're friends.

TROMBONE: You *do* think you're better than me.

FLUTE: Well, you think you're better than me.

TROMBONE: No.

I don't.

I really don't.

FLUTE: I don't believe you.

TROMBONE: Well, it's true. Sorry.

> *Beat.*

This got really *Breakfast Club* all of a sudden.

FLUTE: I've never read it.

> *Beat.*

I'll take your apology now.

TROMBONE: Fine. I'm sorry.

FLUTE: Pardon?

TROMBONE: I'm sorry.

FLUTE: Say it again.

> *TROMBONE walks up to FLUTE.*
>
> *He stands close to her.*

TROMBONE: I'm sorry, Taylor.

FLUTE: Thank you.

> *Silence. They look at each other.*
>
> *Then –*
>
> *TROMBONE tries to kiss FLUTE.*
>
> *FLUTE tries to pull away.*

No, no –

TROMBONE: It's okay, it's okay –

> *TROMBONE keeps his hands on FLUTE, pulling her towards him.*
>
> *FLUTE shoves him.*

What the fuck!

> *FLUTE punches TROMBONE in the face.*
>
> *He doubles over.*
>
> *TROMBONE stands again, and hurls a chair to the ground while turning to face FLUTE.*

You're a fucking BITCH!

FLUTE has grabbed a music stand.

A heavy, black, metal music stand.

She swings it.

HILL runs in.

HILL: No no – !

FLUTE hits TROMBONE in the head. Hard.

TROMBONE drops to the ground.

FLUTE freezes, seeing what she has done.

18. Calls

Chaos outside the school.

KEYS, TRUMPET, BARI, and PERCUSSION make phone calls.

Their phone calls overlap (a / indicates where the next call begins).

KEYS: Mom, can you come get me?
Um.
Something happened at the dance.
I'm okay.
There's an ambulance and a couple cop cars. /
I don't know. No one said.
Yeah, they're with us.
They made us all go outside.
Mom. Mom!
Mom, I'm fine.
Don't freak out.
Yeah, we're all outside now.
I think –

TRUMPET: Mom, can you come get me?
There was an accident at the school. /
Nobody saw it but they're kicking us all out now.
Yeah, they just turned the music off and said –
I don't know.
I guess –

BARI: Hey, can you give me a ride home from the school?
No, that's fine then, I'll just walk. /
The dance ended early.
No, no, I'm totally fine.
They said –

PERCUSSION: Sorry, I know you're at work.
I'm bussing home.
I think –

KEYS / TRUMPET / BARI /
PERCUSSION: – I think somebody got hurt.

19. Home

Later that night. HILL's house.

MATT is waiting up for HILL.

HILL walks in.

MATT hugs him tightly.

They hold on to each other.

A long, tight hug.

MATT: I love you.
Are you okay?

HILL: I'm okay.

MATT: There were so many sirens when you called.
I didn't hear everything.
A girl got attacked?

HILL: I think so.

MATT: Is she okay?
Do they know who did it?

HILL: Yeah.

MATT: That's good.

HILL: No.
It's really bad.

MATT touches HILL.

HILL pulls away.

I'm sorry. I –

MATT: No, it's okay. It's okay.
Did you see something?

HILL: Yes.

MATT: Is she okay?

HILL: Yeah, she's fine.
But she beat the shit out of him.

MATT: Really?

HILL: Yeah.
He looked…
I don't know what he did.
But he's not okay.
It's not okay.

MATT: Oh my god.

          Beat.

Is it bad.
That…
I feel…kind of impressed.

HILL: I think I fucked up.

MATT: No, no, no –

HILL: No. I fucked up.

          HILL curls up.

          MATT holds him.

20. Deserve

          Three days later.

          KEYS and PERCUSSION are in PERCUSSION's bedroom.

KEYS: It's not that fucked up.

PERCUSSION: I didn't say that.

KEYS: It's honestly pretty simple: self-defence.

PERCUSSION: She didn't shove him.
She didn't give him a shot of pepper spray.
This is a girl beating the shit out of a boy with a music
stand.
That is fucked up.

KEYS: He assaulted her.

PERCUSSION: We don't know that yet.

KEYS: Are you kidding me?
You don't believe her?

PERCUSSION: She hasn't said anything yet!
That's just the rumour.
We have *no idea* what happened in there.

KEYS: We're gonna have to listen to his version of it.

PERCUSSION: Yeah. We will. That's how it works.
It's weird being home on a Monday.

KEYS: What time do you have to meet with them?

PERCUSSION: Three.
Are you supposed to dress up for a police interview?

KEYS: What are you gonna say?

PERCUSSION: The truth.
What they said to each other at the water fountain.

KEYS: Are you going to tell them he's a bully?

PERCUSSION: If they ask that.

KEYS: But if not, you'll just leave that out?

PERCUSSION: I'm going to answer their questions honestly!

KEYS: She shouldn't be punished for this.

PERCUSSION: Mmm.

KEYS: I have this reccurring dream where I'm stomping on the
faces of the boys from paddling.
And I just can't do it hard enough.

PERCUSSION: They could have drowned you.
Plus, you're not ever gonna really do that.

KEYS: I think what she did is actually kind of important.
Like it might teach people.

PERCUSSION: That's a really scary thing to say.

KEYS: She clearly felt threatened, so she hit back.

PERCUSSION: Can we just stop talking about this?

Beat.

KEYS: I really thought you'd be on her side.

PERCUSSION: I don't think we should take sides on this.

KEYS: Ugh.

PERCUSSION: What?

KEYS: I just find that attitude infuriating.
It's a terrible excuse for passivity.

PERCUSSION: Do you really think he deserves to die?

KEYS: He's not going to die. He's stable now.

PERCUSSION: Yeah. And partially blind.

KEYS: I just keep thinking…
What if people hit back more often.
What if this was a bigger possibility.
Like if women could carry guns.
And we all knew that.
Would things be different.

PERCUSSION: I think it's been proven it doesn't work like that.

KEYS: Okay, not guns then.

PERCUSSION: Music stands?

21. Statement

FLUTE is being recorded.

FLUTE: No, I asked Mr. Hill to give us privacy.
Yes, I asked Mr. Hill to leave.
So we talked some more and I told him I was ready for his apology.
And he said he was sorry and I said thank you and then he tried to kiss me.
He kissed me out of nowhere and I pulled away but he kept touching me so I hit him to make him stop but he wasn't stopping.
And I didn't know what he was going to do.
And I was scared and he kept coming at me and then he was really *mad.*
I don't know. I didn't know so I hit him.
I, I, I hit him again.
I was just trying to get him to stop.
He wouldn't stop.
I just wanted him to stop.
Anything I tried to say, he wasn't listening to me.
I was trying, but he wasn't listening.
And I was thinking – just make him stop, make him stop so you can get away.
Just – do what you have to do.
So I just – did it.
And I'm glad I did 'cause I don't know what he was going to do.
I don't know.
I don't know.
So I just did it.
I had to.
I'd promised myself
I promised myself
That next time
That I'd just do it
I'd just do it
And I just did it
I did it
I was so mad
I was so mad
I, I –
I'm sorry.
I was really scared.
And I was mad.

22. Stain

> *One week after the dance. The empty band classroom.*
> *BARI arrives for class.*
> *She stops in the doorway and looks at the classroom.*
> *She walks inside.*
> *She stops where TROMBONE fell and looks at the floor.*
> *She straightens the chairs.*
> *She picks up a music stand.*
> *She feels its weight in her hands.*
> *She looks towards the door.*
> *She takes a deep breath, and swings the music stand.*
> *Hard.*
> *TRUMPET walks in.*

TRUMPET: Hi?!

BARI: (*Quickly putting the stand down.*) Sorry!

TRUMPET: ...Want me to go?

BARI: No. It's fine.
I wasn't gonna...(*Mimes hitting him with the stand.*)

TRUMPET: Oh, yeah, no, I know.
I just...

BARI: Don't know how to live in your own skin right now?

TRUMPET: Yeah.

BARI: Same.

TRUMPET: How was your week off?

BARI: I worked a bunch.
Picked up shifts.
I felt guilty having free time.

TRUMPET: Have you seen her?

BARI: No.

TRUMPET: My mom heard he's out of the hospital.

BARI: What's he gonna do now?

TRUMPET: I'd move away.

BARI: Maybe his face is unrecognizable now.

                      TRUMPET looks at BARI.

          Silver lining…?

TRUMPET: You're awful!

BARI: You're smiling.

                      The school bell rings.

                      KEYS and PERCUSSION enter.

                      Everyone is quiet for a bit.

TRUMPET: This is pretty weird, right.
Being in the room.

BARI: There's kind of a stain.

PERCUSSION: What?

BARI: (*Pointing to where TROMBONE fell.*)
There.
You can still kind of see it.

                      KEYS looks.

KEYS: That was always there.

                      TRUMPET walks over to check.

TRUMPET: No way, man, that's a fucking bloodstain!

KEYS: Trust me.
It's always been here.

TRUMPET: You got a heavy flow or something?

KEYS: Just *fuck off!*

                      KEYS leaves.

PERCUSSION: (*To TRUMPET.*) Can you just be nice?
Just be boring and nice. For once.
Don't try to be funny. Don't try to be cool.
Not right now.

TRUMPET: What's he so upset about?
He didn't spend his week being interrogated.

BARI: Did they talk to you?

TRUMPET: Yeah. Apparently, I'm the expert on exactly how drunk he
              was or wasn't and whether he was planning some kind
              of "assault."

                    Beat.

PERCUSSION: Was he?

TRUMPET: He said something about wanting to shake people up.

BARI: Creepy creepy creepy.

                    HILL enters.

HILL: Good morning.

                    Silence.

              I want to start by saying –

                    KEYS comes back in.

KEYS: Hi. Sorry.
              But I just need to say something:
              (*To TRUMPET.*) I can't believe you think it's okay to make a
              sexist joke after what literally just happened in this room.

TRUMPET: It wasn't a sexist joke!
              It was a period joke cause we were fully talking about a
              bloodstain!

KEYS: Stop making excuses! You're exactly what's wrong!

TRUMPET: Dude, I'm sorry you're upset, but I don't think –

KEYS: YOU ARE THE PROBLEM.

TRUMPET: What?

KEYS: YOU ARE THE PROBLEM.

PERCUSSION: (*To KEYS.*) Hey, maybe we should –

KEYS: (*To TRUMPET.*) APOLOGIZE.

HILL: HEY.

KEYS: NO.
              I'm sorry, Mr. Hill.
              But he needs to apologize to me RIGHT NOW.

                    Everyone looks at TRUMPET.

TRUMPET: Sorry.

                    A wave crashes over TRUMPET.
                    He hides his face.

HILL: There are counsellors available in the cafeteria all day today.
You can step out at any time and go talk to someone.
And whatever you're feeling right now, just remember, it's all valid.
Everyone's going to process this differently.
And I'm here, too, if there's anything you want to –

HILL's phone rings.

Sorry.
I should, just in case –
(*He answers.*)
Hello?
Right now?
No, of course. I understand.
I'll come down right now.
Thanks.
Bye.
(*He hangs up.*)
I have to talk to some people at the office.
You can use this as a study period.
Or whatever you need.
I'll – I'll see you on Wednesday.

HILL leaves.

TRUMPET: I think I'm gonna go too.

TRUMPET leaves.

PERCUSSION: (*To KEYS.*) Happy?

KEYS: No.

BARI: I think all the guys are kinda messed up right now.
They're scared.

KEYS: Don't treat girls like garbage and you'll be fine.
It's not that hard!

PERCUSSION: It's still a lot for people to process.

KEYS: It's not though!
Don't assault people.
The end.

Beat.

PERCUSSION: …He tried to kiss her.

KEYS: – And touched her!
And yelled at her!

BARI: OH-kay –

PERCUSSION: (*To KEYS.*) I *know*! What I'm saying is –

KEYS: (*To BARI, re: PERCUSSION.*) She doesn't believe her!

PERCUSSION: LET ME TALK!
I just keep thinking about my brother, okay?
He's 12.
I'm sure he's messed up with girls already and I'm sure he'll do it again when he's older.
Should someone beat him till there's a stain on the floor?

KEYS: Do you talk to him about how to treat girls?

PERCUSSION: Yeah, I teach him to respect everybody.

KEYS: I think it's important to be really specific.

PERCUSSION: I just hate that people are acting like she did something at all good.
She made a mistake too.

BARI: It's not like that!

        Beat.

KEYS: Do you know something?

BARI: I think this was way bigger than a kiss for her.

KEYS: Did he do something else?

BARI: It's not about him.
It's about everybody before him.
All the other guys like him.
I think this was kind of a breaking point for her.
It's like…she took something back.

KEYS: Did something happen at her last school?

BARI: I don't know.

PERCUSSION: Was she…?

BARI: I don't know!
She didn't want to tell me so I didn't dig.
But she said something happened.

PERCUSSION: That could mean anything, though.

BARI: Why do you need to know every little detail?!
So you can decide if it was bad enough?

PERCUSSION: Sorry.

BARI: Sorry.

> *Beat.*

PERCUSSION: I guess she had to do this.

BARI: I'm not saying it was like destiny.

KEYS: But it seems like she had to fight back eventually.

BARI: But she shouldn't have had to.
We all saw what was happening.

PERCUSSION: I didn't see this coming.

BARI: But we all saw how she was feeling.

KEYS: We weren't really friends with her.

BARI: Well, good for you.
I am.

KEYS: You really should not feel bad about this.

BARI: I kind of think we all should.

> *Beat.*

PERCUSSION: I think I'm gonna go – I have an off after this.

BARI: Me too.

PERCUSSION: Wanna walk to Timmy's?

BARI: Yeah.
I want to not be in this school.

> *They start to leave.*

> *KEYS doesn't move.*

PERCUSSION: Want an ice cap?

KEYS: I'm good.

PERCUSSION: Kay.
Maybe you should talk to one of the counsellors.
I'm not teasing you.
But like – I think I keep saying the wrong thing when you wanna talk about this.

BARI: (*To KEYS.*) You can come meet us later if you change your mind.

> *BARI and PERCUSSION leave.*

23. Mom

That night. HILL and MATT are at home.

HILL: They're not going to try her as an adult.

MATT: Good.

HILL: I keep having to explain why I left the room.
They put me on the kid side of the desk today.
Like I was in trouble.

MATT: You did your best.

HILL: I wanted to let her fight her own battle.
She asked me!
She asked me to give them five minutes.
She said they were sorting things out.
I was so proud of her.
I always think about what I'd say if I had one more chance
with the people who fucked with me in high school.
All the things I'd say.
I was so happy for her to have that.

MATT: You did what you could.
And really, it's his parents who –

HILL: Yeah, but his dad –

MATT: I know, I know.

HILL: His mom's whole world was already upside down.
I probably saw him more than she did this month.
God.
I was right there at the door.
I was listening.

MATT: Mhm.

HILL: What?

Beat.

I never thought for a second he was gonna try something,
in a band room, with me literally on the other side of the
door.
It's ridiculous.

This hits MATT hard.

HILL realizes what he's said.

I'm not talking about what happened to you –

MATT: I know.

HILL: I'm sorry, I wasn't thinking –

MATT: I know.
That's the problem.
Nobody thinks about how it actually happens.

HILL: I'm sorry.

> *The doorbell rings.*

MATT: Can we just leave it.

HILL: I think I should check.

MATT: It's late.

HILL: I don't want anyone to think I'm hiding.

> *HILL answers the door.*
>
> *It's a woman.*

Hi.

THERESA: Hi.
I'm sorry to bother you.
I'm Theresa MacKenna.
I'm Tristan's mom.

HILL: We… we know you're going through hell right now.
Do you…do you want to come in?

THERESA: I'm not gonna stay.
I'm sorry to just show up like this.

HILL: It's okay.
How is Tristan?

THERESA: He's home.
They postponed his court date because his balance is still pretty bad.
He's gained another 10% in both eyes though.

HILL: Vision?

THERESA: He's at 40% now.
It might get a little better still, in another month or so.

HILL: That's good.

> *Beat.*

THERESA: I wanted to talk to you about Tristan.

HILL: I'm not sure we should talk like this, without any kind of
            official –

THERESA: It's not about…what happened.
            It's just about Tristan.

MATT: I think Joel is right.
            Maybe we shouldn't go there –

THERESA: He's a good kid.
            Right?
            I know that – all this –
            But that's not him.
            He can be a bit of a loner.
            After his dad…
            And I know he tries to act like a tough guy sometimes.
            But he's a nice boy.

HILL: He's young.

THERESA: He wasn't torturing her, though.
            Or was there something going on that I don't know?
            Please tell me.
            If he was doing something, I want to know.

HILL: It's complicated.

MATT: (*To HILL.*) Honey, you don't have too –

THERESA: Did he say something that offended you?
            'Cause…(*She gestures between MATT and HILL.*)
            That's just how people talk.
            It's not like Toronto. Sorry.
            We just don't meet a lot of –

MATT: I'm from here.

HILL: (*To THERESA.*) I think you should talk to you son.
            Ask him your questions.

THERESA: I did.
            I tried.
            He won't talk about it.
            He won't talk to me.
            So I'm here now and I need you to tell me.
            What did he do?

HILL: It's hard to give an example.

THERESA: Was he mean to her?

HILL: He could be…kind of mean sometimes, yes.

THERESA: What did he do? What did he say?

HILL: Lots of little things.

THERESA: Lots of little things.

HILL: He made her very uncomfortable.

Beat.

THERESA: They said Tristan will have headaches, and dizziness, and chronic pain for the rest of his life.
That sounds pretty uncomfortable to me.

Beat.

MATT: Tell her the rest, then.

HILL: Matt, don't.

THERESA: Tell me what?

MATT: (*To HILL.*) No, I think she needs to hear it.

THERESA: What is it?

MATT: (*To THERESA.*) He tried to force himself on her.

THERESA: He tried to kiss a girl!
He apologized, and then he tried to kiss someone!

HILL: We really can't / talk about this.

MATT: / We don't know what he might have done next.

THERESA: No, I know. I KNOW my son.

MATT: Then where were you while he was becoming the kind of person who does this?

THERESA: (*To HILL.*) Where were YOU?
How did you let this happen?!

MATT: Your son wasn't attacked.
He didn't need protection.
A girl had to defend herself against him.

THERESA: He's not a monster. He's a teenaged boy at a dance.

MATT: Yes, who already thinks the world should give him whatever he wants, or he can take it.

THERESA: No. He didn't TAKE anything.
He made ONE mistake.
Once.

MATT: He doesn't get to learn a lesson at her expense and just walk away.
He hurt someone.
He scared someone.
There are consequences.

THERESA: This is crazy.

MATT: No, this is fair.

THERESA: He can't SEE! He can't SLEEP!
He's having nightmares!

MATT: So will she.
This is forever for her.
She is going to think about your son every day for the rest of her life.
Trust me.

THERESA: She should.

Beat.

HILL: You should go.
This was a mistake.

THERESA: No.
I'm glad we talked.

THERESA leaves.

Silence in the house.

MATT: I only said what was true.
Why didn't you help me?

HILL: She's a grieving mother.

MATT: And I'm your husband.

HILL: This wasn't the time.

MATT: Then you shouldn't have let her in!

HILL: I'm TRYING.
I'm the one in this.
You don't have to get involved.

MATT: Yes I do.
Someone has to say this.
You should have talked to him.

HILL: What would you have said?

24. Friends

BARI calls FLUTE.

BARI: Hey, it's me.
How are you?
Yeah. I get that.
Um, I just wanted to call because…
Because I feel really bad.
That I didn't do anything.
I'm sorry.
I'm really, really sorry.
I know.
I know.
But you told me it was upsetting you, and you told me about the guys at your last school, and I knew you weren't happy, and I just should have been better for you. I just didn't want to annoy you by being around you too much, or asking you a bunch of questions.
I know, but I get that we're *work* friends, not real friends.
(*Beat.*)
Me too!
I think so too!
Oh my god, we're so dumb.
Yeah, I'm okay. I was calling to check on *you* and now you're gonna make *me* cry.
I just want you to know that – I'm around.
Yeah.
And we're friends.

25. Sing

A school hallway.

KEYS has a keyboard, a donation tin, and a sign.

His sign reads:

THE JUSTICE JUKEBOX

REQUEST A SONG! YOUR CHANGE MAKES CHANGE!

(ALL $ GOES TOWARDS THE HRM WOMEN'S SHELTER)

KEYS waits.

> *No one requests a song.*
>
> *TRUMPET enters.*
>
> *He reads KEYS's sign.*

TRUMPET: *Free Bird!*

> *TRUMPET starts to put a loonie in the donation tin. He stops.*

This for Student Council?

KEYS: No.
This is just me.

> *TRUMPET drops the loonie in.*

Thanks.

TRUMPET: Got any requests yet?

KEYS: Two.
For "Free Bird."

TRUMPET: Sorry.
Hey, do you know if those people are coming back to the cafeteria?

KEYS: What people?

TRUMPET: The…the people they had…

KEYS: The counsellors?

TRUMPET: Yeah.

KEYS: No, they were only here for the one day.
Some other school probably needs them now.

TRUMPET: Right.

> *Beat.*
>
> *TRUMPET drops a toonie in the donation tin.*

Can I ask you something and have you not be mad at me?

KEYS: That depends entirely on what you're going to ask me.

TRUMPET: This money goes to help women who've been abused, right?

KEYS: Some of them, yes.

TRUMPET: Are there people who help the men?

KEYS: The men who abuse people?

TRUMPET: Yeah.

KEYS: Yeah.
            Therapists.

TRUMPET: That shit's expensive.

KEYS: If you want to collect money so abusive men can go to
            therapy, go for it.

TRUMPET: Is there a place for that?

KEYS: I don't know.
            Do some research.

TRUMPET: Yeah. I will.

            TRUMPET takes out a ten-dollar bill.

            He pokes it into the tin.

KEYS: …Thanks.

TRUMPET: Do you know what you're gonna do next year?

KEYS: I'm applying to UBC.

TRUMPET: Wow. Far.

KEYS: That's the idea.
            What about you?

TRUMPET: Yeah, I dunno.
            I think I might actually stick around here for a bit.
            My mom would like that.
            And I kinda like Dartmouth.

KEYS: Really?

TRUMPET: Yeah!
            We're scrappy.
            Maybe I'll coach some paddling.

KEYS: Oh.

            Beat.

TRUMPET: Hey, man – that thing I did.
            That was really stupid.
            I should have said something before now.
            But yeah.
            It was stupid.

KEYS: I agree.

TRUMPET: Cool.

KEYS: You'd probably make a pretty good coach.

TRUMPET: Thanks.
I'm actually thinking I might look into like teachers' college eventually.

KEYS: A B.Ed.?

TRUMPET: Yeah, yeah.
A B.Ed.

KEYS: Cool.

TRUMPET: (*Re: the keyboard.*) Hey, can I play something?

KEYS: Go nuts.

> *TRUMPET carefully plays and sings "Lavender Blue" (the 1949 melody by Eliot Daniel).*

TRUMPET: *"Lavender blue, dilly dilly, lavender green*
When I am King, dilly dilly, I'll need a queen
Who told me so, dilly dilly, who told me so?
I told myself, I told me so."

> *A wave of unexpected emotion.*

> *TRUMPET plays something silly to cover.*

That's all I know.

KEYS: My dad used to sing that to me.

TRUMPET: Mine too.

> *Beat.*

KEYS: Okay, I'm gonna pack up now.

TRUMPET: No, no, give it a bit!

KEYS: No one's coming.

TRUMPET: They'll come!

KEYS: I've been here for an hour.

TRUMPET: Then you can't walk away now, man.
You're in it!
We're scrappy.

KEYS: Fine.

                      Beat.

              You don't have to wait with me, you know.

TRUMPET: I don't mind.

KEYS: Do you actually think we're gonna get anyone?

TRUMPET: Yeah.
              Yeah, I think we will.

                      The boys wait together.

                    THE END

Playwright's Note

I grew up in Dartmouth, Nova Scotia (where the play is set) and was an unapologetic band geek. I was bullied as a teenager in insidious ways. I remember explaining it to my grandma: "It's enough that it hurts, but subtle enough that I think I might be crazy." I didn't have the word yet for that specific brand of bullying: gaslighting.

Growing up, I saw depictions of bullying that looked like people being pushed into lockers, or tripped in class, or called names. What I didn't see were the quiet, manipulative, gradual ways we hurt one another – the kind of behaviours that get in your head and make you question your grip on reality.

I hope this play offers a scenario we can dig into to discuss ways of intervening when this kind of bullying is happening. What can we do if we're the target? What if our friend is mistreating someone? What if we're a bystander, noticing the subtle signs? What if we're the one in charge? And what can we do to repair our own mistakes?

A mentor of mine told me a play should be like flipping coin – still in midair, not landing one way or the other yet. Thank you for joining this conversation while the coin is in midair.

Discussion Questions

1. What are some examples of bullying and gaslighting in the play?

2. Bari, Trumpet, Percussion, and Keys are all bystanders. How could they have tried as peers to help Flute or Trombone? What could Mr. Hill have tried?

3. What are some things characters say or do in the play to try to rectify harm?

4. How should we choose when to call someone *out* for harmful behaviour or call someone *in*? (See vocabulary below for more about these terms.)

Vocabulary

Gaslighting: a form of psychological manipulation that seeks to sow seeds of doubt in a targeted individual or in members of a targeted group, making them question their own memory, perception, and sanity.

Assault: an intentional act by one person that creates an apprehension in another of an imminent harmful or offensive contact.

Harassment: unwanted physical or verbal behaviour that offends or humiliates someone. Generally, harassment is a behaviour that persists over time. Serious one-time incidents can also be considered harassment.

Call-Out and Call-In Culture: these terms refer to different approaches to educating or correcting one another, especially in instances of racism, sexism, homophobia, transphobia, or other harmful behaviours. Calling someone "out" typically refers to a response or correction that is public (for example, a post on social media), whereas calling someone "in" is typically done in private, and may include an opportunity or encouragement for the other person to respond or ask questions (for example, a private conversation).

Admissions

Tanisha Taitt

Tanisha Taitt

Tanisha Taitt is a playwright, performer, songsmith, director of both theatre and audiobooks, and teaches 1st Year Contemporary Scene Study at George Brown Theatre School. She was nominated as a director for the Pauline McGibbon Award, and is a recipient of the Canadian Music Publishers Association Award & Scholarship for excellence in songwriting. Also an anti-oppression educator, Tanisha is a two-time nominee for the YWCA Woman of Distinction Award for her commitment to social justice through the arts, most notably for her leadership in activism combatting violence against women. In October of 2019 Tanisha became the Artistic Director of Cahoots Theatre in Toronto.

Photo by Dahlia Katz.

Admissions *is dedicated to every young woman,*
with the hope that she will never forget her worth.

Production History

Admissions premiered at Artscape Youngplace in Toronto, Ontario, Canada on April 24, 2014.

The cast was as follows:

TRISH .... Gabriella Albino

CARLY .... Katherine Cappellacci

GAVIN .... Nirmal Gossai

The director and set designer was Tanisha Taitt.

The stage manager & lighting designer was Carolyn Brennan.

Characters

Scene 1

The present. Toronto, Ontario. A study lounge in a high school. There are three chairs around one table, similar to a cafeteria table, and two standing lamps which are on. GAVIN sits at the table playing a video game on his iPhone. There is a half-empty open bottle of beer on the table, which he takes a swig from intermittently throughout the scene. GAVIN frenetically hits buttons with his thumbs.

GAVIN: (*To the phone screen.*) You are so dead. SO dead... oh crap. Oh sh – oh! Damn it. (*He sighs.*) Okay. One more –

TRISH enters. She turns off the overhead lights, leaving only the lamplight, and sits at the end of the table.

What's with you and darkness?

TRISH: It's not dark. It's ambient.

GAVIN: Well I'm not a mole person. I like light in my life.

TRISH: That's an ugly light.

GAVIN: Light is light.

TRISH: What? Okay first of all, that is blasphemy.

GAVIN: And God said... "Let there be light."...

TRISH: The screen is lit. That's all you ever look at anyway so that's all the light you need.

GAVIN: You are a nyctophiliac.

TRISH: A what?

GAVIN: A nyctophiliac. You love the dark.

TRISH: You made that up.

GAVIN: Yeah, I pulled "nyctophiliac" outta the sky. (*He loses the video game.*) Damn it! Okay, one more... (*He glances at Trish.*) Wiki it.

TRISH: What?

GAVIN:	Wiki it. Nyctophilia. If you don't believe me.
TRISH:	Wikipedia is not a reliable source.
GAVIN:	Wikipedia is the Gospel According to Everything.
TRISH:	I'm nocturnal.
GAVIN:	That too.
TRISH:	Not that other word.
GAVIN:	You're both. It's the middle of the afternoon. The sun is shining outside. And you just walk in and turn the room dark.
TRISH:	There is a difference between "dim" and "dark."
GAVIN:	You're absolutely right. Let's play a game. One of those words describes you, and the other describes this room.
TRISH:	Screw you.
GAVIN:	You're a total nyctophiliac. *Poltergeist* would've sucked if you were Carol-Anne.
TRISH:	Huh?
GAVIN:	You never would've gone towards the light.
TRISH:	Polterwhat?
GAVIN:	*Poltergeist.* We watched it together like six or seven years ago? It's legendary. Really really old, from like, 1982. Directed by Spielberg. I think it's on YouTube.
TRISH:	Ohhh, right. Oh my god you're awful.
GAVIN:	Why?
TRISH:	The little girl from that movie died, for real.
GAVIN:	You're correct. Carol-Anne did indeed go to the haunted house in the sky.
TRISH:	Gavin, that's not funny.
GAVIN:	The older girl died too.
TRISH:	(*In disbelief.*) No way.
GAVIN:	Yep. The *Poltergeist* Curse. I saw it on E True Hollywood Story.
TRISH:	Shut up that's so creepy.
GAVIN:	Totally.

TRISH: So don't make jokes about it!

GAVIN: Who's joking? I mean it. You would've sucked as Carol-Anne.

TRISH: No respect for the dead.

GAVIN: I respect the dead plenty. They had a tough time of it. Things didn't end well.

TRISH: Speaking of which, I admire your valiant effort – I really do – but you're never going to pass Level IV so I don't know why you bother to keep trying.

GAVIN: You keep yappin'.

TRISH: I just don't know why you do this to yourself.

GAVIN: (*Not lifting his eyes from the screen.*) You know what, you should screw your plans and change career direction entirely. Are you sure you don't want to go into motivational speaking?

TRISH: (*Laughing.*) Hey I only speak the truth.

GAVIN: I'm blocking you out.

TRISH: Wait, aren't mole people homeless?

GAVIN: You're ruining my concentration.

TRISH: You said you're not a mole person.

GAVIN: I'm sure you have a point and I anticipate hearing it.

TRISH: Mole people. (*She grabs her cell phone to look up "mole people" in Wikipedia.*) They're homeless. You're mocking the homeless!

GAVIN: Um, Trish, they're not real.

TRISH: (*Finding the definition.*) Um, they are totally real. "Mole people is a term used to refer to homeless people living under large cities in abandoned subway, railroad, flood, and sewage tunnels and heating shafts. These people are also sometimes referred to as 'tunnel people' or 'tunnel dwellers.'"

GAVIN: (*Looking up.*) What?! Where did you read that? Oh crap! (*He loses the game he is playing, again.*) Okay my brain just exploded. I was sure they were an urban legend. I totally want to meet some.

TRISH: (*Laughing.*) Wikipedia. The Gospel According to Everything.

GAVIN: You are so annoying.

TRISH: But, once again, right.

GAVIN: Why do I love you?

TRISH: You can't help it.

GAVIN: Annoying and vain. Is there any virtue you don't possess?

TRISH: Why don't you just admit that you're obsessed?

GAVIN: With what?

TRISH: With beating my score.

GAVIN: Whatever.

TRISH: Yeah whatever whatever. It's eating you up.

GAVIN: Whatever you need to believe.

TRISH: I don't believe it. I know it.

GAVIN: Delusion 101.

TRISH: The truth is hard to swallow.

GAVIN: White noise babe.

> *TRISH pulls a textbook from her bag and plops it on the table.*

TRISH: I swear to god this is gonna be the death of me.

GAVIN: No it won't.

TRISH: I don't care about parsing sentences. Why does it matter?

GAVIN: I don't even know what parse means.

TRISH: Look it up.

GAVIN: Oh for heaven's sake just tell me.

TRISH: No. We're a lazy, spoon-fed society. Look it up.

GAVIN: No. I'm lazy, just like you said. Stop complaining. Don't you want to be smarter than me? Or smarter than I?

TRISH: I think they're both accepted. I think. Maybe.

GAVIN: Ah... but "accepted" is one thing and "right" is another.

TRISH: Leave me alone. And I'm already smarter than you.

GAVIN: Really.

TRISH: Really.

GAVIN: I presume you have evidence to this effect.

TRISH: It must be hard to never see Level V – isn't it?

> *GAVIN rolls his eyes and shakes his head. He turns off his phone. TRISH laughs and flips through the pages of her textbook.*

Why didn't they teach us this? Education FAIL.

GAVIN: I'm pretty sure they did. I don't think we were paying attention though.

TRISH: Huh?

GAVIN: Point made.

TRISH: No, they didn't. I think Grandma tried to though. Bless her heart. I remember her sitting me down a few times with some old tattered book when I was about nine. Of course she always did it during *Hannah Montana,* which sucked.

GAVIN: Now you can't be doing that to Miley…

TRISH: Honestly, I wish I'd listened. Carly is so good at this stuff.

GAVIN: Well if you want to be a writer…

TRISH: I am a writer.

GAVIN: Yes you are. But the competition is tough. If you want to get into that program –

TRISH: Yeah I know. I should've just stuck with Creative Writing. I'm totally creative.

GAVIN: True.

TRISH: It's not Grammatically Perfect Writing. That is NOT what it's called.

GAVIN: Equally true. But you chose to apply to both so deal with it.

TRISH: Thank you for that.

GAVIN: Hey, I only speak the truth. Journalism is a different game. If you were a novelist or something you could break all the rules – get all your tenses wrong and everything and they'd call you a maverick prima donna. If you were busted you could just call it "poetic licence."

TRISH: None of that made sense. And I do not get my tenses wrong. (*She sighs.*) I could be another Brontë.

GAVIN: Aren't there like eight of them?

TRISH: Close. Three.

GAVIN: Never pegged you for a chicken, though.

TRISH: Excuse me?

GAVIN: You tossed your hat into both rings and you're second-guessing your decision. Comfortable with Creative Writing, but Journalism scares you. (*TRISH looks briefly down at her shoes but does not respond.*) A little fear is good. It keeps things from being boring. I know you. You'd be bored out of your mind doing something that didn't freak you out sometimes. The Grammar thing is a challenge but you live for that stuff. Remember when you learned how to fix the DVD player? (*Pause.*) Okay not the same thing but my point is that you're super smart, you're a quick study and you're gonna do great. Don't let it get the best of you.

TRISH: Thanks. So, you're my analyst now?

GAVIN: Just telling you what I see.

TRISH: You see someone who's irritated and busy.

GAVIN: Sure. And scared. You're afraid of not acing the exam so you're acting like it's dumb. That's like, Avoidance 101.

TRISH: Is that the period before or after Delusion 101?

GAVIN: I'm just telling you that you're pulling As in both.

TRISH: I don't actually recall asking, but whatever.

GAVIN: I would think you'd be all over this, just so you could correct me for the rest of your life.

TRISH: I'd have to learn it all first.

GAVIN: Well then consider that your incentive.

TRISH: I admit to finding that more than a bit appealing.

GAVIN: You'll hear from Creative Writing any day now, so at least soon you'll only be worrying about one of them instead of two.

TRISH: Aren't you worried at all?

GAVIN: For what? To get an ulcer? I did what I could do. I busted my butt in my classes, and now I wait it out like a good little boy. It's out of my hands. Yeah I could worry 24/7 but there's no point. It's gonna be what it's gonna be. I'm going to grab some chicken after practice. You want me to get you some?

TRISH: I'm broke.

GAVIN: I'm asking if you want some. I'll get it.

TRISH: Oh!

GAVIN: You don't have to be so shocked.

TRISH: Well I'm not just going to assume. Thanks. I didn't realize you were swimming in cash. Things must be good in the world of frozen yogurt.

GAVIN: Oh but they are. And fruity. And nutty. And refreshing.

TRISH: And decadent.

GAVIN: Should I get the chicken or not?

TRISH: Now I want yogurt.

GAVIN: So come by the shop later.

TRISH: You won't be there.

GAVIN: So?

TRISH: So then I have to pay for it.

GAVIN: Holy freeloader, man! It all comes clear. I think I'm starting to understand why you sent me the job posting.

TRISH: No comment.

GAVIN: If you wanted free yogurt why didn't you just apply yourself?

TRISH: Have you seen your uniform?

GAVIN: Ohhh. That's below the belt, man.

TRISH: Sorry dude.

GAVIN: You never seem to mind my uniform when you have a spearmint watermelon cone in your hand. How do you even combine those anyway?

TRISH: First of all, it's peppermint cantaloupe. Second of all, it is a cacophony of flavour on my tongue that is beyond delicious. Thirdly, you in this job has been a means to an end for me, the end being "delicious." And finally, seeing you in that uniform amuses me.

GAVIN: (*Laughing.*) Bitch.

TRISH: Hey man, you gotta do what you've gotta do.

GAVIN: Okay last call. Jesus Christ, do you want the chicken or not?

TRISH: Chalet or KF?

GAVIN: Chalet.

TRISH: No thanks. That gravy is gross.

GAVIN: It's good! And, um, KF's coleslaw looks radioactive.

TRISH: It's good! The colour is to make it distinct.

GAVIN: Oh it's distinct all right.

TRISH: That gravy would not get past the first round on *Chopped.*

GAVIN: I think their shareholders would say that they're doing just fine without *Chopped.*

TRISH: I don't want brown saltwater disguised as gravy. I want peppermint cantaloupe.

GAVIN: We just took a sharp left turn away from chicken.

TRISH: Dessert is always more interesting than dinner.

GAVIN: They're both more interesting than this conversation.

TRISH: Ouch.

GAVIN: I'm just sayin'...

TRISH: You're just bitter.

GAVIN: Or better.

TRISH: Why do I love you?

GAVIN: You can't help it.

> TRISH *makes a face at him.* GAVIN *picks his backpack up from the floor and puts his phone in it.*

           I've gotta jet.

TRISH: You're not gonna stick around to say hi?

GAVIN: Can't. I've got practice like, now. (GAVIN *puts his beer can on the floor beside his chair and stands up. He picks up his backpack.*) Don't stress so much, okay? Carly is amazing and so are you. She'll have you reciting that textbook in three other languages before you know it.

TRISH: Then I could capture the international market.

GAVIN: I mean it, I'm not worried about you. I know you're gonna kill it because that's what you do. (*Jokingly.*) You're good enough, you're smart enough, and doggone it – people like you. Seriously, we all need a dose of humility to shake us up sometimes. This is yours. You can't always coast. But you do need to have some faith in yourself. Your essay was amazing and you're going to slay this test. Okay?

TRISH: Okay.

GAVIN: So no chicken?

TRISH:	Not unless it comes with fluorescent slaw.
GAVIN:	Yeah… no chicken.
TRISH:	Fine.
GAVIN:	Fine. (*He plants a kiss on her head.*) See you later.
TRISH:	See ya. (*GAVIN begins exiting.*) Oh, and Spielberg didn't direct *Poltergeist*.
GAVIN:	Yeah he did.
TRISH:	(*Calling out after him.*) Wiki it!

> *GAVIN exits. TRISH reluctantly pulls her textbook toward her.*

Scene 2

> *The remaining scenes all take place in the same location. TRISH meticulously sets up her study space on the table.*

TRISH: (*Reading aloud to herself.*) "A dangling participle is a participle or participial phrase, often found at the beginning of a sentence, that appears from its position to modify an element of the sentence other than the one it was intended to modify." (*She sighs, frustrated.*) What? "As in 'Plunging hundreds of feet into the gorge, we saw Niagara Falls.'"

> *TRISH buries her head in textbook in exasperation. CARLY enters the room unbeknownst to TRISH.*

Or as in "Plunging hundreds of feet into the gorge, Tired Trish didn't have to write this test."

CARLY: (*Walking towards the table.*) Drama Queen. As long as I don't have to scrape you up from the bottom of the gorge. You're actually making it harder than it needs to be. It's a participle intended to modify a noun that is not present in the text.

TRISH: That would all be well and good if I had a handle on participles.

CARLY: We did this.

TRISH: I know. Shoot me now.

CARLY: Think. You know it.

TRISH: A participle is a word…

CARLY: Yep?

TRISH: That's all I got.

CARLY: Trish –

TRISH: All right all right. A participle is a word formed from a verb, like "going" or "gone" from "go," that can be used as an adver- no, an adjective.

CARLY: Examples?

TRISH: Working woman. Boiling water. Rising sun.

CARLY: Good. Now a sentence with a dangler.

TRISH: Um… "Swimming in the lake, the moon shone brightly."

CARLY: Oh my god.

TRISH: What, is that wrong?

CARLY: No. (*Wistfully.*) That sounds amazing.

TRISH: I know, right? Well, except for the missing subject.

CARLY: Ooh, look at you.

TRISH: Good tutor.

CARLY: Good student.

TRISH: A swim in the lake right now would be heaven.

CARLY: Only a month 'til summer.

TRISH: Yep. This part actually makes sense.

CARLY: It all makes sense the moment it makes sense.

TRISH: Uh huh.

CARLY: That'll make sense too.

TRISH: Why did I put myself in the position of having to write an exam *and* an essay? I'm such a masochist.

CARLY: It wasn't an essay, it was a story. You love writing stories.

TRISH: Not when they decide the next four years of my life.

CARLY: It's a competitive program. They want the best. There's no reason why that can't be you. Your story was awesome; they always are. They'll love it.

TRISH: Thanks. (*Pause.*) It took me two weeks to decide what to name the horse.

CARLY: More like five or six. First it was Brandy…

TRISH:	Hey, it was Brandy for a whole four days. No other name lasted that long. "Priscilla" only stuck for ten minutes.
CARLY:	That's because Priscilla is either Elvis's wife or the Queen of the Desert. Priscilla is not a horse.
TRISH:	Hence the ten minutes.
CARLY:	So what happened to Brandy?
TRISH:	She dies at the end. It's 25 degrees out, aren't you hot in those sleeves?
CARLY:	No I'm not and I know she dies, you nutbar. I read it, remember? I mean why'd you change the name?
TRISH:	Oh, I don't know. It was fine for four days and then one afternoon I typed it and it felt wrong coming out of my fingers. Just totally wrong.
CARLY:	Good choice in the end.
TRISH:	Thanks, I think so.
CARLY:	Jezebel's a cool name for a horse.
TRISH:	Isn't it? Jezebel's mane shone. Intransitive.
CARLY:	Indeed.
TRISH:	Do you ever think of what you'll do if you don't get in? Like, anywhere?
CARLY:	Yeah, of course.
TRISH:	I think about it every night. I don't sleep much.
CARLY:	That's not going to happen.
TRISH:	I don't know that. You don't know that. (*TRISH gets up from the table and begins slowly pacing.*)
CARLY:	What is with all this worry all of a sudden? You're probably going to get into CW. Pass this exam and you're a shoo-in for Journalism too. You're just nervous. Everyone is.
TRISH:	I handed in the story before I started studying for this test. There were things I didn't know when I handed it in... what if there's a participle dangling somewhere?
CARLY:	Stop worrying.
TRISH:	Yesterday I was feeding Henna. Same as I do every morning, same as I have every morning since I was, like, ten years old. Half of a cup of dry food, half a cup of moist, some water and some honeydew.

CARLY: I thought it was cantaloupe?

TRISH: That's the frozen yogurt I like.

CARLY: Right.

TRISH: So I gave her the cantaloupe –

CARLY: Honeydew.

TRISH: Right. And went upstairs and took my shower, like I always do. Then I came back down and fed her. Again. As in, all over again. Fifteen minutes later. Dry, wet, honeydew. All again. Absolutely no memory that I'd already done it. How do you feed a dog twice in twenty minutes and not remember? That's crazy. That's like, dementia.

CARLY: I think you can rule out dementia.

TRISH: It's like this stupid test and the story and these applications have literally – figuratively – eaten away at my brain. I don't know. It's weird. I don't really feel like myself. I feel like… I can't describe it. A chrysalis maybe.

CARLY: I would've said pupa, or larva. Not pretty words. You? "Chrysalis." That's why you're the writer, and I'm the architect.

TRISH: You did build amazing forts in Grade 7.

CARLY: That is some truth, right there.

TRISH: I think I'm freaking out a little.

CARLY: The cocoon is nice. I get it.

TRISH: Yeah.

CARLY: One morning about two weeks ago I'm eating cereal. Cereal's been pretty much a daily occurrence in my life since I was two. I sit for ten minutes, eating it, and when I'm done I look down at the bowl and it's totally empty. Not a flake left. I didn't realize that I'd eaten it. At all. An entire bowl in my mouth and down my throat and I didn't notice. I know exactly what you mean.

TRISH: I hope it wasn't Froot Loops because that would be sad.

CARLY: Shredded Wheat.

TRISH: Your brain did you a favour. Ew.

CARLY: We were out of Corn Flakes. And my mom ate all the granola.

TRISH: Whoever invented that stuff should be exiled. Christ, it's like eating a barn.

CARLY: Pretty much. We're all preoccupied. Everyone's trying to look calm when everyone's freaking out. You think I'm sure about what I'm doing? I know that I want to be an architect. I think I'd be good at it 'cuz I like building. And I like buildings. I like looking at buildings and wondering whose lives are unfolding inside them and imagining what stories they would tell. But does that mean anything? Not really. It's all speculation until it isn't. I think I'll get in. I think I'll spend four years mind-expanding and come out the other end ready to design the most stunning building that ever was, but I'm just hoping. We're all just hoping. And trying. And believing in a future because we have to.

TRISH: Crap. Now I want Froot Loops.

CARLY: (*Looking around.*) Who am I talking to?

TRISH: Sorry.

CARLY: Split infinitives. Go.

TRISH: Uh… something about adverbs. Can I look at the book?

CARLY: No.

TRISH: I'm going to look at the book.

CARLY: Then why'd you ask me?

TRISH: 'Cuz I'm polite. (*She flips the page to the section on split infinitives and reads aloud.*) "A split infinitive is a grammatical construction in which an adverb or adverbial phrase comes between the marker 'to' and the bare infinitive form of a verb."

CARLY: I don't think you need the book.

TRISH: "An example of a split infinitive is 'To generously sprinkle,' because 'generously' splits the word 'to' from the word 'sprinkle.'"

CARLY: Most famous example?

TRISH: *Star Trek.* "To boldly go where no man has gone before."

CARLY: Splits are good to know about in case they ask but –

TRISH: The rule is barely enforced anymore and they've become accepted now.

CARLY: You *know* this.

TRISH: I humbly thank you for the vote of confidence.

CARLY: I mean it, you know more than you think you do.

TRISH: A few boys have told me that... Seriously though, how do you know all of this stuff?

CARLY: I learned it really young.

TRISH: But how do you remember?

CARLY: What is the Pythagorean Theorem?

TRISH: Huh?

CARLY: The Pythagorean Theorem. What is it?

TRISH: The square of the hypotenuse is equal to the sum of the square of the other two sides.

CARLY: How do you know that?

TRISH: I don't know. I learned it and it's stuck in my brain.

CARLY: Exactly. That's it. You learned it. Once you learn something you might forget it, but you can never unlearn it. It's always in there somewhere.

TRISH: I can write without knowing all of this stuff.

CARLY: That's true. You can.

TRISH: People make amazing music without knowing theory.

CARLY: They do.

TRISH: You don't care what I'm saying, do you?

CARLY: Not much. If you can know more, if you can know that what you're writing or saying is not only eloquent, but correct – why wouldn't you? Besides, it's fun.

TRISH: In what universe?

CARLY: Stop whining.

TRISH: (*Quite obviously whining.*) I'm not whining.

> CARLY *gives her an irritated look.*

            So... you excited about prom?

CARLY: I guess.

TRISH: I hear the food's gonna be yummy.

CARLY: For the price of the ticket it'd better be.

TRISH: Do you have your dress?

CARLY: No. You?

TRISH: I don't even have a date, much less a dress.

CARLY: What?? Since when?

TRISH: It's his aunt's wedding. The same night. She met a man while on retreat in Kathmandu and came back engaged. She's like 55 and everyone in their family's been waiting for her to get married since the 80s so it's a huge deal. He can't get out of it.

CARLY: Oh man. I'm sorry hon. Do you still want to go? Someone else will ask you I bet.

TRISH: I don't know. He invited me to the wedding but I've never even met this aunt and you only have one senior prom, you know?

CARLY: He should understand if you still want to go, with a friend. As soon as you tell people you're going alone, someone else will ask you I'm sure.

TRISH: I'm not sure of that at all.

CARLY: Oh please. You're smart and you're pretty. Someone will ask you.

TRISH: You have an amazing date!

CARLY: He'll do.

TRISH: I don't feel smart. I open this damn book and I feel stupid.

CARLY: Because you're smart.

TRISH: I knew you were going to say that.

CARLY: The curse of eight years of friendship. You're smart. You skipped a grade, and even a year younger than the rest of us you still get really good marks and you're a great writer. You're not used to asking, you're used to knowing. Now you don't know and it's uncomfortable. It's a classic case of –

TRISH: Let me guess – Ego 101.

CARLY: Ha! Sort of, yeah. Is that a Gavin diagnosis?

TRISH: Uh huh. I won't have room for any electives now that I have to fit Ego 101 into my schedule along with the other 101s.

CARLY: Which are?

TRISH: Delusion and Avoidance. Clearly my brother thinks I'm a very sound, pleasant person.

CARLY: I don't know if I can argue with the second one. We have 45 minutes and you spent three of them talking about the prom.

TRISH: I should've written my story about my prom plans. It would've been short.

CARLY: Your story was great. When Jezebel gave her last exhale I freakin' lost it.

TRISH: I think it's good. I do. Of course, it might be full of grammatical faux pas.

CARLY: I doubt it. And if it is you can't do anything about it now. When you submit your next one, it'll be a syntax paradise. Comma splices. Go.

TRISH: "A comma splice is the use of a comma to join two independent clauses. Comma splices often arise when writers use conjunctive adverbs to separate two independent clauses instead of using a coordinating conjunction." Well at least I know what a conjunction is.

CARLY: Good. A coordinating conjunction is one of these seven words: for, and, nor, but, or, yet, so. A conjunctive adverb is a word like furthermore, however, or moreover.

TRISH: As in "Furthermore, I don't give a damn."

CARLY: Like hell you don't.

TRISH: "A conjunctive adverb and a comma, or a conjunctive adverb between two commas, is not strong enough to separate two independent clauses and creates a comma splice."

CARLY: Right. So what do you need?

TRISH: "Only semicolons and periods are strong enough to separate two independent clauses without a conjunction."

CARLY: Which are?

TRISH: For, and, nor, but, or, so.

CARLY: And?

TRISH: I already said and.

CARLY: No I mean you're missing one.

TRISH: I can't remember it.

CARLY: You didn't even try!

          TRISH struggles to recall the missing conjunction but can't.

Yet.

TRISH: Ah! Yes. As in "Are we done with comma splices yet?"

CARLY: Uh, no – to that example and to your question.

TRISH: I'm just playing. I get these, I do.

CARLY: (*Getting out of her chair.*) Let's make sure.

> *CARLY goes to the chalkboard. She writes a sentence with a comma splice in it on the board. She then holds out the chalk for TRISH to take.*

Correct it.

> *TRISH walks to the chalkboard and looks at it for moment. She picks up the chalk and corrects the sentence, then looks at CARLY.*

Okay, we're good. Why don't we do a quick review of transitive and intransitive verbs?

TRISH: Why don't we do a quick review of lunch? I'm starving.

CARLY: I have a protein bar.

TRISH: I'll take it.

> *CARLY reaches into her bag and hands TRISH a protein bar. TRISH unwraps it and takes a bite. She speaks with her mouth full.*

Maybe I should've gone for the chicken.

CARLY: You turned down chicken?

TRISH: But I hate that gravy.

CARLY: Then don't have gravy. You act like it's baked into the chicken.

TRISH: I messed up. I should've said yes and asked for ketchup.

CARLY: Ketchup works.

TRISH: As Gavin would say, "My stomach is having a conversation with itself."

CARLY: It's telling you off. That's what happens when you turn down chicken. Okay, transitive verbs.

TRISH: Verbs that have an object to receive that action.

CARLY: Full definition.

TRISH: Seriously?

CARLY: Full.

TRISH: Transitive verbs are action verbs that have an object to receive the action.

CARLY: In a sentence?

TRISH: Gavin ate the chicken.

CARLY: Good. Give me an intransitive verb in a sentence.

TRISH: Trish's stomach grumbled.

CARLY: Never say no to chicken.

TRISH: It's not fair that someone going into architecture is such a grammar guru.

CARLY: Damn it – now *I* want some chicken.

TRISH: And Froot Loops.

CARLY: Oh god yes.

TRISH: But not together.

CARLY: I wouldn't rule it out.

TRISH: Do we have to do any more of this today?

CARLY: We kind of just started.

TRISH: I know, I'm sorry. My head's just not really in it.

CARLY: You're thinking of food.

TRISH: And frozen yogurt.

CARLY: You've been thinking of food constantly since you were 11.

TRISH: Puberty made me extremely hungry. I make no apologies.

          CARLY picks up her phone to check the time and sees a new email message.

CARLY: Jesus. Another reminder about prom tickets. We know already.

TRISH: So is it a suit or a tux?

CARLY: Suit I think.

TRISH: It's in two weeks! When are you getting your dress?

CARLY: I haven't had any time. I've been more interested in studying for finals than comparing satin and taffeta.

TRISH: You want me to go with you this weekend? I have to study on Saturday but Sunday's good. I can live vicariously. I hope all the good stuff isn't gone.

CARLY: I think the whole prom thing is totally overblown in our society. It's just a party. A very expensive party that leaves teenagers feeling even more stressed than they already feel.

TRISH: I don't know, there's something kind of nice about it, I think. You don't?

CARLY: I didn't say that. I just think that it might be more of a hassle than it's worth. It's that one final ritual that solidifies, just in case anyone forgot, who's actually the koolest. Can't we all just be equal at prom?

TRISH: When is anyone ever equal at prom? There's no equality when you graduate and everyone knows it. There's a valedictorian. There's a king and queen. Some of us graduate with honours and some don't. Some will get into university and some won't. Some kids have full scholarships, some will be working in frozen yogurt shops for the next four years.

CARLY: And… we're back to food.

TRISH: I'm right. Equality only actually exists in principle before we're born. It disappears the minute we come out. One baby's born poor, another's born rich. One's born black and another's born white. The whole idea of a level playing field is bogus. We try to convince ourselves that we can achieve it but the fact that some people aren't even born on the field means that we can't.

CARLY: All the more reason to be annoyed with the prom thing. If you know you're going to be on uneven ground for the rest of your life, the last thing you need before stepping out onto it is to take part in some bizarre ritual that we all know is about having the dress and the shoes and the waistline and the hair and the cleavage and the date on your arm that will make everyone in the room jealous.

TRISH: Okay, but maybe it could be a fun diversion from the other stuff. And romantic.

CARLY: We'll see.

TRISH: Well it kind of has to be. Did you forget this year's theme? "Love Is In The Air."

CARLY: They don't hold back on originality on the prom committee.

TRISH: Hmm. Love. Or semen.

CARLY: Ew.

TRISH: You know it's true.

CARLY: Well at least the theme is subtle. Why didn't they just name it "This Prom Will Be Romantic, Damn It."

TRISH: Hershey's Kisses on every table, I hear.

CARLY: And a condom in the gift bags.

TRISH: Get. Out.

CARLY: Damn that was a great movie.

TRISH: Condoms?

CARLY: They were told no but I hear that they're going to sneak them in at the last minute.

TRISH: Shut up. Principal Heller's gonna go ballistic.

CARLY: I'm thinking that's the point.

TRISH: Ah but you're wrong. The point, dear Carly, is that Love Is in the Air.

CARLY: I hope we're not paying for those gift bags in the cost of our tickets.

TRISH: Of course we are.

CARLY: Those things are for 10-year-olds' birthday parties.

TRISH: Minus the condoms.

CARLY: Who knows? They're starting young these days.

TRISH: That's gross.

CARLY: Am I lying?

TRISH: I still don't get why you need to apply to a program halfway across the country. It's so much more expensive and everyone in your life is here.

CARLY: Which is exactly why I think it might be a good idea to go.

TRISH: You seriously just said that.

CARLY: Trish, Dalhousie has a great architecture school.

TRISH: Yeah, in the freakin' Atlantic. If you don't want to stay here I get it, sort of, but Waterloo is good too.

CARLY: I don't want to live in Waterloo.

TRISH: Okay then McGill. They have a great program there and at least we could visit.

CARLY: We can't visit if I'm in Nova Scotia?

TRISH: I mean driving.

CARLY: It's possible to drive to Halifax.

TRISH: You know what I mean. You know how far it is to drive to Halifax from here? I checked. 1,100 miles. That's a thousand miles, and then another hundred. How often could we do that?

CARLY: Why can't you just be happy for me that I know what I want? Why is that so difficult?

TRISH: Because it came out of nowhere. You never said a word about leaving town until a week before applications were due and suddenly you're all about the Maritimes.

CARLY: Yeah, I am. I want the ocean, and lobster, and Acadian men.

TRISH: Pardon?

CARLY: Nothing. I'm kidding. Look, you want to study here and I'm happy for you. I'm really really happy for you. I want something else.

TRISH: Do you think I didn't think of leaving? I thought of leaving. Do you know that? For a nanosecond. But then it was like "Of course I'm not leaving. My family is here. My best friend is here." I never considered it after that.

CARLY: So I'm supposed to feel bad? Is that the point of that story?

TRISH: No.

CARLY: Maybe I won't get in and you'll get your wish.

TRISH: That's not fair.

CARLY: Then what is it? You considered leaving. You made a decision. I considered leaving, and I made a different one. Be happy for me. That's what friends do.

TRISH: That is what friends do. You're right. (*Pause.*) I thought you were my sister.

CARLY looks away and says nothing.

I know you don't want to live in Waterloo. But McGill... you'd still be in a different province if that's what you need –

CARLY: That's what I need.

TRISH: – but close.

CARLY: Maybe I don't want to be close.

TRISH is clearly stunned. She closes her notebook.

TRISH: Wow.

CARLY: Trish –

TRISH: Have I done something to hurt you? Have I upset you in some way that I don't know about?

CARLY: Of course not.

TRISH: Are you sure?

CARLY: You haven't done anything, Trish. Do you think I'd be tutoring you if you had?

TRISH: I don't know, maybe, I have no idea. If someone had told me a couple of months ago that you'd leave Toronto – I would've said "No way." So I'm not really sure about anything.

CARLY: I would tell you.

TRISH: I'd hope so.

CARLY: When was the last time I was pissed at you and you didn't know it? I would tell you.

TRISH: Okay. (*Pause.*) Oh. I get it. That comment, about Acadian men.

CARLY: That was a joke.

TRISH: Was it?

CARLY: I was kidding.

TRISH: No you weren't. That wasn't a joke. That's why you don't really care about the prom. You're going to break up –

CARLY: I need some space.

TRISH: Wow. Why would you not –

CARLY: Trish, please.

TRISH: I'm hungry and I can't talk any more right now. I need to eat. I've got to go.

> *TRISH stands and picks up her books and purse. As she starts to walk towards the door, she fails to notice when she accidentally drops her pen.*

Scene 3

> *CARLY notices and moves from her chair to pick it up.*

CARLY: (*Walking towards the pen.*) Hold on. Your pen.

> *TRISH stops. She turns around at the very moment that CARLY bends down to pick up the pen. As CARLY bends over, her blouse falls forward and TRISH notices something strange on CARLY's right arm, just below the shoulder.*

TRISH: What's that? (*CARLY hands TRISH the pen.*)

CARLY: What?

TRISH: On your arm.

> *CARLY stands up quickly and adjusts her blouse.*

CARLY: You know, walking away because you don't like what I'm saying is pretty lame.

TRISH: What *is* that?

CARLY: Nothing.

> *CARLY turns to head back to the table.*

TRISH: What's on your arm?

CARLY: Trish just go. Our session's done and it's pretty clear that you don't support my decision for my own education – based on you walking away and all – so hey, just keep going. Leave. You're welcome for picking up the pen.

TRISH: It's not just your education. It's your whole future.

CARLY: Yes it is. Mine. And yours is yours.

TRISH: (*Taken aback.*) Point taken.

CARLY: I appreciate that.

TRISH: But I think you're wrong.

CARLY: Because you want me to stay.

TRISH: That's not the only –

CARLY: (*Under her breath.*) Like there's nothing else I could be doing…

TRISH: Pardon?

CARLY: Do you honestly think that there is nowhere more exciting that I could be right now than here going over grammar rules with you?

TRISH: I didn't ask you to do that. You offered to do that.

CARLY: Yes I did. Because you're my friend. Because I want you to succeed. However you choose to. I want for you what you want for you.

TRISH: I don't know what I'm supposed to say.

CARLY: There's no "supposed to."

TRISH: I'm sorry that tutoring me has kept you from more exciting things.

CARLY: I'm not trying to be a bitch. I'm not.

TRISH: I'd hate to see you trying.

CARLY: Weren't you leaving? Weren't you hungry?

TRISH: It can wait.

CARLY: Oh I see. I believe I was speaking to you and you walked away in the middle of it because you were hungry. So go, stuff your face. Knock yourself out.

TRISH: What's on your arm, Carly?

CARLY: Oh for heaven's sake just go.

TRISH: Did you fall and land on your arm?

CARLY: You really do need to eat. You're seeing things.

TRISH: I saw something there.

CARLY: I rest my case.

TRISH: Did you burn yourself with your curling iron or something?

CARLY: Go. Eat some Fruit Loops. Although perhaps you've been eating too many.

TRISH: Did you crash into something on your bike?

CARLY: No.

TRISH: Then what was that?

CARLY: I don't know, it must've been a shadow or something.

TRISH: A shadow. Really. So if I turn on the light it should disappear then.

CARLY: You can stay if you like. I'll go.

> *CARLY picks up her knapsack with her right arm and then quickly transfers it to her left; as if uncomfortable. She begins walking away.*

TRISH: What happened to your arm, Carly?

CARLY: Okay, yes, I lost control of my bike and crashed into a parking meter. Are you happy now? It's totally embarrassing.

TRISH: I thought it was a shadow.

CARLY: I lied. I feel like an idiot. I was riding on the sidewalk which I shouldn't have been doing, because I'm a wuss and I was scared of traffic. I swerved to avoid a cat that crossed in front of me and I ran into a parking meter.

TRISH: Are you okay?

CARLY: Yeah I'm fine.

TRISH: Then that's kind of hilarious.

CARLY: I'm such a loser.

TRISH: You're not a loser, (*Pause.*) you're a liar.

CARLY: It's a bad idea for this to continue.

TRISH: You would've texted me 10 minutes after that happened. You would've called me that night laughing hysterically.

CARLY: Is it so impossible that I didn't tell you something? There's that ego again. Maybe I was in pain and I didn't find it funny.

TRISH: What happened to your arm, Carly?

CARLY: I'm out of here.

TRISH: Avoidance 101. I have an A in it, remember? Can smell it a mile away.

CARLY: Don't forget, you're an ace at Delusion too.

TRISH: What happened to your arm?

CARLY: I already answered that question.

TRISH: What happened to your arm, Carly?

CARLY: Get some dinner, Trish.

TRISH: What happened?

CARLY: Have a good night.

TRISH: What happened to your arm, Carly?

CARLY: Enjoy your chicken.

TRISH: Did a man do that to you?

CARLY: Back off, Trish. Just back the hell off.

TRISH: I get it. Oh my god – it's why you don't want to go to the prom, why you haven't tried to get a dress. It's why you want to leave. But you don't need to be embarrassed. You didn't do anything.

CARLY: What? You're damn right I didn't do anything.

TRISH: I think I understand.

CARLY: I'm dying to hear your theory.

TRISH: You did not ride into a parking meter. I know that much.

CARLY: You think you know a lot.

TRISH: I know your story is BS.

CARLY: I said back off Trish or I'm going to go to places you don't want me to go.

TRISH: Like Dalhousie?

CARLY: Ha! Yes.

TRISH: That's better than here?

CARLY: It's better than hell.

TRISH: I knew it. A man did this to you. Let me see –

> *TRISH reaches to pull down CARLY's collar, partially revealing a bruise.*

CARLY: I said BACK OFF!

> *TRISH is stunned and almost loses her balance at CARLY's bark.*

I can appreciate that you enjoy playing detective, but Nancy Drew is long behind us.

TRISH: Can I just ask you, please, one question?

CARLY: You can ask whatever you like.

TRISH: That you'll answer.

CARLY: You can ask whatever you like.

TRISH: The man who did this to you… are you seeing him?

> *CARLY just stares at her.*

Are you seeing him?

> *There is a long pause.*

CARLY: Yes.

> *TRISH looks at CARLY before speaking.*

TRISH: Okay. (*Pause.*) Now it makes sense.

CARLY: Trish, it would be really smart for one of us to leave right now.

TRISH: No. That's why you wouldn't tell me.

> *CARLY is silent as she turns away from TRISH. Finally she speaks.*

CARLY: How could I?

TRISH: I just want to help. I'm not mad at you.

CARLY: Wha – at me? Why the hell would you be mad at me?

TRISH: Because of… you know.

CARLY: No I don't know. Why would you be mad at me? You already said I didn't do anything wrong.

TRISH: And you didn't. I mean not to get hit. No one deserves to be hit by someone even if she's cheating on somebody else.

CARLY: WHAT? (*Silence.*) Is that why you think I didn't tell you that someone – that someone was – was hurting me? Because… because I'm cheating?

TRISH: Isn't it?

CARLY: Trish… no.

TRISH: What do you mean no? I'm sorry but I'm totally confused. You said that you're seeing the person who did this to you.

CARLY: I am.

TRISH: But that would be Gavin –

> *TRISH stops dead in her tracks and stares at CARLY. There is a dialogue-free exchange between the two of them, during which it becomes clear that TRISH realizes that CARLY is identifying Gavin as the man who inflicted the bruise. CARLY realizes that TRISH is overwhelmed.*

CARLY: Trish –

TRISH: Be quiet.

CARLY: I have never –

TRISH: Don't speak.

CARLY: I have never – not even once – cheated on your brother.

TRISH: You… you're – no, no.

CARLY: It's true. (*Pause.*) Why couldn't you just let me leave?

TRISH: I'm sorry…

CARLY: Me too.

TRISH: … but I don't believe you.

> CARLY *walks across the room and sits down. There is a heavy silence.*

CARLY: I knew you wouldn't. Or perhaps more accurately, I knew you couldn't.

TRISH: I don't believe it.

CARLY: That's why I was just going to leave. So I wouldn't have to see the day when you said that to me.

TRISH: No. I believe what you said before. About the parking meter. I believe that.

CARLY: That wasn't –

TRISH: I can totally believe that. You've always been such a klutz, as long as I can remember. I can see you crashing right into it.

CARLY: Trish –

TRISH: And I get that you'd be embarrassed because no one wants to admit that they can't ride their own bike without crashing into things, on the sidewalk no less.

CARLY: Trish –

TRISH: No, sorry – singular pronouns – that he or she can't ride his or her own bike…

CARLY: Trish –

TRISH: Oh, but "their" is now used as a singular pronoun too –

CARLY: Stop! Trish… stop.

TRISH: Or it was a shadow like you said. The light played tricks on me maybe.

> CARLY *shakes her head.*

CARLY: Then turn on the light. Like you said before, it should disappear.

TRISH stands still.

TRISH: Gavin wouldn't hurt a fly.

CARLY: Maybe so. I'm not a fly. Turn on the light, Trish.

TRISH doesn't move. CARLY begins to take off her blouse.

TRISH: What are you doing?

CARLY: There's more than one.

TRISH: Don't. Please.

CARLY rebuttons the blouse.

CARLY: That's what I said to your brother.

TRISH: Shut the hell up. You're saying... you're saying that Gavin... Gavin... oh HELL NO. Carly, what is wrong with you? What the hell is wrong with you? This is insane. Dear God, you're insane.

CARLY: I was just going to leave. I was going to Halifax.

TRISH: Because – because my brother... my brother... beats you. That's what you're telling me? That's your story.

CARLY: Stories are your thing Trish.

TRISH: Don't be smart with me, bitch. I don't know why you're saying this. I don't know how you could protect the animal that's doing this to you, and throw my brother under the bus. I don't know how you can look in the mirror and do this, how you can call yourself my friend and do this. You have known us for years, you know how we were raised. You do this to my mom? To my dad? They adore you. You've sat at their table, ridden in their car, slept in their house. You say this about their son?

CARLY: I wish I didn't have to.

TRISH: You don't. This other man – the one you're protecting? Why? Who is he? Is he married?

CARLY: No one hates that I'm saying this more than I do.

TRISH: I can guarantee that that is untrue. Is he one of our teachers? Is he blackmailing you? Tell me. Does he have video or just snapshots?

CARLY: I should slap your face.

TRISH: Why don't you?

CARLY: Because then I'd be no better than your brother.

TRISH: Don't you say another word you little whore.

CARLY: How could you.

TRISH: ME?

CARLY: Yes, you. How DARE you. How dare you say that to me? So now I'm a tramp? Is that it? Who am I cheating with, Trish? Who did this? Our principal? The janitor? The parish priest?

TRISH: I don't know.

CARLY: Well I DO KNOW. What you saw on my arm was put there by YOUR brother. Whom I *love*. Whom I have tried for months to love through this charade. It wasn't like this the whole time. For a whole year it wasn't like this. Gavin can be an incredibly sweet person. He's held my hand through a lot of crap and all I want is for him to be who I know he can be all the time.

TRISH: (*Barely audible.*) None of us is perfect.

CARLY: What? WHAT? Okay – I know that you love him but I don't give a damn anymore. Thank you for that brilliant piece of insight Trish. I didn't realize that the only two options were perfection or violence! You know me Trish. You know me. I don't want Gavin to be perfect! I want Gavin to not hit me!

TRISH: You say I know you. I know HIM.

CARLY: Some of him.

TRISH: Don't say that. Don't say these things. I need to get away from here.

CARLY: So do I. I just need to get further.

> *TRISH remains silent.*

It's happened four times.

> *TRISH says nothing.*

Your brother has beaten me four times.

> *TRISH stares at CARLY, silent. She walks the garbage can and picks it up. TRISH sits back down and positions the bucket in front of her, then leans over it.*

TRISH: Go on.

CARLY: Are you sure?

TRISH: Go on, or get out!

CARLY: (*As if reliving.*) He grabs my arms so tightly and it hurts so much, like he's trying to cut off the circulation... He squeezes until they bruise and digs his nails into them... He shakes me – really hard – and it feels like I'm having a seizure... That concussion from the soccer ball wasn't from a soccer ball... He pushes me... He shoves me into walls... He jabs me with his knees. I have a huge bruise on my shin from the last time... A kick – the first one – He'd never kicked me before... I decided to go to Dalhousie the day he kicked me.

TRISH: I don't know whom you're talking about... I can't listen to any more.

CARLY: I love your family, Trish. I do not want to hurt any of you. But I didn't do anything to Gavin. He did it to me, and he sure as hell wasn't thinking about what it might do to you or your parents or ME when he did.

TRISH: I don't understand. I don't. My brother has always worshipped you.

CARLY: You've got it confused. Gavin doesn't worship me. *You* worship Gavin.

TRISH: I've never met that person. That person is a stranger to me.

CARLY: Gavin began a relationship with me. And then Gavin began another relationship with which I cannot compete. He drinks too much. Gavin drinks too much. You know that. We all know that.

> TRISH *says nothing.*

           We argue sometimes like every couple does. We disagree. But if he's been drinking, the disagreements turn into fights, those fights are scary and I end up with "shadows."

TRISH: He's been drinking less recently. A lot less. He really has.

> CARLY *points to the beer can under the table.*

CARLY: Yours?

> TRISH, *again, says nothing.*

           In the school.

TRISH: It was after school.

CARLY: Let's add Denial 101 to your course load. You're not allowed to have beer in school Trish!

TRISH: So I'm just supposed to believe you, is that how it goes? You tell me my brother's a monster and I just believe you.

CARLY: I'm not that naïve. I knew you wouldn't know what to do with this. I get that. But I also know you can tell when I'm lying, and you can tell when I'm not. Your brother has had some horrible, horrifying moments. But he's not a monster. He needs help dealing with some things and he needs it now, very very badly, before he cracks some poor girl's skull open.

TRISH sits perfectly still.

TRISH: When we were little he protected me from the bullies.

CARLY: Life is full of contradictions.

TRISH: He has stood up for me my entire life.

CARLY: That I do know.

TRISH: You have no clue what you're asking of me… what are you asking of me?

CARLY: That I don't know. I can't tell you exactly what to do. All I know is that he needs help.

TRISH: You're afraid… of Gavin. You're afraid of Gavin.

CARLY: Yes. But I'm more afraid of becoming okay with Gavin. (*She pauses.*) Trish, if it was anyone else I would've been gone after the first time. I know I would've. Then, after the second time, I adopted a "three strikes and you're out" policy. They were very hard strikes.

TRISH: You said it happened four times.

CARLY: Which is what happens when you ignore your own policy.

TRISH: How could you – sorry, nothing.

CARLY: How could I let it? Because he burst into tears after every time. Because I convinced myself that if the drinking stopped, when it stopped, that it would never happen again.

TRISH: I really don't think it would.

CARLY: Maybe. But that's a hypothesis that I'm not willing to collect any more bruises to test. I was never going to say anything. And I know that that might make me a really, really bad person, because I was willing to run to Halifax and bury it and leave him here to do it to someone else.

TRISH: Why didn't you tell me?

CARLY: Are you kidding? Because of THIS. Because you adore him. And even though my love for myself was greater than my distaste for him, my distaste for him was never greater than my love for you.

TRISH: I don't know if I can keep talking about this right now Carly. I just…

CARLY: Do you need –

TRISH: No.

CARLY: You have to talk to your brother. Or you have to tell your folks and they have to. He has to get some help. Now. Because the next girl won't be torn. He'll go to jail, Trish. And he'll deserve it.

TRISH: I never saw anything. I never noticed… anything.

CARLY: That's the way it usually goes.

TRISH: … not anything.

CARLY: You can spend the night at my place if you don't think you can go home. (*Trish doesn't respond.*) I need to go to the bathroom. If you'd rather I didn't come back, tell me right now and I won't.

> CARLY *waits to see if* TRISH *speaks; she doesn't.* CARLY *exits.* TRISH *turns off one of the lamps and sits alone in silent contemplation. Suddenly,* GAVIN *unexpectedly re-enters the space. Wearing his knapsack, he holds a plastic bag in his left hand, and a small paper bag and a smoothie in his right.* TRISH *is shocked.*

GAVIN: Hey! Great you're still here.

TRISH: What? What are you –

GAVIN: (*Walking towards her.*) Nice to see you Bro? Nice to see you too Sis? How was practice? Well it was great, Sis, thanks for asking! Were you nice enough to bring me a frozen yogurt smoothie? Why yes, yes I was.

TRISH: Why are you back?

GAVIN: Hey do you want this or not? Cantaloupe Peppermint. It's gonna melt. How did your session go? Did you learn to parse? I looked it up, by the way. And not on Wikipedia.

TRISH: I thought you were going straight home.

GAVIN: I thought so too but I figured you guys might work late and I know you wanted yogurt and Carly hadn't eaten so I swung by. Don't be too happy to see me or anything.

TRISH: Thanks for the smoothie. I just – I didn't expect you.

GAVIN: Well I'm all about surprises. Hey where's my girl? Damn it, tell me she didn't leave already. I brought her some chicken.

TRISH: She went to the washroom. I need to go too –

> *At that moment CARLY re-enters. She is behind GAVIN, facing TRISH. He does not see her.*

GAVIN: She, unlike you, appreciates the Chalet.

> *CARLY, looking directly at TRISH, begins to slowly take off her blouse. Standing facing her friend, she reveals her arms, both of which are bruised. She remains unseen to GAVIN. TRISH stifles a gasp as GAVIN puts down his knapsack and takes a boxed dinner and a bottle of juice of out of the plastic bag, which he places on the table. Then, from the paper bag, he pulls out a can of beer.*

I was thinking about how much you've been worrying about getting into school and you know what? It doesn't matter. You get in, great. You don't, you can work for a year and try again. There's a spiffy uniform in your size at the shop, eh? Seriously, I don't care if your participles dangle. Nor do I care what that means. I'm gonna like you anyway 'cuz I kinda can't help it. (*He laughs.*) Anyway, I stop off at home after practice and guess what's in the mailbox?

> *GAVIN puts down the beer. He opens his knapsack and pulls out two large envelopes which he waves in the air.*

Woohoo babe! One pour *moi*, and one pour *vous*. (*He holds out an envelope towards her.*) Department of Creative Writing. For you. Admissions.

> *TRISH looks at CARLY. GAVIN, realizing that TRISH is looking past him, turns around. CARLY stands there, bruises exposed.*

CARLY: (*Cold and sarcastic.*) Hey babe.

> *GAVIN is stunned. He looks at her, then at TRISH, then slowly backs up against the wall as if cornered. Trish, unable to look at him, grabs the beer can from the table. GAVIN appears to quickly reach inside his jacket for a moment, but stops short. TRISH sees this, reaches into his inside breast pocket and pulls out a small flask. She looks at him in dismay. CARLY glares at him, not breaking her gaze. GAVIN slowly walks over to the chair beside the lamp and sits silently, like one awaiting trial. TRISH opens the flask and empties it on the floor.*

TRISH: One day, *that…* that's going to be someone's blood.

> *TRISH walks out, forgetting her envelope. GAVIN and CARLY stare at each other. For a moment GAVIN looks like he might speak, but says nothing. CARLY exits. GAVIN stares at his envelope and then, without opening it, slowly rips it in two and tosses it in the wastepaper basket. He eyes TRISH's envelope, picks it up, and holds in both hands, looking at it. He reaches into his knapsack to put the torn envelope inside it, and pulls his hand back out holding another can. He reaches towards the lamp and turns out the light. In the darkness, we hear the sound of a beer can opening.*

THE END

Afterword

Violence against women often starts sooner. When women are girls and when men are boys. It starts with boys not taught how to feel their emotions fully. Or perhaps more accurately, taught to NOT feel their emotions fully... the one exception being rage. Everything tied to vulnerability – fear and uncertainty and sadness – is cloaked in fury. Anger belies weakness. Anger feels strong. "Manly." What does that mean? In control, I think. Yet at its root, anger is unmanaged hurt and unbridled insecurity. Hurt people hurt people.

I wrote *Admissions* because I want girls to know that they are so much more than receptacle or dumping ground, or fountain of forgiveness for undeciphered male wrath. I wrote *Admissions* because I need girls to know that our love for one another as women, as sisters, as human hearts is so much bigger than the rancid residue of angered tangled spirits. So much bigger than the wounding words, the blistering blows, the provisional contrition and makeshift make-ups. You will always be bigger. You will always be more. You are freedom and force and ferocity and future. You are fire. You are fierce.

Tanisha Taitt, October 2019

Discussion Questions

1. While discussing the prom, Carly and Trish have a conversation about there not being "a level playing field" at the end of high school. Do you agree with this? Why or why not?

2. Would you characterize Gavin as a villain? Explain your answer.

3. How do you feel about Carly's initial decision to leave town quietly?

4. Do you think that Carly and Gavin should reconcile if he is able to quit drinking? Why or why not?

5. If you had to write another scene after the end of the play, what would you have happen next? What should the plan of action be for each of the three characters?

Who Killed Snow White?

Judith Thompson

Judith Thompson

Judith Thompson is a playwright, director, actor, and artistic director of RARE theatre, a company which serves the needs of communities rarely heard and seldom seen on our stages. She is also a Professor of theatre studies at the University of Guelph. She lives in Toronto with her husband, Gregor, two dogs, a cat, and adult children who come and go.

Photo by Bizerka Livaja.

*I dedicate this play to all young people who
are being or have been assaulted or bullied,
and publicly shamed through the internet.*

*There was no internet in 1970, but I was bullied for two
years almost to death, in the sense that it triggered a nearly
fatal seizure, so I understand what you are going through.*

*I promise you, it does get better. You will leave it all behind,
and you will always be a person who empathizes with those
who are suffering. I guarantee you that you will be valued
as the treasure you are. Hang in there, the day will come.*

Foreword
by Cynthia Ashperger

Canada's brilliant playwright Judith Thompson invited me to the *Who Killed Snow White? (WKSW)* journey in 2013. It took five years to bring this breathtaking play to its first full production; the journey to the opening night was a thrilling rollercoaster ride from start to finish, and I had the privilege of participating in it as Ramona. Up the rollercoaster went, and after numerous twists and turns, we landed for the first professional production in the summer of 2018 at 4th Line Theatre. For those who have been to "the farm" I need not describe this mystic, dreamlike theatre in Millbrook, Ontario. The sweetness and purity of it enveloped the heartbreak of *WKSW* in a healing embrace.

Three generations of female characters and their various entanglements through love attachment, desire, ignorance, joy, jealousy, betrayal, hatred, compassion, generosity, and forgiveness have been a constant in the ever-changing *WKSW*. The first *WKSW* workshop presentation was part of Groundswell Festival at Nightwood Theatre. The play was then set in an urban setting and my character Ramona was a super smart Gloria Steinem–like feminist who gave a hilarious university lecture about the etymology of the taboo word that describes the female genitals. That Ramona mourned the fact that she never had a child, while trying to save her favourite female student from self-destruction. Crack cocaine was omnipresent in the first version and many characters ended up on it, including the grandmotherly Babe. Babe spoke beautiful monologues about her late husband. Their romance was set against the backdrop of World War II. Meanwhile the young protagonist, Fancy, railed against feminism while feminist Ramona adopted her as if she were her own, only to be betrayed.

The second iteration of *WKSW* in 2015 saw the birth of new characters as it was in development with 4th Line Theatre. Demonic and hilarious Uncle Silas burst onto the stage as well as his disciples Dodge and Pratt in contrast to tender Riley. Ramona had a teenage daughter, Serena, and was married to a good man. The character of Babe was still alive, but Fancy was changed – she was now a best friend to Serena, who was the protagonist. Serena was a beautiful but shy soul – and her best friend Fancy still had a tendency to betray. The draft started with Ramona's "Furies" monologue that takes place during a sleepwalking revenge dream. Reading that first monologue out loud, I experienced waves of strong goosebumps and all of a sudden I felt transported into Ramona's mind – a feeling I've only ever experienced when speaking Judith's words. There I was, hooked once again by Judith's virtuosity with dramatic imagery: *I tore them, tore them apart with my teeth. My my hand was the axe the axe that we chop down our Christmas tree every year out at the Christmas tree farm. The axe that Jay chops the firewood with. I am…in blood now I am standing in their blood I am wading in their blood. And there is no turning back.* Yes, this second version was thick with violence and this Ramona was so full of contradictions. Strong, compassionate, smart – and yet righteous and vengeful. I fell in love with this larger-than-life warrior woman, and according to the author, I said that "more Mother" would be a good thing for the play. Indeed, the next draft got more Ramona.

And then it was 2018, and *WKSW* was getting its production at 4th Line Theatre under the confident direction of Kim Blackwell. In this version, Ramona is living out in the country and is a brilliant storyteller, too. This mother tells the story of her daughter Serena's young life. The character of Serena is played by three actors with a focus on the older teenager (played beautifully by Judith's daughter Grace Thompson). In my mind now it is a ghost story and Ramona, too, is a ghost. Ramona takes the audience through her daughter Serena's young life with passion as well as heart-breaking tenderness. Hilarious Babe (a star turn by Maya Ardal) tells us of the importance of female friendships for young women and recounts how she intervened in a disturbing instance of bullying during her days in high school while giving lessons in cruelty to her granddaughter.

"Cyberbullying" was the keyword for our discussions, a container for other important themes such as childhood, coming of age, coming out of the closet, love, self-discovery, family, friendship, fitting in, be-trayal, community, patriarchy, and suicide. Already an epic work when we started, the play was daily sharpened and shaped by the author herself. We were so lucky that J.T. was in the house, never missing a rehearsal, sitting in her seat, making copious notes. "That's the most fun," she explains. "I don't want to be sitting in a room alone all the time. I want to come to rehearsal. I don't want to miss the best part!"

WKSW is not an "issue play." It is not a theatrical sermon which tells us what to think, but rather, as with all Judith's work, it is a large and uncompromising reflection of society. The light falls on the subject gazing at herself in the mirror from many angles, and what's reflected back is deeply poetic, but also realistic. Written in the genre of magic-realism, in which characters' innermost desires, secrets, and sorrows will be revealed and manifested, this is a major work created by Canada's top dramatist at the height of her powers.

So now it is your turn to get on the rollercoaster... Fasten your seat belt – it will be a memorable ride!

October 2019

Production History

I would like to acknowledge the extraordinary contribution of 4th Line Theatre, specifically the artistic director, Kim Blackwell, to the play's development. Kim believed in this play from the very beginning, and guided me through many revisions.

Each of the actors and the designers inspired me daily to make this play into the play that deserved their talents.

Who Killed Snow White? was first produced at 4th Line Theatre, Millbrook, Ontario, August 6 – 25, 2018.

Creative Team

Written by Judith Thompson

Director	Kim Blackwell
Original Music Composition and Musical Director	Justin Hiscox
Costume Designer	Meredith Hubbard
Set & Props Designer	James McCoy
Sound Designer	Esther Vincent
Choreographer	Monica Dottor
Fight Director	Edward Belanger
Director Intern	Lisa Ryder
Apprentice Assistant Director	Lindy Finlan
Auditing Director	Simone Georges
Dance Captain	Cassandra Guthrie
Production Manager	Scott Banks
Stage Manager	Alanna Wrenshall
Assistant Stage Manager	Christine Mepstead
Production Assistant	Monica Prendergast
Site Manager	Tristan Peirce
Assistant to the Costume Designer	Katrina Fletcher
Wardrobe Manager	Samantha Baljet
Props Builder/Scenic Painter	Tristan Cruise
Musicians	Justin Hiscox, Mark Hiscox, Saskia Tomkins
Carpenter	Bruce Kennedy

Cast

RAMONA: .... Cynthia Ashperger

SERENA: .... Grace Thompson

FANCY: .... Cassandra Guthrie

RILEY: .... Tom Keat

JAY: .... Mark Hiscox

Uncle SILAS: .... Christian Lloyd

BABE: .... Maja Ardal

PRATT: .... Steven Vlahos

DODGE: .... Andrei Preda

DOREEN: .... Saskia Tomkins

ARWEN/CHORUS: .... Angel Haines

JESS/CHORUS: .... Maggie Grant

CHORUS/Young SERENA: .... Maude Rose Craig

CHORUS/Young FANCY: .... Jalen Brink

Younger SERENA: .... Meah McGahon

CHORUS/Young PRATT: .... Lev Khaimovich

CHORUS/Young DODGE: .... Alexis Mantler

CHORUS: .... Freyja Adams

CHORUS: .... Kiana Bromley

CHORUS: .... Asha Hall-Smith

CHORUS: .... Amelia Hansen

Mrs. W (alternate)/CHORUS: .... Emilee Henricks

CHORUS/Boy #2: .... Vlad Khaimovich

CHORUS: .... Emma Khaimovich

CHORUS: .... Aiden Playford

Mrs. W (alternate)/CHORUS,
Boy #1/Extra #1: .... Joseph Roper

CHORUS: .... Emma Wilson

Setting

The play is set in the present in and around Peterborough, Ontario. If you are producing the play, you may substitute the name of a local town (and hockey team.)

The premiere production was set in a field, and a barn, and through trees – but obviously this will not usually be possible. There are multiple settings in this play indoors and outdoors, but the set should invoke the natural world as much as possible, through sounds, lighting, or any other means.

Ramona's dream had Serena riding in on a white horse and because we were in a rural setting for the first production, we did have a horse, but most productions will not be able to do this. Therefore, the director is invited to use their imagination, and employ any theatrical means to give the illusion of Serena arriving on a horse.

Scene 1

A field, a barn, trees.

Music.

As the music plays, between twelve and twenty young females, and a few young males (the EXTRAS) arise from the long grasses or emerge from the trees, or the roofs, one by one.

It is dawn. RAMONA emerges from her house, in a white nightgown, searching for her daughter, SERENA. At first she walks quietly through the grasses and around the trees; she does not see the ghosts, she is looking for SERENA, but she soon walks faster and faster, and then breaks into a run, and then even climbs a tree or a roof to call for her.

RAMONA: Serena?
Serena?
Serena!
Serena.
(*And now from the roof or treetop:*) Sereeeeeeena!!!

ALL: SERENA. (*Singing.*) Sereeeeeena. Sereeeena. Sereeeena.

They sing her name in harmony, beautifully, which lulls RAMONA to sleep.

SERENA rides in on a beautiful white horse. Some young women help her off and guide her to the centre of a circle they have created. Then they dance a subtle, beautiful, welcoming dance, and then she is placed on a rock or something, which elevates her, and each of them silently greets her.

Then, slowly but steadily, they all disappear but SERENA, who goes to her mother, RAMONA, and gives her a flower.

Then she moves away, about twenty feet, and watches.

RAMONA wakes up, and sees the flower. She touches it and wonders. She looks at the horse. The horse runs away.

RAMONA: I had the dream again.

You know, the dream that all of our girls and boys arose from the dead; they were in the long grasses and the branches of maple trees, they were on the roof of the barn, and in the still pond, they were waiting. For Serena. And she arrived, on a huge white horse and they welcomed her, into the fold, their fold, their silvery arms...stretched towards her to bring her into their warm world; they were singing, these wounded angels.

Singing.

I only ever have that dream when I am here; when I walk in the dawn looking for answers to what happened, in my bare feet; and then fall asleep here, out of doors, on the rough ground. I am oh so glad I had that dream; though it shakes me to my core – I haven't had it in so many months, why did I have it again?

Maybe it's the gods telling me not to be angry anymore. But I am still angry. I have not forgiven.
I imagine them, those "golden boys" who are free, yes, free! and laughing at her grave, I
imagine them
in the dark and cold cells they should be in, if there was any justice in this world,
eating themselves alive. But of course they would not be able to eat their own hearts because they have no hearts. There is an empty space where their hearts should be. On the night they attacked my daughter their hearts
became gravel.

Sorry, I am morbid and vengeful but if you were where I am? I think you would be the same.

So, I am here and you, you people are there and though I know this is also a dream, me having an audience, at dawn, in a hay field...
Ha ha – the last time I had an audience was my wedding; one hundred beautiful friends and family all so very happy for me. Not one of them suspecting what lay in wait.
I need witnesses now, and so I thank you.

I need to tell you. So that I know it's real.

I am here to tell you her story.

Maybe you can spot the moment it began.

Maybe you can feel that moment and then, maybe we can learn from that, maybe …maybe this won't happen to other girls, or boys, yes it will, no, it doesn't have to! It doesn't have to, does it?

You tell me. I want you to tell me.

I am going to tell you the story of Serena.

I warn you, it is not easy to listen to,

but the truth must be told, don't you think?

Her father cannot tell it with me, as he cannot utter it, he cannot think it.

He cannot hear it and he cannot say it.

> *JAY appears.*

I tell her story for all the lost children.

The well-fed children, living in our peaceful and prosperous country, the healthy and happy children who are driven, driven to their graves.

Do you think your dead hear us? When you say their names, when you think about them? When you imagine them in their favourite chair? I don't know. I vacillate between "Yes, of course they hear me," to "Don't be an idiot, the dead are the dead are the dead. DONE. Forever done.

It depends on the day.

So we tell her story for them, for all of them.

We will begin at the beginning.

> *SERENA disappears.*

Scene 2

The sound of a baby crying – if there is an available baby, someone dressed as a nurse hands the baby to RAMONA.

Her spouse, JAY is there.

RAMONA: Oh my God oh my God oh my God my God she is soooo beautiful, you are so so so beautiful my little angel…

JAY: Hello! Hello there, beauty! Hey! Look at all that gorgeous hair!

RAMONA: Oh yes, yes, my furry little hedgehog, you do, you do have a lovely head of hair, don't you? Just lovely! Oh my goodness the smell, the smell of her head, Jay.

JAY: I. Wow. I just…I can't believe the…you know, the-the-the

RAMONA: Miracle of it?

JAY: Yeah. Like, there was just us and I thought you were great and gorgeous and…now…

RAMONA: There is her!

JAY: And she…is…she just IS, isn't she?

RAMONA: Oh yes, she…she certainly is. You are, aren't you, baby, you just are you, just…

JAY: All that…explosive…potential…like…like our pumpkin seeds, right? They were just seeds and now, now, a field of these huge…

RAMONA: Is he calling you a pumpkin? Who's calling you a pumpkin; you're not a pumpkin, are you?

JAY: Oh look, she's rooting for milk, look at that!

RAMONA: And she's getting it, oh yes she is, oh my, you are very. Very, very skilled my precious…a powerful suck! Such a powerful suck, she's really getting it!

JAY: Amazing.

RAMONA: Amazing. So fragile and yet so powerful.

JAY: You know. It almost makes me believe in God.

RAMONA: For me? She is God.

JAY: Yeah. Oh yeah. She is most definitely divine.

Scene 3

As RAMONA talks, the chorus moves in some way.

RAMONA: That is scene one, of course.
Do you remember your scene one? I am sure you do.
But do you remember scene two? I don't think I do. Or scene
three? Maybe scene ten but not forty-five, or forty-six. Our
memory, it skips around, we miss so many days, don't we?
I would like to show you every single day of her fifteen years
but the sad truth is that you would be bored and I do not
remember every day. I wish I did.
I want to show you
What I do remember;

What I was there for,

But also what I was *not* there for.
Because there is much in even a child's life that we are not
there for.
They have another life, outside of us.
A life that only their friends know
and also
A life inside.
That only they know,
And even they only know that one...
What does the Bible say? "Through a glass darkly."

I will show you what I know, as well as
What has been told to me, and
What I have imagined, or re-constructed.

Because I must take you by the hand and lead you
Down the path
To the water
Where:

I like to think she dived deep into the pond and she
Emerged on the other side
Into a most beautiful, peaceful...

She points to the pond.

There are many twists and turns along the way.
I am dearly hoping that one of you will have the answer.
The answer to
The question.
How...how...how did this happen?
Please.
Please.
When you have seen everything.
Will you tell me?
How?

Scene 4

First Day of School.

(*NOTE: Whenever the EXTRAS speak as a chorus, the director may decide which actors will speak particular lines.*)

EXTRAS: Once
Upon
A time
There was
A girl
Named

SERENA: SERENA

ALL: SERENA

EXTRAS: And
On the first
Day
Of Kindergarten
She was scared.
Because she missed

SERENA: My mother.

EXTRAS: We all missed our mothers.
Except I missed my dad.
Me too.
I missed both dads.
And I missed both mums.
And I missed my sister.
And I missed my granddad.
And I missed my auntie.
But Serena.
Serena
She
Missed

SERENA: My mother.

RAMONA: And I stood outside the classroom door and I watched through the little window and I saw her opening and closing her mouth, as if she couldn't get enough air, as if she needed me to breathe into her.

>*The classroom is created with all the "EXTRAS" that open and close their mouths, about three times.*

But I what I did is I walked away because she had to know that she would be fine, she could do it, she could spend the whole day away from me and she would be fine.
And she was fine. Our Serena was resilient! A gorgeous elastic band.
It was me who was not fine.

Jay said:

JAY: What? What is your problem? She'll be fine! Let go, Ramona, she needs to fledge! Let the girl FLEDGE.

RAMONA: Is that a verb? To fledge? I don't know, it sounds funny to me. But he was right. I needed to let her…fledge, though she was only five. *Five!*

Dodge and Pratt perform Don McKay's poem and lay on the charm.
Photo by Wayne Eardley, Brookside Studio.

Scene 5

SERENA runs into her mom's arms.

RAMONA: How was your first day, Serena? Was it nice? Was the teacher nice? What did you do? Did you make a friend?

SERENA: Ummmmm....

RAMONA: Well?

SERENA: (*She opens and shuts her mouth a few times.*) I don't know.

RAMONA: You don't know?

SERENA: I want an orange Popsicle. (*As a teen.*) I didn't want to disappoint her. She so wanted my first day to be perfect.

RAMONA: She was such a shy little girl. And that is heartbreaking for a parent, because there is nothing we can do but send them out there, into the world. And the world is...overwhelming for a shy child. But we cannot keep them cloistered; they must dive into this mad world.

Now I wish I so wish we had lived upon a mountain somewhere, in the middle of Bolivia, or Nepal, or the Rockies; somewhere there were no other people.

SERENA: (*Young.*) There are always other kids, Mum. (*Teen.*) There are always, always other people.

Scene 6

RAMONA, EXTRAS.

RAMONA: I keep asking myself is there anything we could have done to prevent what happened?
Anywhere we could have lived?
Or was it.

EXTRAS: 1. Written
2. Fated
3: In the stars
4. Done
5. Unavoidable
6: Written
7. Fated
8. Fated

RAMONA: From the moment she was born?

And what about them? The boys?

The golden boys with souls like rotten fruit. True, they weren't there when she walked into the water, they might as well have been. They might as well have held her head underwater – for they were there, in her head, oh they were there.

They must have been sweet little baby boys, at one time, all babies are pure.

What happened? What happened to them?

And what happened to those perfect days? Those endless days of pure imagination that went on for hours and hours and hours until we called for them to come home

RAMONA is spent.

Scene 7

Young SERENA and FANTASIA (Fancy), nine or ten,
playing together in the barn/woods.

SERENA: Sister, sister!

FANTASIA: Sister, oh Sister!

SERENA: Sister, where are you? Are you hiding in the trees with the birds? Are you hiding in the barn with the chickens?

Are you hiding in the pond with the fishies?

FANTASIA: Sister, oh Sister, HELP! Help me! The wolves the she-wolves are holding me captive! Heeelllp!

SERENA: Oh dear sister, I will save you because I...am...Super Girl. super super GIANT bluebird girl

Will SWOOP into their wolf nest and and...grab you by your hair and and FLY you right out into the air!

FANTASIA: the blue blue air

SERENA: and the white white clouds

FANTASIA: and and where will you fly me to?

SERENA: The star. The NORTH star of course!

FANTASIA: Hurry. Hurry Super Girl, they are growling and moving closer and and snapping their teeth.

SERENA: DON'T be scared! I am here!! Da da daaaa!

FANTASIA: Oh thank you, super girl. You have SAVED me!! And we're flying!

I love this flying through the air.

They are running about.

SERENA: Flying, and flying faster and faster!

BOTH: Whoooooo!

FANTASIA: And here we are! On the North Star! (*On a roof, or up a tree.*)

SERENA: It's nice here. Nice and warm, and…green! I didn't know it would be green!

FANTASIA: Nice and warm and green. And…there's Smarties!

SERENA: AND sour keys!

FANTASIA: Thank you, Super Girl, for saving me!

SERENA: You're welcome, Star Girl. I am glad you are back on your home star.

FANTASIA: The North Star.

SERENA: Yeah. OUR homestar.

FANTASIA: Fingerlock?

SERENA: Fingerlock.

FANTASIA: Best friends

SERENA: 4 ever!

FANTASIA: 4 ever.

RAMONA: Sereeeena!

BABE: Fantasia!

Scene 8

RAMONA/BABE.

RAMONA: And that friendship, that best best friends forever friendship – that was everything to Serena!

BABE: Oh my, and to Fancy too!

RAMONA: You know how obsessed young girls get with their female friends!

BABE: Oh yes! Yes, friendship is a passion for young girls. A frankly sensual, profound... I was deeply in love with my friend Pixie, we would skip out on French class and smoke stolen cigarettes on the tennis courts until Sister Antonio would come for us with the strap. "Sinners, sinners," she would shriek. We laughed so hard that Pixie actually urinated through her kilt. Always had a weak bladder, Pixie. I think that's what finally killed her. It's apparently quite a pleasant way to go.

RAMONA: It's often the most important relationship a woman will have.

BABE: Our girls relished every moment together.

RAMONA: Sleepover every weekend night.

BABE: Gobbling up the same dreadful foods, drinking the same fizzy red drinks.

RAMONA: They even thought the same thoughts!

And meanwhile, those boys, those boys were growing up, in the same neighbourhood.

They were growing from cute little cubs into...

(*With sheer hatred.*) Is there a word? Is there a word for what they became?

Scene 9

Uncle SILAS, DODGE, and PRATT – hiding behind a bush, with shotguns, hunting birds, in face masks. Boys are eight or nine.

SILAS: Okay boys, what we gotta do? Is keep low, keep still and most of all keep hidden. Do NOT start fidgeting. A lotta newbies they miss right out 'cause they get bored and they start moving around or: they take the shot too early. BIG mistake. Range of a shotgun? Forty metres – you shoot from any farther away alls it does is scare 'em off.

PRATT: Can we take these stupid masks off?

DODGE: It's itchin' my face, Uncle Si!

SILAS: Are you kiddin' me? The mask is your most important hunting accessory, guys, apart from the gun; if the birds see your fool faces they are gonna FLY – you follow them with the eyeballs only: eyeballs ONLY.

PRATT: How do you follow a bird with your eyeballs? Eyeballs see, they don't follow.

DODGE: But really truly, how can you follow with your eyeballs, Uncle Si?

SILAS: Watch. Watch, look, and listen.

DODGE: I don't want to shoot birds. I like birds. And anyway I'm cold. Lookit, my teeth are chattering.

SILAS: We are HUNTING GAME, Dodger. One of the most ancient pastimes of guys and their uncles.

PRATT: Dodge is such a loser. I wanna get me some BIRDS, oh yeah. Come on, birds, come on and get KILT, you suckers! I wanna see you drop from the sky.

DODGE: Why, Pratt? Why do you wanna kill them?

PRATT: Because. It's cool.

SILAS: What's your problem, Dodge? You feel sorry for the birds?

DODGE: No.

PRATT: Oh yes he does. He doesn't even let me step on ants! "Ants are very intelligent," he'll say.

DODGE: It's true.

PRATT: He is such a girl, he puts the birdseed out for Mom on Saturdays.

DODGE: No, I don't.

PRATT: Yes, you do, you liar. LIAR. I've SEEN you.

SILAS: SHUT UP, you guys. (*Sound of geese.*) Hear that? Hear that? They are comin' our way, you ready? Now watch, you just watch your Uncle Si.

Sound of geese, he shoots.

PRATT: Hah! You missed, Uncle Si.

DODGE: Yessss!

SILAS shoots again.

SILAS: Got him. Crafty bugger, but I shot the life outa him, didn't I? Didn't I, boys?

PRATT: Good job, Uncle Si.

DODGE: Stupid.

Scene 10

> *DOREEN is comforting DODGE; PRATT is looking on,*
> *sneering/jealous.*

DOREEN: No, my angel, you do not have to shoot birds if you don't want to!

DODGE: But Uncle Si said…

DOREEN: Nonsense. Uncle Si just wants some special time with his special nephews.

PRATT: Dodger is such a scaredy-cat! Mew. Mew.

DODGE: I am not. I just don't like to shoot, that's all.

PRATT: I'm gonna call up Dad and tell him, he's gonna hate you!

DODGE: No, please don't tell him!

DOREEN: Pratty, you will do no such thing. Oh, you are full of shit. Now come here, both of you. Shake hands. SHAKE hands.

That's right. Remember, boys, you've only got one brother.

Scene 11

RAMONA: Serena and Fancy learned about life together, stumbled around until they found their own cobbled-together child-brain answers.

> *SERENA and FANTASIA, as kids, about eight.*

SERENA: Ewwwww. I'm not EVER doing that. EVER.

FANTASIA: But you have to.

SERENA: No you don't, you don't have to.

FANTASIA: If you get married you do. That's what you have to do to have babies.

SERENA: EWWWW.

FANTASIA: My grammy says it's beautiful. If you love somebody. If you love somebody it's like flying to the moon. Or…swimming. But if you don't? It can be horrible. Like drinking sour milk.

SERENA: I hate sour milk.

FANTASIA: And she said that…*it's* a treasure. That our stinky smelly you know what? Is a treasure.

SERENA: That's stupid. Rubies and diamonds are treasures. And gold and and sapphires. Not vaginas.

FANTASIA: Unless it's a sapphire vagina…

> *They laugh uproariously.*

You know what my grammy told me? That most of us will die a terrible, painful, horrible death.

SERENA: What? That is not true, some people die in their sleep. My gramps died in his sleep.

FANTASIA: But most people don't. Most people die in hospital, screaming in pain. That's what Gran said. Or in a car accident, or a train runs over them!

SERENA: Well, not me. I am going to die at 100 years old, in my rocking chair. On my porch. With my cats around me.

FANTASIA: Me too.

SERENA: Maybe we will be on that porch together!

FANTASIA: I know we will. We will!

SERENA: Fancy? You are my best friend in the entire world.

FANTASIA: You too.

SERENA: And we're not gonna die a terrible painful horrible death.

FANTASIA: No way. Not us! Never.

JAY: I wake up in the middle of the night reliving every moment of her childhood, scouring it for reasons for…how we are to blame, for bad choices we made, for casual things we said that might have…caused her to crumble…

> *Movement piece in which the younger girls hand off the roles to the older girls.*

Scene 12

SERENA, RAMONA, and JAY.

SERENA: Dad! Daddy, wake up, it's the best part of the movie!

RAMONA: Oh, the poor man is so tired.

SERENA: But he's the one who chose this movie! Dad!! Daddy.

RAMONA: Uh oh!

JAY: (*Pretending to be a monster waking and tickling.*) Whoaghhhh haghhh! Roarrrrr!

> *SERENA screams with delight.*

SERENA: Daddy! Daddddy! Stop! Don't tickle me! Pleeeeze!!

RAMONA: Jay!!

JAY: (*In monster voice.*) Now it's time to tickle big mama!! Where is big mama? There! You, girl creature, you need to help me tickle her into oblivion!!

SERENA: Yes!! Oh yes yes, its tickle time, tickle tickle

RAMONA: No, mercy. Oh have mercy, please!

> *They tickle her; she screams, but in a semi-delighted way.*

Jay, we were happy! Remember? We were a really, ridiculously happy family of three... Serena was shy, yes, but she was a happy kid.

JAY: I thought she was. But maybe there was something underneath, you know what depression can be...

RAMONA: She was loved. She had us, she had her best best friend Fancy, lots of other friends too, but then...

JAY: When she was about thirteen... that distressingly awkward transition into puberty...

RAMONA: Everything changed. Radically! Horribly! Almost all the other kids turned on her –

JAY: Like a pack of demons.

Scene 13

> *EXTRAS ignore SERENA, whisper about her, etc. She tries to walk through them, around them, but they jostle her, insult her, and leave her in a heap on the ground.*

RAMONA: For the whole of Grade Eight she was tormented. Apart from Fancy, she had no friends. She did not go to a single birthday party, or skating party, or pizza after the soccer games, nothing. And the social media – there was this diabolical site – ASKfm? Where kids were able to make anonymous comments? I could not keep her away from it. But then her life-saver, her very best friend in the world, her last hope –

Scene 14

FANTASIA and SERENA.

FANTASIA: So the thing is, we are fourteen now, and frankly, you are a little bit embarrassing to have as a friend. You don't really know how to dress, you don't know what to say, and...I hate to tell you this, but none of the other girls like you. So it's not fair to me that I should be...well...lumped in with you, get it? I don't want Chari and them to think that they have to invite YOU if they invite ME. We are NOT the same person, and just because we were friends as kids does not mean that I owe you anything. Okay? And I don't think it's nice that they call you names and spit in your hair and stuff, I do not like that, but they keep on doing it and okay, I was laughing the other day but you don't have to tell your mom that! She is just going to upset my gramma. I was laughing because you had your sweater on inside-out and you looked SO WEIRD and I thought how could this sad person have been my friend–so I wanted to let you know that although I still sort of like you in a way, like I don't *not* like you, I am not inviting you to my birthday party. Nobody else but me likes you and if they knew you were coming they wouldn't come.

RAMONA: Was this part of it...of how she became...a target? When her best friend betrayed her? Did this weaken her foundation...in some way? Bullies know, they sense someone who is...easy to demolish. Demolition is their game.

BABE: When she came home and told me what she had done I turned away.
I turned away from her and continued preparing my vichyssoise. I asked her to take the scissors and cut some chives for sprinkling on top, I could not even look at her. I could not believe that my granddaughter – me, who was the social secretary for the Governor General, who was sought out for guidance on good manners by diplomats, would have a grandchild who would commit such an egregious social felony.

FANTASIA: But no one would be my friend if I stayed her friend, Gramma. I had to do it. Anyway, I feel bad enough, so just stop.

BABE: I am sorry you feel "bad" but truly, there is never a need for such brutality. I understand that your feelings about Serena may have shifted, this happens with many friendships. There are ups and downs, there are certainly shifts. But you did not need to break the girl's heart –

FANTASIA: But isn't honesty the best...

BABE: Hush. You hush and listen. Fantasia. All you needed to do was a slow distancing. I have done this many a time when a friend began to bore me: the solution is busy: busy busy! You have dance, you have Guides, you have skating, and you have mathletes.

FANTASIA: Mathletes? I hate math, Gramma!

BABE: Shush! See her for a short time once every few weeks, and then once a month, and then every two months and so on and so on and eventually, she will tire of it and give up.
               What you did was cruel. Cruel and unusual. I do not understand you. Please explain. With eloquence.

FANTASIA: Gran. You even said you like it when I'm popular. You were the most popular girl at your school! You tell me that every day.

BABE: Goodness. Not every day.

FANTASIA: Do you want me to sink to the bottom with her? Because if I remained her friend we would both sink, right? Into the sludge of the least popular kids in the school.

BABE: Fancy. Do not refer to human beings as "sludge."
               Tell me something. Why have the others turned on her? She is a perfectly attractive young girl, sweet, smart, and even persuasively dressed. She is from a most respectable family, and...

FANTASIA: I don't know. Its...kinda...no reason, It's...because ... maybe they get how sensitive she is? She is sensitive about everything. Always saying she's ugly or whatever. And... well...she is a little – different. She doesn't have cool clothes. And she won't listen to me.

BABE: Mmmm... Yes. I suppose I can...empathize with your predicament. There was a girl at St. Hilda's... Ungainly thing. She was a scholarship girl; father was a little teacher somewhere, mother a sack of potatoes. Well, this Libby, and that name alone: Libby! she was always just...not one of us, her uniform was never right: untucked shirt, skirt an inch too long, baggy socks and – well... I tried to be kind to her when the others would have nothing to do with her because she smelled of carbolic soap – I did try, but then she clung to me like a burr, and I had no choice but to gently remove her. Very gently. What you are doing is not gentle.

FANTASIA: I am a terrible person, I know. The worst! But another few days being seen with her and they would start throwing rocks at me too, snotty Kleenexes.

BABE: Kleenexes? Why were they doing that?

RAMONA: WHY?

FANTASIA: I don't know. I don't know. It's terrible and they just won't stop. I just. I just have to save myself. Can you forgive me? Do you hate me now?

RAMONA: Have any of you had to see your child go through that kind of rejection?
The friend rejection? There is nothing you can do, there is no way to fix it.

JAY: I have to admit when I see Fancy on the street I just...well I pretend I don't see her. I know she is a kid, but...hey, anyone who hurts my child....

Scene 15

RAMONA and SERENA.

RAMONA: Serena? I know you don't want to talk to me about it. Especially to me. I understand that. But…I

I do know a little of what you are going through. When I was thirteen?

I was…so different from the other girls,

I had just come to this country. I was terrified of all of them. They were so confident, and stylish, and they laughed all the time, with such a cold look in their eyes. They had expensive makeup and earrings and designer jeans and I had nothing. We lived on the 14th floor of a shabby apartment building on the edge of town.

I would wear my bra till it was grey. I only had one. Because I didn't know! My mother died in a car accident when I was nine, as you know, and Dad, your granddad, he had terrible hygiene himself, loony physicist that he was, he didn't know anything about girls; I had no one, no one to guide me…

SERENA: Mom! I would never ever wear a dirty bra! Gross! I have ten bras and they are always always clean.

RAMONA: I know, I know you wouldn't! You are far more sophisticated than I was. Serena, my love. Look, I want to say be fearless, but I know it's not easy. I know how much it hurts. One day, you will forget about those vampires. Because I can promise you, they are nothing; they will be making breakfast sandwiches in the Tim Hortons until they drop dead.

Scene 16

RAMONA: (*To audience.*) Was that too much? Sorry, I am a mother, not a saint.

JAY: But then! After that year of hell, everything changed.

RAMONA: It was like spring after a terrible winter!

JAY: She made a friend!!

CHORUS joins in with the word "friend." EXTRAS clap or cheer.

Scene 17

SERENA and RILEY.

SERENA: Ryan? Is that what you said?

RILEY: Yeah. It's unbelievable. They named me Ryan Ryan.

SERENA: Oh my God. Really? Why?

RILEY: Because that's their sense of humour. Truly. I mean, I love my moms, both of them, but Chernelle is in the Forces, she is a colonel, and a top-of-the line sniper, she was in Afghanistan and she was a hero, much more about that later over poutine, point being she needs to laugh, gotta have comic relief, and my name is the comic relief, and Ronnie, she is a midwife, so she doesn't get much sleep. I think they thought it was "cute." I am so not into cute. Any old how, I changed my name to Riley!

SERENA: Riley Ryan. I like that. Sounds…

RILEY: Like a fictional character?

SERENA: Yeah. On a comedy show. With a laugh track. You're new here, right?

RILEY: Yeah.

SERENA: Where'd you come from?

RILEY: Timmins.

SERENA: Timmins. That's way up north, huh?

RILEY: 'Bout four hours north. Yup. And yes, Shania Twain comes from there.

SERENA: Oh, I don't really know her…music…

RILEY: Biggest records sales of all time. I know, scary.

SERENA: How do you like it here?

RILEY: It's…fine.

SERENA: It's awful. Right?

RILEY: It's not so bad. Kinda boring, maybe. Not as bad as Timmins.

SERENA: There are real assholes in this school.

RILEY: Yeah?

SERENA: But you don't have to worry. I'm their target.

RILEY: Really? Why?

SERENA: I'm…not sure. I guess I'm gorky. Different.

RILEY: Gorky is sweet. And Different is essential. You are sweet and essential.

SERENA: My best friend, Fancy, dumped me last year, because she was scared of being associated with me. I don't blame her, actually.

RILEY: That sucks.

SERENA: So…I will totally understand if you wanna keep your distance now that you know I'm a loser. A "pariah."

RILEY: A pariah! Ohhh, I looove pariahs!

SERENA: In middle school, I was crying at the computer, and my dad he looked at the screen before I could change it and he saw these horrible toxic comments and ran across the street to her house and confronted her parents.

Scene 18

JAY talks to audience as if they are Hank, the neighbour.

JAY: Ahh hi Hank,
I'm doin' fine; well, not really, I have to ask: Hank: do you know what your Jessica is doing?
Yes. Well, do you know what she is doing on that computer? You don't. Privacy. Well, as a friend I would like you to go down to Jess's room right now.
And sneak up behind her and read what she is writing.
Because I just read it on my daughter's screen.
Death threats. YES. Horrible, cruel, brutal, nasty words, words to make someone feel like NOTHING. NOTHING. I am asking you to stop this. To stop this happening. NOW.
I want to watch you go down to your daughter's room and cut the cord to her computer. NOW.
You trust her. Oh, that's rich. You think I am exaggerating? My daughter is hysterical, she is crying hysterically wanting to give up on everything – she is thirteen years old. Do you think that's okay?
I am asking you. If You Think That's Okay.
Okay. Yeah. Okay, I'll stop "bothering" you…fine.
By the way, our friendship is over.
I hope you burn in hell forever.

Scene 19

RILEY: You have an amazing dad.

SERENA: Yeah. Both my parents are pretty great. So. Enough about my tribulations. Who's your homeroom?

RILEY: Miss Rush.

SERENA: Can you believe how long her hair is? I'm always worried it will get caught in something.

RILEY: What colour would you call that?

SERENA: Auburn?

RILEY: No. Not auburn. More...chartreuse...

          She's really sweet. Was so welcoming to me. And funny. Without meaning to be.

SERENA: She says the most...

RILEY: Wack

SERENA: Crazy

RILEY: Wild

SERENA: Things. Like "Serena, you look like a fountain today."

RILEY: She told me I had a "wild rose" feel... I took it as a compliment.

SERENA: Do you notice she always wears something yellow? Even if it's just a ring, or a hair elastic.

RILEY: It's the yellow cult! And the way she has the same thing for lunch every day?

SERENA: An apple, cut into four slices.

RILEY: With a giant spoonful of peanut butter.

SERENA: Every day.

RILEY: Of her life.

SERENA: So where're you going after high school?

RILEY: Travel for a year. Asia, Australia, Andalusia.

SERENA: All those As...

RILEY: Yeah. Wanna come?

SERENA: Sure.

RILEY: I think we might be soulmates.

SERENA: Really? That would be…amazing. A soulmate.

I mean I look at you and…and that jacket!! It's just so. Is that designer?

RILEY: You like it? Take it.

SERENA: Wow. Thank you. I mean, no, I couldn't…I…

RILEY: It's a policy of mine. Don't worry. Just take it.

SERENA: Thank you.

RILEY: So, I have to ask, is it okay to be queer…in this high school? Is there, like, an LGBTQ group?

SERENA: Umm…well, we do have a Gay-Straight Alliance. We meet on Thursdays.

RILEY: Won't be a problem then, with the bros?

SERENA: I don't think so. I mean, there are asshats for sure.

RILEY: I noticed.

SERENA: And they do call each other "fag" all the time. Or "ladies."

And say things they don't like are "gay." And kinda wrestle each other.

RILEY: Superb. SU-perb.

SERENA: They look at me sometimes like I'm a cockroach.

RILEY: Cockroaches are sublime. They walk through walls and wires. They survived the ice age and they would survive a nuclear ex plosion. Can I be your cockroach best friend?

SERENA: I'll get tee shirts made! Here's to the next four years of hell!

RILEY: But cockroaches can survive anything, right?

SERENA: And grow bigger every time!

Scene 20

RAMONA and JAY.

RAMONA: I was told she started to speak up in class, to express herself.

JAY: And we noticed a big difference at home. She actually smiled.

RAMONA: She had an appetite again!

JAY: We thought it was over.

RAMONA: We really thought…everything would be fine.

Scene 21

Classroom: PRATT/DODGE/RILEY/SERENA.

PRATT: So ahhh. Good morning, boys and girls, Miss Rush. We are doing our project here, on the poetry of a local gentleman.

DODGE: Well, not local-local.

PRATT: Fairly local.

DODGE: So the twins who are not twins.

PRATT: Monsieur Pratt.

DODGE: And Mr. Dodge.

PRATT and DODGE: Present:

DODGE: Wait for it:

PRATT and DODGE: Mr. Doooooon... McKay!!

PRATT: So: you wanna know if we are prepared? You wanna know what prepared is? We have memorized the poem!! WE LOUTS have actually memorized!

DODGE: You ready for some real Canadiana? Its about...da da daaaa: birds!

PRATT: The birds that are all around you! Singing, and swooping, and eatin' birdseed and earthworms, and red berries. Ready, everyone?

DODGE: Be prepared to be blown away.

DODGE and PRATT alternate lines:

"Concentrate upon her attributes:
the accipiter's short
roundish wings, streaked breast, talons fine
and slender as the X-ray of a baby's hand.
The eyes (yellow in this hatchling
later deepening to orange then
blood red) can spot
a sparrow at four hundred
metres and impose
silence like an overwhelming noise
to which you must not listen."

PRATT: Pretty interesting – rhymes that don't rhyme, right?

DODGE: "And the silence is like an overwhelming NOISE," right?

PRATT: What do you think that means? Class? Does nobody have any thing to say?

Silence.

TEACHER: Class, try to engage. Think about it for a second. These boys have done a lot of work here. And very good work it is!

SERENA: Well, um…isn't it…that moment before the kill? The silence? And, like, we think of birds as just these…beautiful, graceful, peaceful creatures, and their singing as…our entertainment, when really, the singing is either about territory, or mating, or where the good earthworms are.

DODGE: Like us. As in, what did you have for dinner last night?

FANTASIA: Lamb. We are totally killers.

PRATT: Baaaaa. Dodge here won't eat lamb 'cause it's a babe.

RILEY: Birds have to kill to survive. Birds of prey kill mice and rabbits, even robins kill worms. They don't kill: they die.

PRATT: And so us killing them is no big deal. It's the same thing.

DODGE: We are like the birds, hunting their prey. Except we don't eat the birds we kill.

PRATT: We just like killing them.

DODGE: You like killing them. He gets, like, all excited.

PRATT: While you're there cringing like a girl.

SERENA: You shoot birds? For fun?

PRATT: Absofrickinlutely. Over a hundred.

RILEY: Soooo cool.

PRATT: And yeah, Serena Beena Feena Meena, it is fun. Lots of fun. You should come out.

DODGE: Riley. New kid. Funny boy. What do you think the poem means?

RILEY: I…honestly don't know.

PRATT: But I thought fags loved poetry…

TEACHER: Hey!! Homophobia has no place in this school. You will apologize this instant. And then you will report to the vice principal.

PRATT: Sorry. I was just kidding.

TEACHER: Now go.

PRATT: What's the point? He'll tell me I was wrong and I should apologize and I just did. It's a waste of time. Anyway, like I said: I was just kidding.

TEACHER: Pratt, you need to go report to the…

PRATT: Make me.

DODGE: Not cool, bro.

TEACHER: Well, as long as you apologized.

RILEY: Queer is the word we like.
Q.U.E.E.R. and some of us like poetry and some of us shoot birds.
But about the silence…silence… can be very, very – dangerous.

PRATT: On the other hand, it can be: An overwhelming noise, to which you should not listen. Like when idiots are talking, it's just all white noise.

SERENA: We need to listen to the idiots most of all. Because they are the dangerous ones.

DODGE: So! In conclusion, Mr. Don McKay's poems are all about creatures in the woods. Insects, birds, badgers, all of it. And my opinion is that he sees these creatures…

PRATT: As a metaphor..

TEACHER: For?

Scene 22

RAMONA: I was just so glad, can you imagine? As a mother? The relief I felt knowing she finally had a friend?

And they were inseparable.
Formidable.
The bullies, they tried to bring them down,
but Riley and Serena together? Were a powerhouse.

Scene 23

EXTRA: Oh look, it's the gay and the turd he pooped out this morning.

RILEY: Did you hear that sound, Serena?

SERENA: Yes, Riley, I did…I think that is the sound that bacteria makes, isn't it?

RILEY: It IS.

EXTRA: Bacteria? Ohhh, that is lame burn. Where's your boyfriend?

RILEY: He lives in Ottawa, actually. But he's coming for the weekend, wanna meet him?

EXTRA: No, I guess you two will be busy.

RILEY: That's right! We will be very busy. Expressing our love for each other. Wanna join us?

ALL EXTRAS: EWWWWW

RILEY: Oh Sam, I could introduce you to a lot of nice guys…take you to a gay club; they'd be all over you.

EXTRA: Get out of my face, man!

RILEY: Your face is red, it's turning really really red!
            Like a stop sign!

EXTRA: Go to hell!

SERENA: And he's melting. Right in front of us, like the Wicked Witch of the West.

RILEY and SERENA: MELTING.

Scene 24

RAMONA: And even when the bullies pushed them, attacked them, physically, Riley, surprise surprise, learned to fight on the streets of Timmins, He was a dancer and was as tough as an alley cat, and my Serena, did you know that she was a black belt? Oh yes! Because I had taken her to judo since she was five years old. I was so happy when my kid fought back; she and her friends fought back and crushed those bullies!! They crushed them until they were smears on the sidewalk!

Scene 25

Music over a choreographed "fight" in which the EXTRAS attack SERENA and RILEY... FANTASIA (Fancy) appears, and after an internal struggle, joins SERENA and RILEY – the three win and the bullies slink off.

FANTASIA: That was FUN!! Did you see Hansen? He just crumbled!

RILEY: Replay! I want a replay!

FANTASIA: Crumbled like a cookie! And Martin and LaChance? See La Chance bleeding from his ugly mouth? I did that! I did that!

SERENA: And Martin bent over like an old man! Riley, you were awesome.

RILEY: I did that! a good punch in the solar plexus, no problem!

FANTASIA: Loved every minute. Whooo!

SERENA: Fancy. Uh...Wow. You were... super girl. Thank you for helping us.

FANTASIA: Well, all that rugby had to be good for something.

RILEY: You killed it. Killed it.

FANTASIA: So, are we friends again? We're friends again, right!

SERENA: I don't know, Fancy. I don't know what to think.

FANTASIA: Oh, you sound so SERIOUS!

SERENA: Just...you know...you said you didn't want to be seen with me.

FANTASIA: I was a stone-cold mean girl.

SERENA: It was really hard.

FANTASIA: I was fourteen. I was half formed. I wasn't even...a person. That was a year and half ago, in kid time that's a lifetime. We're good now, right? Now that I put on my Super Girl cape and came to your rescue.

RILEY: Hey. We didn't need...

FANTASIA: I know, but I helped, didn't I? Didn't I?

RILEY: It's completely up to Serena. Threes don't always work out.

SERENA: But um...we haven't really talked about how bad it was. You really really hurt me.

FANTASIA: It's over. As of now! Like my Gran says:

BABE: Less said, soonest mended!

FANTASIA: Lets mooooove onnn. Onward and upwards! Ima parta your army now. And I am sorry. I mean I am really really really sorry. It was bad. Oh, it wasn't that bad. Maybe it was.

SERENA: The stuff online was…like being knifed, over and over, every day. Just like, six months ago.

FANTASIA: That was Hadley, she was…crazy. I don't know. There was something going on at home. I think it was her parents' divorce.

SERENA: But you were hanging out with her. You didn't stop it.

FANTASIA: I tried. I actually truly said to her, "The online stuff stops now. NOW. Because it's wrong and you'll go to hell for it – she is very religious – But I wasn't there when she was… actually… writing those…

RILEY: But you saw the posts.

FANTASIA: No!

SERENA: Did you?

FANTASIA: I was a coward. I could have done more, you're right. I just desperately, stupidly wanted to fit in with those girls, I wanted to go to their parties, the games, the city, and I thought that losing you would…

RILEY: Did it?

FANCY: Yes.

RILEY: Was it worth it?

FANTASIA: None of those girls are my friends. And even if they wanted to be? They only talk about makeup and weight and guys. That is IT. If you talk about anything else you are labelled as WEIRD. So, can I hang out with you guys now? Would you take me back, Serena? Please? Pleeeeze?

RILEY: What do you think, Snow?

SERENA: Snow?

RILEY: Snow White. And I'm the seven dwarves.

FANTASIA: Huh. I like that.

SERENA: Yeah. Okay. A nickname. I always wanted a nickname, but I wasn't popular enough to have one! Snow White.

RILEY: General Snow.

SERENA: Colonel Cockroach?

RILEY and SERENA: Private Fancy.

> *Beat.*

> *RILEY and SERENA extend their hands to FANTASIA, who reaches her hand out to touch theirs.*

Scene 26

RAMONA: So now they were a trio! Yes, they were formidable, like cartoon superheroes, indestructible! Bound together, by "invisible hoops of steel," to borrow from Shakespeare! They were either at our house, or Riley's or Fancy's grandmother's! The mythic three-headed guard dog. Guarding their dignity, guarding the good, but they were not exclusive! Oh no! They welcomed all the outsiders into their fold, with open arms.

BABE: I can't tell you how relieved I was when my Fancy came to her senses.

Scene 27

FANTASIA: And so I don't even need to do your distance thing, Gram, because the truth is, she has always been my best friend and she always will be. I was just a stupid coward, who cared more about being popular than I cared about real friendship. So now we are closer than ever, and her new friend Riley, he is totally cool and he is my other best friend.

BABE: Have you been ostracized? From social events? Not invited to parties?

FANTASIA: Funny thing is, we *are* all invited now, but we don't go! Those "events" are so boring! Everybody competing for status? We have way more fun with each other. Not just each other, but all the other outcasts!

BABE: The drama club?

FANTASIA: Exactly! And the astronomy club, and the geo-political club and the school paper, all of it! Outsiders are the real insiders.

BABE: A pungent observation. (*Hugs her.*) Fantasia, I love you more than words can express.

Scene 28

RAMONA: And there was something she began to understand about herself. Only she couldn't tell us, so she shared it with her new friend.

RILEY and SERENA.

SERENA: Here's the thing.
And don't tell anyone; I mean anyone.

RILEY: Even Fancy?

SERENA: Even Fancy.
I am – okay, oooh this is soo hard to say, don't know why... but.
Um. I am...struggling...with my...

RILEY: Sexuality.

SERENA: Yeah. Wait. How did you know?

RILEY: Because...of how you... I know you. I watch your eyes.

SERENA: It's not just about sex... I sometimes wonder if... I even... have any...

RILEY: You do. You do you do you do we all do.

SERENA: I have these girl crushes. NOT Fancy. She is my friend, and that's all.

RILEY: ARWEN.

SERENA: No.

RILEY: Hah! I've seen the way you look at her. You are totally in love. And lust. Both tangled into one beautiful crush.

SERENA: There is something about...the way she...moves. And the words she uses. So simple, and yet...to the point, like arrows. The way her eyes are so green... And her hands. Have you noticed her hands?

RILEY: She's steaming hot.

SERENA: And her voice. Oh my God. I just want it wrapped around me like a blanket.

RILEY: Well? Why don't you...

SERENA: Oh, she would NEVER even consider – and anyway, I don't think she...

RILEY: I don't know. I get a kind of Ellen vibe from her.

SERENA: Yeah?

RILEY: Go for it. GO FOR IT.

SERENA: What would I do, though? Ask her out?

RILEY: Go for coffee.

SERENA: But how would I actually…ask her…like, would I say "Um…I was wondering…

RILEY: If you wanted to go for coffee."

SERENA: Oh, that's so lame.

RILEY: Can't say lame any more.

SERENA: Oh yeah, Danny says it's offensive, because he is actually lame. He's right. But it's so hard to stop.

RILEY: Like saying "that's so gay." Even I said it.

SERENA: It's hard NOT to say.

RILEY: So, coffee. "Hey Arwen, would you care to join me for…an extra whip, extra hot?"

SERENA: She would know how I meant it and if she said no I have to be at that school the rest of the year. And then even after that I would run into her in town, at the market, the skating rink, swimming in the river, whatever, till we're like FIFTY!

RILEY: True. Because what I have found is that even if they are gay, it does NOT mean they like YOU.

SERENA: That happened to you?

RILEY: Yeah. I really liked this guy, Reza, in this semi-pro singing group we had in my last school, Smash? He had an amazing voice, and he is really hot, and funny, so funny, and so I said, "Wanna hang out sometime?" And he's just like "I have a boyfriend in Toronto." I wanted to die. I had to see him every day. I just shrank whenever I saw him.

SERENA: I really don't think I will ever…
          Be with…
          Anyone.
          I told my mom that. She laughed and said:

RAMONA: Of course you'll find someone, darling.
          You're perfect.

SERENA: I'm like "MOM, I am so not perfect, just stop." Some people are meant to be alone. Alone with their turtle.

RILEY: That's ridiculous. People who are alone? Are people who want to be alone.

Scene 29

RAMONA: Sometimes, of a Sunday, we would all gather for a scrumptious dinner at Fancy's place. A dinner created for us with gusto by her antique and quite unique grandmother, Babe: but this Sunday we had a reason:

> *RAMONA, BABE, SERENA, RILEY, JAY, and FANTASIA.*
> *The roast chicken dinner.*

BABE: Will anyone have more of my autumn mash?

RILEY: I will, thank you!

JAY: Thanks, it's great.

BABE: Oh I do like to see a young man with an appetite. Serena??

SERENA: No, thank you.

BABE: Have a little more. You're such a tiny thing.

FANTASIA: Nanna made it with her own hands.

RAMONA: It's very good. What did you say was in it?

BABE: Sweet potato, purple potato, P.E.I. potatoes, turnip, and parsnip. With cinnamon, maple syrup, turmeric, and…oh that other pumpkin pie spice, the name escapes me.

RILEY: Nutmeg? Cloves?

SERENA: Ginger?

BABE: Perhaps cloves.

JAY: This is the best orange mash I have ever tasted. Amazing!

RAMONA: Fantastic.

BABE: Fancy?

FANTASIA: No, thank you. I ate all this ice cream this afternoon and then I puked it up so feelin' kinda…

BABE: Oh dear! I don't think that's a public conversation, my darling.

FANTASIA: Oh Nan, everyone has bulimia now. It's cool to talk about, it, we can't be hiding these things.

BABE: Fancy! Discretion!

FANTASIA: Why?

RAMONA: If we have no discretion, we are –

BABE: A bull in a china shop!

FANTASIA: A bull…in a… huh?

SERENA: Breaking every tiny crystal thing, right, Mum?

RAMONA: Breaking… people's…

BABE: Delicate feelings! Their…sensibilities!

SERENA: But…that's one of the things we love about Fancy.

RILEY: She tells the hard truth.

FANTASIA: Well, now I do. Now that I'm not lying to myself anymore, being a DOUCHE.

BABE: I beg your pardon? Did you just say what I think you…

FANTASIA: A douche. An asshat. You know.

BABE: Last I heard a douche was a sort of squirty feminine hygiene product.

RAMONA: Not anymore!

JAY: Oh boy.

FANTASIA: Grammy, it just means jerk now.

BABE: Oh, these words!

RAMONA: So. Be that as it may. We are gathered for a reason tonight!

BABE: Yes. Yes. And it was an excellent one. What was it?

FANTASIA: To devise…a war plan!

RAMONA: No! Not a war plan; rather, a…

BABE: Strategy. Is that the correct word?

RILEY: To talk about the situation at school?

SERENA: In which we got in big bad trouble for fighting back. After WE were attacked.

FANTASIA: Suspended! SO much fun. That's why I got to hang out with you all week, Gran, watching *Ru Paul's Drag Race*.

RILEY: For five fabulous days. I wrote an opera.

SERENA: While the bullies…

BABE: Oh, the bullies always float free. And then they take over the world.

JAY: They become president of the United States.

FANTASIA: Bets he was a bully in school.

RILEY: Indisputably.

BABE: I have found that the bullies always get away with their
                nasty deeds. Unless someone stands up to them. And that is
                what you marvels did. I triple salute you.

JAY: But the trouble is, Mrs. Lancashire, that our kids are the ones
                in trouble.

RAMONA: And we will not let that stand.

BABE: No!

RAMONA: So the school suspends them, and the bullies have kept
                up their campaign of cyber-terrorism. Did you know that,
                Babe? The threats, the crude online harassment?

                          *RILEY hands phone to BABE who reads the nasty
                          tweets.*

EXTRAS: (*All on phones.*)
                We'll get you.
                Watch your backs, uglies.
                You are not safe anywhere!
                Not in your beds.
                Not in your bath.
                Not in the classroom.
                When you least expect it.
                A knife in your back.
                Destruction.
                We will follow you everywhere.
                And we will kill you. Slowly.
                And your families. With big knives.
                Your life is over.
                So you should kill yourself now.
                Why don't you hang yourself?
                Or we will cut off your fingers and your hands.
                Then we will cut off your ugly faces.
                You watch your backs, bitches!
                Because we are…
                Everywhere.

Back at dinner at BABE's.

BABE: "Big Knives"? "You should kill yourself"? "Hang yourself"? Threats of amputation? Good Lord. We must report this to the police.

RAMONA: Exactly.

JAY: Tonight. Now. While we're here together.

RILEY: No.

FANTASIA: No. No!

JAY: Serena?

SERENA: I don't know. No. I don't think so. We'll be labelled

RILEY: As snitches.

FANTASIA: Which is the worst.

BABE: They shaved the heads of the collaborators in France, those women who had consorted with the German soldiers in exchange for stockings and chocolate, they shaved their heads and they stoned them and…

FANTASIA: Gran!! We did not consort with German soldiers!

RAMONA: Reporting serious and threatening harassment to the police is hardly…

BABE: I know, oh dear God, I know that, I was just reminded…

FANTASIA: Gram.

JAY: We cannot let them get away with this.

SERENA: But Dad…

FANTASIA: The police won't do anything. Nothing. I had a friend who went through this at her school, and she reported it and there was a big investigation and all they got was a finger wagging and "no computers for a week." We were like: "Are you kidding me?" My friend had to switch schools! The cops make it much, much worse.

RILEY: Much much worse. Always.

JAY: Not always. We have to put some trust in our police.

RAMONA: Surely with all this talk in the media? With the schools all claiming they take this seriously, they will listen.

FANTASIA: You will only make it worse for us. We're here to tell you.

SERENA: It's true, Mom.

BABE: Perhaps you could all attend Neuchatel, in the Swiss Alps.

JAY: Why not? That's what a line of credit is for. Let's do it.

FANTASIA: The Swiss Alps? No way. I like my teachers. Especially history, Mrs. Tantoni? Is a beast about history.

SERENA: And the astronomy. And drama club! All my new nerd friends this year.

RILEY: And I'm basically the star of choir, we are going to travel to Europe.

SERENA: Same with drama! Kitchener! Sears Drama Festival!

RILEY: And track, Mr. S. says I could be recruited. Top schools in the country.

FANTASIA: And they are not kicking us out of our school!

RILEY: That's letting them win.

SERENA: We will not let them win. We will –

RILEY and SERENA and FANTASIA: NOT LET THEM WIN!

BABE: But really, you don't you think the police...?

RILEY and SERENA and FANTASIA: No!

BABE: But the threats!

JAY: I am going to each and every bully house.

BABE: And I will accompany you. With a hockey stick.

RILEY: It really doesn't matter to me. I've seen it all my life. Empty threats. I had those threats every day up in Timmins!

>   *Beat.*

SERENA: The thing is, guys, we have each other.

FANTASIA: And we are unbelievably powerful!

RILEY: And unbelievably weird.

SERENA: Right?

BABE: I don't know, I don't think you should underestimate the power of evil.

RAMONA: I think it will be fine. I think these three will create a...

RILEY and SERENA and FANTASIA: Snowstorm!

Intermission

Scene 30

RAMONA: So. The Party; The party that ended in the pond.
"Party."
What an extraordinary word for that desecration.

Scene 31

JESS, EXTRAS.

JESS: No, I really want you guys to come.

EXTRA 2: Totally! It's gonna be lit!

EXTRA 3: And Riley, we were hoping you would play for us!

EXTRA 4: And that Serena, you would sing. My friend in choir says you are an awesome singer.

EXTRA 5: And Fancy can dance, right? I hear you are a wild dancer!

JESS: Honestly, nobody is gonna be a douche, we have talked about it, and they feel really really bad for what they've been doing online to you guys. They know they started it and everything. And there was that assembly all about cyber-bullying? With that play? And we all know how wrong it was. Seriously… This is a way to make peace, right? To make things better. My mom is a Buddhist and it was her idea, to have you all over. She won't be there, she's at a conference in like…Copenhagen. So come. Please? We really want you to come… We're making margaritas in the bathtub!

EXTRA: Oh, and Drake might be coming!

JESS: Seriously, he has a cottage near here, next to Megan's, and her cousin's best friend was his sound guy before.

RILEY, FANTASIA, and SERENA look at each other, debating.

Anyway, it's my birthday and I would really like it if you guys were there. We want to make it up to you, we really do. Serena, remember all the birthday parties when we were kids? We used to be such good friends, remember? All the play dates? Picnics with our moms? I hate it that there's such a distance now.

Scene 32

RILEY: Hah. Drake is definitely not coming.

FANTASIA: That is hilarious. Do they really think we'd be suckered in by that? *Drake?*

SERENA: I don't know. I thought she was…kinda genuine. Besides the Drake thing. And we did used to be friends.

RILEY: I think I'm gonna go. Just for the adventure. I am sure Jordan, your star quarterback, is gay. And I think he likes me.

FANTASIA: Let's just go, and see what happens, right? I got to know Jess when I was a mean girl and I think she was genuine.

SERENA: I got that vibe too. I think it will be fine.

RILEY: But Drake will SO not be there.
He does NOT have a cottage near here. His cottage is up in Muskoka.

SERENA: Right?

FANTASIA: But the margaritas in the bathtub? I'm down.

RILEY: Yeah.

SERENA: Yeah?

RILEY: But I'm not playing.

SERENA: And I am definitely not singing.

FANTASIA: I'll dance, though. I'll dance my freaky face off.

SERENA: Anyway, I'm not afraid of them. And maybe the online stuff will stop. Maybe she was telling the truth.

RILEY: And, most importantly, Arwen's going to be there…

FANTASIA: Arwen? What?

SERENA: (*Shoots RILEY a look.*) How do you know that?

RILEY: We do track together. She told me.

SERENA: Really?

FANTASIA: What, do you like Arwen? So cool! Oh, I would love to see you two together!

SERENA: It's nothing like that, just –

FANTASIA: Serena, stop, just stop right now. (*Beat.*) So we're gonna do it?

RILEY and SERENA: We are, we are!

FANTASIA: Anyway, if it IS some kind of trap,

RILEY: We're ready for anything, right?

FANTASIA: Because we are the three-headed dragon. Grrrrrr!

RILEY: In-de-structible.

SERENA: Yeah! And anyway, I'm sure it will be fine. Actually, I have a really good feeling about it.

Scene 33

The Party.

An outdoor party. Crowded with the EXTRAS, improvising "party talk." Many people dancing. A DJ plays music. It is very loud. Lights are pulsing. RILEY and SERENA are together. SERENA is already drunk. Staggering. FANTASIA is dancing wildly. Later, RILEY spots ARWEN.

SERENA: Whoaaa. Look at Fancy. She is fancy-dancing! Whoooops! Oww!

RILEY: Serena, I told you all that pre-drinking was a bad idea.

SERENA: What? It was only rum and Coke.

RILEY: And rye and ginger, and gin and orange juice. And some weird old liquor your parents had at the back of the cupboard. You're an idiot.

SERENA: But now I'm not scared at all!

RILEY: You were scared? Of those idiots? (*Pointing inside to party.*)

SERENA: No ! (*She whispers.*) AR-WEN. Seeing Arwen!

RILEY: What? There is nothing to be scared of. She's cool.

           Just…be true, you know? Be yourself.

SERENA: Hey! Look at Fancy!! Fancy!! Fancy!

                    FANTASIA waves.

FANTASIA: Dance parteeeee!!

EXTRA: So you think you can dance!

EXTRA: Right! That girl is merked.

RILEY: She's so high. So high.

SERENA: Looks like everybody's high. What's going around? MDMA?

DODGE: Hey, birds. How goes the night?

SERENA: Hi there, poetry guy!

RILEY: The bird shooter.

DODGE: When's the last time you ate chicken?

RILEY: Okay okay, point taken.

DODGE: Now Pratt, he is the killer. I've seen him twist a chicken's head off.
Shoot a deer for no reason. Whatever.

RILEY: What a silverback. Double-A alpha male. So impressive.

DODGE: Hah. He thinks so.
By the way you are looking beautiful tonight., Serena. You... wanna dance?

SERENA: Ummm...thank you, but...I'm not really a dancer.

RILEY: So where is the alpha male tonight?

DODGE: Out there vomiting into the pool.

RILEY: Nice.

SERENA: Aren't you gonna take care of him? He could drown. He could totally drown! Dodge! Take care of him!

DODGE: You know what? You gotta point! Stay sexy, you! Stay sexy for me.

                          DODGE leaves.

SERENA: That was weird.

RILEY: I think he's hot.

SERENA: Why is he being nice to us?

RILEY: I don't know. But why not trust it? He thinks you're beautiful.

SERENA: But it's not him I am interested in, Riley.

RILEY: I know, I know, but it's flattering. Enjoy it.

            Ahhhh! Look. I told you she would be here.

SERENA: Oh my God. I think I'm going to faint.

RILEY: Let's go over.

SERENA: No! No way! Looking at her would be like looking at the sun.

RILEY: Well, take my sunglasses. Here you go.

SERENA: No. No. I'm leaving, I'm…

RILEY: (*Pulls her.*) Come on. Where's your liquid courage?

SERENA: Oh my God, Riley. No! I said no!

RILEY: Hey, we don't have to. She's coming over to us.
If you run away, it'll look really, really bad.

SERENA: I'm not running away.

ARWEN: Hey Riley. How's it going? Serena, isn't it?

SERENA: Yeah. I'm in choir with you. I joined late.

ARWEN: Oh. How come you weren't on the New York trip?

SERENA: Had my wisdom teeth out. How was it?

ARWEN: It was sick. We performed in Brooklyn with three other
schools, and everybody said we were the best. But the other
schools were good, you know, very well trained. Just… a
little too slick. I liked our choices way better. Everybody was
really friendly too, not stuck up at all. We found these all-
ages clubs, so, after the concert we were out all night. It was
like ten a.m. when we went back to the hotel. The teachers
were frantic. Poor Mrs. W. was sobbing. I had to calm her
down.

RILEY: Did you literally dance all night?

ARWEN: Yes. And everything else you can imagine. And in
Manhattan.

SERENA: I love New York. Such a great city.

ARWEN: You've been?

SERENA: Oh yeah. A few times. We always stay in the East Village
at this friend of my mom's. It's so cool. We go for the art
exhibits. Well, my parents do. I just love walking around.

RILEY: My moms take me for the musicals. Even though they're
actually better in Toronto.

ARWEN: What? Toronto? No way. I mean Broadway…

SERENA: It depends, right? It depends on the cast.

ARWEN: So, how do you like the partee so far?

RILEY: Looks like folks are having fun.

ARWEN: Nice place. On the river? Gotta love that. And the margaritas
aren't bad.

RILEY: Yeah. I'mona go get me one.

SERENA: Uhh…no thanks.

> *RILEY goes, they look out the window at the river.*

ARWEN: Yuh. If I lived here I would swim that river every day of the year.

SERENA: Even in winter?

ARWEN: Wetsuit. You can swim in any temperature in one of those things.

> *Beat.*

SERENA: I saw you run.

ARWEN: Huh?

SERENA: At the track meet. You were…incredible.

ARWEN: Was a good race. How come you were there?

SERENA: Riley.

ARWEN: Oh, right. He did pretty well himself.

SERENA: Yeah. But you – you killed it… in the 100 metres…you… were so far ahead…of the others!

ARWEN: Yeah. I know. Something took over.

SERENA: Like a lion.

ARWEN: Huh?

SERENA: Well, that's what I thought of when I saw you run, that you were…like a lion…chasing after…I don't know.

ARWEN: A mouse? No, it would be…one of those little deer animals they have in Africa…. Do you run?

SERENA: Oh no, I'm pathetically slow. Pathetic.

ARWEN: It's not everyone's thing.

SERENA: You're beautiful.

ARWEN: Huh?

SERENA: I just said: I think you are beautiful.

ARWEN: Oh. Well, thank you.

SERENA: And…amazing. Amazing too.

ARWEN: Yeah? Okay, I'll take amazing. Anyway, I gotta find my friend.

SERENA: Wait.

ARWEN: What's up?

SERENA: I have to tell you.

ARWEN: What?

SERENA: I think about you a lot.

ARWEN: What? What do you mean?

SERENA: I'm…I think – I love you.

ARWEN: What? What the hell? Girl, you don't even know me.
Go throw up or something.

ARWEN takes off. RILEY and FANTASIA observe this.

Scene 34

JESS and DODGE and PRATT and EXTRA.

JESS: Oh my God, look…look, she was totally hitting on Arwen
and Arwen totally dissed her. Look at her face!

PRATT: I love that in porn, two chicks and a guy? Actually it's the
most popular.

JESS: Ewww, Pratt, shut up.

EXTRA: Serena! Thinking Queen Arwen would be into her? Arwen
has been recruited by the top schools in the country for track.

DODGE: Well…to be fair, Serena is very, very smashed.

EXTRA: She looks ridiculous. Look at her stumbling around.

DODGE: What, are you jealous? She looks amazing.

PRATT: Little Miss Perfect, smashed? Cool! Maybe we could make
her a little less perfect.

JESS: I'm gonna go see if I can help her. Get her water or something.

PRATT: Finish this sentence: The drunker the girl…the…

JESS: Pratt, you're weird. And I think you're pretty drunk yourself.

EXTRA: The drunker the girl the…softer the ground. For, like,
planting. Get it? Planting?

JESS: You're an idiot.

PRATT: Poor little gay virgin. We should help her out!

Hey! Jesse. Would you do something for me?

JESS: Depends what you do for me.

PRATT: You know I'll do anything, baby, I got no shame.

DODGE: That is true.

PRATT: I got two vials of a very special potion in the red pencil case in my backpack. By the back door. Go get one, pour it into a cosmo; she is already wasted, she's gonna go for the Cosmo, guaranteed. Drunk people always want more to drink.

DODGE: You are not serious, Pratt.

JESS: Are you talking about R? That is disgusting, Pratt. It's illegal. What the hell are you doing with that stuff?

EXTRA: Chill, Jesse.

PRATT: Jess. It was just a joke. I wouldn't even know where to get it.

JESS: Not funny.

DODGE: Not funny

JESS: At all. If you want to hook up with someone, do it the old-fashioned way!

PRATT: Sure. Sure. I was just kidding, Jesse. You can go check my pencil case! All that's in there is weed! Really!

JESS walks away in disgust.

JESS: Whatever.

DODGE: Were you kidding?

PRATT: What do you think?

DODGE leaves, disgusted.

EXTRA: I'll help you out, Prattster. I mean, look at her? That girl Serena? She is looking for love big time. Time for her to join the club, right? Time for the Snow to get dirty. You say your pencil case is red?

PRATT: "Time for the Snow to get dirty," I love that. You are too much, weirdo!

We see EXTRA pouring R in a drink.

Scene 35

FANCY and RILEY go to SERENA.

FANTASIA: Oh my God, what happened?

SERENA: Nothing.

RILEY: Did you ask her to hang out? What did she say?

SERENA: What?

FANTASIA: What did she say?

SERENA: Nothing. Nothing happened, Fancy. Nothing happened. You guys are so nosy.

RILEY: Oh. I get it. None of our business.

FANTASIA: Everything is our business! We are the triumvirate!

The gang of three! No secrets!

RILEY: Shhhh.

SERENA: Oh my God. You two are such nerds.

FANTASIA: I am really sorry she hurt you, Serena. But I'm really proud of you for trying.

RILEY: There's no shame in it! We all get rejected. Part of life. Makes us stronger.

SERENA: I didn't get rejected! I'm not some big loser.

> *FANTASIA and RILEY embrace SERENA, she begins to lose her composure, cries.*

I was so rejected. Like a dead bug. It couldn't have been worse.

FANTASIA: So let get really, really, drunk.

RILEY: Wasted.

FANTASIA: Blotto.

RILEY: Falling down, stupid-ass…

SERENA: Whoooo! Let's DO IT. And I'm gonna dance,

FANTASIA: DANCE DRUNK!

RILEY: Drunken dancing!

SERENA: Oh YAH!

> *They join a group doing "shots" and chanting something like "Ole Ole Ole Ole." Everybody cheers when SERENA downs three or four shots in a row. ARWEN looks disgusted and leaves. DODGE, PRATT, and EXTRAS watch. EXTRA 1 pours the R in the drink and hands it to SERENA. Nobody sees this except PRATT.*

Ramona's dream: the angels guide Serena to heaven.
Photo by Wayne Eardley, Brookside Studio.

Ramona's dream: the angels all hail Serena!
Photo by Wayne Eardley, Brookside Studio.

Scene 36

> SERENA, FANTASIA, and RILEY are all dancing in the big crowd.
>
> EXTRA takes SERENA's hand, pretending to be her friend, dancing with her. DODGE joins in, and PRATT too. SERENA looks happy. She is extremely drunk. FANTASIA begins to make out with another person, and RILEY gets lost in conversation with a guy, who he begins to dance very closely with, and, if possible, kisses.
>
> The music is cranked up. PRATT puts on strobe lights.

PRATT: Hey beautiful! You look like you are going to fall down!

SERENA: Wayyy too much...tequila... wayyyy too much...ohhhh... would you help me? I am feeling really really srange. Did I just say "srange?" I mean...strange. Oooh. I really need to lie down.

PRATT: Sure thing. Just come on with me, you can go lie down on Jesse's bed. There's a nice feather duvet there, just waiting for you.

EXTRA 1: Don't worry, I got you. You're gonna be just fine. Do you need to throw up?

SERENA: No, no, just just...maybe lie down.

EXTRA 1: So that is exactly where we are taking you.

PRATT: Jess even said, "take her to my bed!"

SERENA: Oh yes. Jess? She's so nice. A feather duvet? Oh yes, yes – I –

> PRATT picks two other guys and they follow him and SERENA and EXTRA. They are all grinning.
>
> DODGE sees what is happening and does not like it.

DODGE: Hey. Hey, Pratt. What are you doing?

PRATT: She said she is going to pass out. I'm just taking her to Jesse's room so she doesn't fall down.

DODGE: Serena? You all right?

SERENA: Yeah. Thanks. You're really sweet. I just...want to lie down. Need to... fall down...to...oh. Oh my God – that...that tequila is really...

DODGE: Pratt. You didn't put any of that stuff into...

PRATT: Dude! No!! I told you I was kidding about that!

EXTRA who did put the R in the drink smirks.

SERENA is really stumbling and has to be supported by two guys.

SERENA: Thanks for helping me, you guys are the best. Thank you so much.

The music becomes distorted, with a very sinister sound, perhaps slowed down dramatically – and possibly the party/dancers move into a slow motion dance. They lead her off – a choreographed sequence in which the beginning of the assault is expressed in a very abstracted way.

Scene 37

Rape Scene.

A highly stylized choreographed abstraction of four boys raping an unconscious SERENA is played out. One of them is recording on his iPhone. DODGE enters. He tries to pull them away, they throw him to the floor.

DODGE: Hey! Hey! Whoa. Dudes, this is not cool. Hey, guys, she's unconscious. Come on, dudes… you have to stop… you have to STOP!

EXTRA: Get out!

The guys push him out roughly, possibly down the stairs. He is drunk. SERENA is passed out. They take pictures.

The party is continuing; DODGE is frozen: he won't call police, or tell on his brother, but he cannot stop it.

DODGE: What do I do? What do I do here? If what is happening is what I think is happening I – I should – It can't be happening, right? No, it is, it is happening, I think it is happening but, but – I know, I'm weak, I'm pathetic, I'll burn in hell for this but…I can't…report my brother, my flesh and blood;

Beat.

My dad would never forgive me.

Scene 38

> *RAMONA speaks. SERENA's dad, JAY, is there, silent, unable to speak.*

RAMONA: Where was God?
Where was God?

Where was I? I was at home asleep, snoring in my swivel chair in front of a crime show, and her dad, he was asleep on the couch in front of Sport News, his laptop on his chest. He was waiting up for her, as he always, always did. We were happy that she had gone to a party; her social life was looking up, we sensed no danger, she was with her friends, her best friends, they would watch out for her.
I have wished every moment of every day that I was there. That I could have seen what was happening and I could have...stopped it. I would have torn them apart with my hands.

JAY: Where were the others? The others who just stood by, who knew exactly what was happening, and did nothing to stop it. Nothing... Why, why, why did nobody stop it?

Scene 39

> *DODGE.*

DODGE: Family first. Family first. Loyalty is the greatest quality a man can have, my dad he always says that, he would say that to us every day growing up. He was in the Canadian Forces, he was in Afghanistan and loyalty to your fellow soldiers came before everything, everything. You had their back and they had yours. No matter what. He says the lowest form of life is a squealer... even when you know something is not right, you cannot...I cannot. Inform on my family. I cannot do what I know I should do, I cannot do what I know to be right because to do that we would be wrong. More wrong.

Scene 40

> *A car driven by PRATT on the road. It stops. PRATT and DODGE pull out unconscious SERENA. They dump her in the field.*
>
> *In car.*
>
> *Silent in the car.*

PRATT: FUNNY.

EXTRA 1: It was funny.

PRATT: It was funny, right?

EXTRA 2: Even she was laughing!

PRATT: And she's fine; she'll sleep it off in the long grass. Wake up to the dawn. She loved it, she was totally laughing she was…

EXTRA 1: Laughing. Everyone was laughing! It was a joke.

PRATT: She was smiling, right? She was puking out that window and she was smiling: like, "Bring it on!"

EXTRA 2: She said that, I heard her say that.

PRATT: "Bring it on, Pratt," so I put my hand on her hip…

EXTRA 1: And something somewhere else. And she's gonna be fine, right? She was breathing and everything, right. It was…

PRATT: Awesome. Like hunting deer. That feeling? When the bullet hits, and the deer goes down? Like lightning inside you.

> *Beat… beat.*

It was funny, right?

Scene 41

> *RILEY and FANTASIA are looking for SERENA in the fields.*
>
> *They call out her name.*

RILEY: Sereeeeena!

FANTASIA: Serena! Where are you?? Serena??

Oh my God. Oh my God how did you…

RILEY: What are you doing here? Serena? Serena, wake up!

FANTASIA: She's…oh no. Oh no. Something's wrong. Something's very very…

> *SERENA wakes up.*

Serena! Serena what happened to you? Serena?

SERENA: Just…who…am I…is this a dream? Where…where… I want my mother. I want my mother…

Scene 42

> *DODGE/PRATT/Home.*

DODGE: Pratt! What did you do?

PRATT: Oh, chill, bro. It was nothing. We took her to Raven's field so she could sleep it off.

DODGE: What did you do to her? What were you guys…

PRATT: You going to the game later?

DODGE: She was unconscious.

PRATT: The Kingston Frontenacs are totally gonna lose. The Petes are killing it this season.

DODGE: Did you hear me?

PRATT: Listen. She was into it. She's fine.

DODGE: Liar. I'm your brother and I know when you are lying. Your lip does this twitch thing, every time you lie, and it just twitched.

PRATT: Hah. That's funny. You're funny, Dodge. But you don't know what you're talking about.

DODGE: I think you… Did you….

PRATT: You gonna call the cops?

DODGE: I didn't say that.

PRATT: Go ahead. Think I care? Think they're gonna do anything? Think they won't laugh?
Call them, little girl. You be a good little girl and call them.

> *PRATT punches DODGE. DODGE punches back. A fight.*

Are you still my brother? Are. You. Still. My. Brother?

Scene 43

RAMONA with JAY, FANTASIA, RILEY.

RAMONA: We were all the next day at the hospital.
It was clear she had been – assaulted.
But Serena did not remember who, what, or where. Serena did not remember anything.

SERENA: Nothing.

RAMONA: Nothing?

SERENA: I was drinking, yes, way too much, yes, and dancing, and then…nothing. Nothing. What happened? What happened to me?

RAMONA: She asked us not to go to the police. She wanted to forget about it.

FANTASIA: I should have noticed. I was totally into this guy, so I…it was like there was nothing else.

RILEY: I was in the dancing zone, and I didn't even see anybody else.

FANTASIA: I can't believe I was not looking out for my best friend.

RILEY: Yeah.

FANTASIA: And that nobody saw anything.

RILEY: Or if they did…

FANTASIA: Yeah.

Scene 44

PRATT: (*To EXTRAS 1 and 2.*) The story. The story.
Just in case it gets out. We want to be safe. So.
The same story. Word for word.

EXTRAS: WORD FOR WORD.

PRATT: She was very drunk. But not unconscious.
Never unconscious. NEVER.

EXTRA 1: Do they know about the R?

PRATT: You tell anyone about the R and you are dead. Dead, you hear me?

EXTRA: Did we get rid of the vials? I don't know what happened to the vials.

PRATT: I took care of them. They're at the bottom of the river.

EXTRA 1:   It's her fault for being so drunk! Why did she get so drunk?

PRATT: She was looking for love.

EXTRA 2:   She was all over us. Kissing us. Grinding against us.
           Undoing our belts.

PRATT: She said she wanted to lose her innocence.
           That night, that place. That's what she said, right, boys? "I
           want all of you, boys." That's what she said.

EXTRA 1:   "Give me everything you've got."

PRATT: That's what she said.
           If either of you brats says a word to anyone – and I mean any
           one at all, consider yourselves dead. Got it?

EXTRA 2:   Yeah!

EXTRA: You know it.

Scene 45

BABE/FANTASIA.

BABE: I'll tell you something in absolute confidence: what happened
           to poor dear Serena happened to several girls I knew growing
           up, but we spoke about it only in low whispers. Nobody dared
           make it public, let alone go to the police; the police would
           have laughed us out of the station. We just regarded these
           events as one of the perils of being a girl: we were the antelope
           in the Savannah, with the lions roaming about. I knew what
           happened to my friends was wrong, I was burning with
           anger, but I never dared take any action whatsoever until it
           happened to a blind girl in my dorm at McGill. Leonora. They
           kept her underwear pants and flew them like a victory flag
           out of their disgusting dorm room. Well, I marched into their
           rooms with an ice hockey stick and said, "You are nothing
           more than the scum of the earth: a disgrace to your gender
           and if you don't take Ms. Roberts' personal property down
           this second and hand it to me I will smash every thing in this
           revolting room, and report every one of you to the Dean."

FANTASIA: And did they? Did they do what you said?

BABE: Without a moment's hesitation.

Scene 46

About a week later.

SERENA comes home.

SERENA: Hi, Dad. What are you doing sitting in the dark?

JAY: Waiting for you.

SERENA: Oh. You didn't have to do that.

JAY: I don't mind. It's peaceful here; I was worried about you.

SERENA: I was…just at choir practice.

JAY: Good. Good. How was it?

SERENA: Fine. Fine. Well. I'm going to bed.

JAY: G'night then.

SERENA: G'night, Dad.

JAY: Serena?

SERENA: Yuh.

JAY: You okay?

SERENA: It's nothing, Dad. I just got really drunk and yes what happened was bad, but I am coping, okay? I've been online and there are so many girls this has happened to, and…well, it helps to talk to them. A lot. It's really not a big deal.

JAY: You know, there are really good counsellors who deal with this situation all the time. We have made an appointment for Tuesday with the finest psychiatrist in Peterborough. Everybody says she works miracles, Sere.

SERENA: I really have not connected with any of the counsellors I've seen so far. I just…didn't like them, and they didn't get me. I can totally handle this myself, Dad. I'm fine… Really!

JAY: Serena, you don't have to pretend.

SERENA: What the hell, Dad. I said I'm fine. Look at me, I'm resilient, I'm your basic elastic band, your bouncing ball, I AM FINE! Just leave me alone.

> *SERENA leaves – JAY feels utterly defeated. RAMONA enters.*

JAY: Hey.

RAMONA: Hey. How was she?

JAY: I wish…I could help her somehow. I feel like she's…sinking.

RAMONA: No. No! She is not sinking, she is as well as can be expected, Jay; she is –

JAY: (*Cannot meet RAMONA's eyes.*) I'm just so scared she might –

RAMONA: Jay! You stop that right now! Don't ever ever even imply – what's wrong with you? Why are you – catastrophizing? Serena is strong, unbelievably strong, and she will survive.

Scene 47

Other EXTRAS all getting the video on their phones.

Laughing, and forwarding to hundreds of others. improvising reactions, laughing.

"Oh my God." "What?" "No!" "Look at that." "Isn't that his…" "Ewww!" "So gross." "So funny!"

EXTRA 3: Oh my God. O.M.G. did you see what Martin posted?

EXTRA 4: You won't believe it you will NOT it's disgusting oh my God!

EXTRA 3: It's that girl, whatsername you know, the one they called –

EXTRA 4: Snow White! Lol, 'cause she was like so pure…and in the video she is wasted and she is naked, like at a party, in someone's bedroom!

EXTRA 5: That's Jess's bedroom. Her party two weeks ago! And there's all these guys in there all over her…and –

EXTRA 6: Who are they? Nice guys, SMH…

EXTRA 5: Their faces are blurred out. But hers isn't. Whoaaa.

Scene 48

EXTRAS 1 and 2, PRATT.

EXTRA 1: Dude! There are like 50,000 likes!

EXTRA 2: No way. You can't see it's us, though.

PRATT: What a nightmare. A freaking goddamn…

EXTRA 2: See? I didn't really do anything. Look at me, I'm just…

PRATT: You did. And so did I. And Morris. And Robinson. And Rohan.

EXTRA 2: No NO. I was way too wasted.

EXTRA I: Nobody cares. This happens every day. I'm tellin' you, 50,000 likes. Oh look, we're up at 62. And anyway, everyone's shared it… It's out there now…

PRATT: You stupid, pathetic little weasels. I don't know you. We don't speak. Ever. And if it comes to a court case – it was all you. I was trying to stop you. Me and Dodge, we tried to pull you off.

EXTRA 2:   Whaaaa?

PRATT: What you did. Is disgusting. We are done.

            Takes their phones and smashes them.

Scene 49

            SERENA, FANTASIA, RILEY.

            SERENA and RILEY and FANTASIA find the post on You Tube.

            SERENA starts screaming. RILEY turns it off.

SERENA: No. No. No. Oh my god, oh my god.

RILEY: We're going to the police.

SERENA: NO. Oh my God I had thought it was only one, I thought… I didn't know… oh no. Oh no. I don't want them to SEE this. I don't want my mother or my father to see this, are you kidding? We have to get rid of it, is there a number, is there someone we can call, computer experts, like Anonymous?

FANTASIA: You will survive this, look at all the Hollywood stars and their sex tapes, nobody cares.

SERENA: But this isn't a sex tape, this is…

RILEY: Assault, multiple assaults.

SERENA: I think I'm going to faint.

RILEY: Here, sit down. Sit down. Drink this.

FANTASIA: Well, the cops will see this, and that will be the proof they need.

RILEY: I don't know. I don't know. You can't see their faces.

SERENA: Oh this is so bad. This is so bad.

RILEY: Okay. I agree. It's bad. But Fancy's right, it might be proof. It might be. Maybe they can unblur their faces. And their voices. Do you…recognize their voices?

SERENA: No, yes, kind of. I don't know. I have to go, I have to get out of here.

RILEY: But where, where will you go?

SERENA: Anywhere, I don't know. My cousin's farm in Windsor?

RILEY: But there's internet everywhere.

FANTASIA: There is no getting away; you have us. You have us!

SERENA: What about, like the mountains, or up north, sometimes there is no internet at our cottage, maybe I could just go break into a cottage, or or –

RILEY: You have to face it head on. You have nothing, nothing to be ashamed of, Serena.

FANTASIA: They raped you. You need to go to the police. This is mass rape, Serena. A big felony, they will get serious time in prison for what they did.

SERENA: WHO? Their faces are blurred, their voices are changed. Who, who was it? I have to get out of here.

Musical bridge.

Scene 50

SILAS: Tell me it wasn't you two. Pratt, there is a rumour going around it was you and the Dodger leading some kinda gang bang at a house party, some unconscious girl. And I am telling them there is no way, no damned way; I told the guy I would kill him if he said another word; these boys are the best and the brightest, they are headed to med school, they come from fine families, my sister's family, an old Peterborough family, they vacation in Hawaii and Whistler, they volunteer at the Food Bank, they love their moms…they are even kind to beggars in the city. And the guy said: "Watch the video." I want to get the truth from you boys first.
Holy shit. You aren't saying anything…Pratt? D? Talk to me. TALK TO ME.

DODGE: Don't look like that. I wasn't there.

SILAS: Are you telling me the truth?

PRATT: Girls now? They are all about making YouTube videos or Tumblr movies of themselves, naked, whatever, showing everything, sending it to everyone, they think it's funny!

SILAS: I am NOT buying, Pratt, what you are selling. 'Cause it's lies.

PRATT: You wanna see my phone, Uncle Si?

DODGE: Si, I knew the girl was passed out, so I was trying to get her to a taxi. Ask anyone. That is why you'll see me in the background, I'm trying to get her out of there. God's truth.

PRATT: She was into it, Si. Seriously. You gotta believe me.

SILAS: Pratt. Wake up, man. You need to wake up.

PRATT: You need to wake up.

SILAS: You little shit. (*Slaps him.*) This is a part of you I don't even know. I feel like I'm talkin' to strangers, here. Aliens disguised as my nephews.

DODGE: I am telling you I was not part of…whatever it was.

PRATT: Hey, you're the one who got us hooked on porn, Uncle Si.

SILAS: Oh come on, that was *Playboy*, that's not even porn! Anyway, this is real, dudes, real girl, real life. And a crime. If this is true, you are criminals and I am ashamed to call you my nephews. And me a cop.

PRATT: She was totally cool with it, Si. We were hooking up, that's all it was. An innocent hookup.

DODGE: I am not a criminal. If you want to know who the criminal is…

PRATT: (*Attacks him.*) You are no longer my brother.

Scene 51

The mother of PRATT and DODGE.

DOREEN: They were honestly, honestly? The sweetest little boys on the planet: curious, and kind, and oh so smart. Pratty, he wore his Spiderman cape every day for a year when he was seven; he wouldn't even let me wash it! Dodge, he was the sensitive one, even rescuing baby birds that had fallen out of the nest? He would bring them home, and give 'em water with a dropper. He would put the soft cat food on his finger, and the bird would open its yellow beak wide and there would be Dodge, feeding his baby. Now Pratty, he would go after Dodger about his baby birds, even gave one to the neighbour's cat just to see Dodger cry; I told Dodger, if you had left it on the grass the cats would have got it anyway! That is the cycle of nature! Oh, Pratt loved to tease his brother, you know how boys are – and Pratt, oh he was all boy from the moment he was born. Always into something, always had to be first, and had to have the most. That is just the kind of kid he was and his dad, well his dad always said, "Doreen, let him be. He'll have to be tough to get anywhere in this world. The kid is gonna be a leader, and I will not have you get in his way."

Now that he's in Florida with *her*, he never bothers to see them at all; so it is all on me. But I promise you:

I have never taught them to disrespect a woman or a girl.

And though it is true that their father would get cranky with me, if his dinner was late or if I looked a mess, he rarely laid a hand on me.

> *Beat.*

My boys are good boys. I know them better than anyone else in the world and I know they are good.

I know…they…are…GOOD.

Scene 52

> *SERENA and RILEY and FANTASIA are communicating in the middle of the night.*

SERENA: I can't take it. I can't take it, Riley, I am freaking out freaking out. It's…it's all coming back to me, flashing back, and and I keep throwing up when I think of it, because I can see his face, their faces in my mind, their eyes in my head are burning through me… I can feel what they did. What they did all night to me and…it is so intolerable that. I'm losing my mind, I'm losing myself, I don't know what to do I don't know what to do I just don't know what to do…

RILEY: It's three in the morning. Try to sleep.

SERENA: I am never never going back to school.

RILEY: You don't have to. But if you decide to? You come and you hold your head up high. I will be right there beside you.

FANTASIA: Me too.

SERENA: I feel like I am in a horror movie; their faces are filling my head and their things and their smell in my nose and and I can't I can't control it anymore guys; they are taking over. I have to – I have to somehow –

> *She runs into the night.*

RILEY: Sere?

FANTASIA: Serena!!

Scene 53

RAMONA and SILAS.

SILAS: Ramona Gordon, how are you?

RAMONA: Not well, Silas, In fact, very very worried. My daughter. You remember Serena? I think you taught her judo at the Community Centre.

SILAS: Sure, Serena: black belt, right?

RAMONA: She…wasn't in her bed this morning, or at school… and it's just not like her…

SILAS: I wouldn't worry about that, Ramona. Happens all the time. How old is she? Fifteen, sixteen?

RAMONA: Just turned fifteen, Silas, and this does not happen with her.

SILAS: Yeah. but you know, teen girls are…

RAMONA: Silas! I know my daughter and she has been very depressed… something…very serious has happened in her life and… maybe you know about it –

SILAS: Nope. Haven't heard anything.

RAMONA: Well. You may hear eventually, people talk. And because of this…she has been under an enormous amount of stress, and… we are scared, Silas, we are very very…worried about her. She left…in the middle of the night, she was not in her bed this morning. Do I need to go above your head?

SILAS: I'll look into it.

RAMONA: You will?

SILAS: Yeah. Of course. I'll look into it. Right away.

RAMONA: How? How are you going to look into it?

SILAS: I…we have our ways. We're gonna find her, okay? I promise. Just…leave it to me. You stay home, in case she shows up.

RAMONA: This is my daughter, do you understand? This is my daughter. You are a police officer. DO. YOUR. JOB.

                   He looks at it for another moment, peering to see if it is his nephews, and shuts it with disgust.

Scene 54

RAMONA's dream.

Middle of the night. Ramona finds herself in the water.

RAMONA: Is this hand real, this blood, my voice? Am I in the middle of the woods in the middle of the night all alone with blood, blood on my hands?

That isn't me this can't be happening it can't be true
I am dreaming of course I am yes YES, silly, I can wake up at any time, ANY time.

But where am I? where am I? why would I be standing in the river
In the night
Oh, oh, oh yes yes I know I know it now
I am the FURIES. I am the FURIES, the avengers,
I am all of them, all two thousand of them
Inside me the power of all of them I AM the FURIES
Watch out for me, boys, watch out for me oh yes
I tore them, tore them apart with my teeth. My my hand was the axe the axe that we chop down our Christmas tree with every year out at the Christmas tree farm.
The axe that Jay chops the firewood with
I am...in blood now
I am standing in their blood I am wading.
in their blood.
and there is no turning back.

> *RAMONA wakes from her dream. She is outside, on the ground.*

(*To audience.*) Yes, yes. The dream again. The revenge dream. It's a different revenge every night. Some nights, I cut their heads off. Some nights, I feed them to the dogs... Some nights, I hang them from the highest trees. And look! I am sleepwalking. I haven't done that since I was a child, and my mother died. Here I am on the cold ground.
I need to find my child.
I need to make it better. Will this blood on my hands make it better?
I need...to find...my child.
Is she lost? Tell me. Is she lost forever?

Scene 55

EXTRAS gossip.

5. Did you hear…oh my god. Did you hear about Serena Wales?

6. She's missing.

7. Missing? What?

8. Her mom hasn't seen her for two days…

10. She was here yesterday, wasn't she? NO. She was not here yesterday.

11. I saw her, I saw her at her locker, around seven o'clock after choir rehearsal.

12. You couldn't have.

13. I did. No, maybe that was her friend…

14. Did you speak to her?

15. No, maybe it wasn't her.

17. It must be because of that video: did you see that video?

18. Everyone saw the video.

19. It's disgusting.

20. Harsh.

1. Really harsh.

2. I would DIE.

3. Me too, I would punch myself in the face till I died.

4. I would disappear. I totally understand the disappearing. Have you seen it?

5. It's disgusting. DISGUSTING. She is like throwing up, and the guys are… I can't even –

6. You watched it?

7. It came onto my cell phone.

8. I tried to turn it off, it was too late.

9. It's disgusting.

10. But she's missing, dude!

11. Maybe she…

12. Just went to the city, right?

13. Or the States or something. To get away.

14. Or boarding school. Remember that other girl? That's what she did.

RILEY: You know that by watching it you are part of it, right? You are part of it when you are watching it.

1: What?

2: Who are you?

Scene 56

> *DODGE and PRATT and SILAS. SILAS grabs them both, hard.*

SILAS: You low-down dirty ANIMALS.

PRATT: Whooaa. Si!

SILAS: You should be burning in HELL.

DODGE: Not me, Si. I swear to God. I swear to God.

SILAS: She is missing! She is missing, you rodents, did you know that? She left home in the middle of the night and nobody knows where she is; you did that; YOU are responsible.

PRATT: Oh no…That's terrible, Si!

SILAS: And you will PAY, I will see to it that you PAY.

DODGE: She's probably just at a friend's house. I mean, where would she go?

SILAS: Where would she go? Where would she go? What is wrong with your BRAIN, boy? Do you have a BRAIN? Do either of you have a BRAIN in your HEAD?

PRATT: Si, man, if she took off somewhere that is unfortunate, but it is nothing whatever do do with our hookup.

> *SILAS smacks PRATT, or possibly tackles him to the ground.*

SILAS: Hookup? Hookup? Listen to me and listen hard. Pratt. I need you to acknowledge that it's everything, everything to do with what you did. Say it.

PRATT: Get off me.

SILAS: EVERYTHING. Say it. EVERYTHING.

> *PRATT squirms away, breathless.*

PRATT: GET OFF ME. That's assault, Si, I could have you charged, man.

DODGE: Si, like I said: I was trying to help her. I swear on my mother's grave. I wanted to get her into a taxi. I don't do those things, they make me sick, they –

PRATT gives his brother a dirty look and hisses.

SILAS: Her mother has reported her missing. To me. And I'm sick. I am sick with worry that – I can't even say it. And by the way, be prepared for a long, long time in prison.

PRATT and DODGE alone.

PRATT: (*Hand gesture of triumph, laughing.*) YES.

DODGE: Yes what?

PRATT: We are in the clear, bro.

DODGE: But he said –

PRATT: Hah. He's just trying to scare us. He's family, Dodge. Family. Be happy. We're free.

DODGE: But…where do you think she is?

PRATT: Not our problem.

Scene 57

RAMONA and JAY, searching. Running. Yelling.

RAMONA and JAY: Serena!! Serena!! Serena!

RILEY and FANTASIA join them.

Scene 58

BABE.

BABE: Oh this is a terrible turn of events. I don't like it one bit. I have a very, very bad feeling the same way I did about that child up the street from me in Toronto in 1979. I had that spiny fear feeling in my belly all night and it did not turn out well.

Fancy is always out looking for Serena. She is out with the team day and night and night and day, inch by inch, scratching at the earth, diving through the murky river, she is determined to find her friend.

Because she is feeling…I am afraid, responsible in some way. Because she was dancing, having fun, whilst all of it was happening. But how was she to know? How? How are any of us to know?

A tiny, old-fashioned part of me thinks if a girl is going to get into bed with a fella, and she's been drinking the rum and the whiskey, what on earth does she expect? Hail Marys?? I mean why? Why didn't her mother warn her? We have to understand men to survive in their world. Men are wild, they are wolves, they are hungry wolves, they are pack animals. With very few exceptions. Women of my generation, we understood men. We understood, that they need to be managed. They – Oh God have mercy.

We have not slept an hour since she disappeared. We are fearful; we are filled with fear, fear, and that spiny creature of fear is growing by the hour inside all of our stomachs – but we always have hope.

Beat.

There is always hope.

Scene 59

Search party.

RAMONA, JAY, SILAS, BABE, FANTASIA, RILEY, EXTRAS, DODGE, PRATT, DOREEN, all searching inch-by-inch through the long grasses.

Scene 60

SERENA walks into the pond.
She addresses the audience.

SERENA: I am here. Here I am! I am here, but I am hiding. I am hiding
so they can never ever find me.

I know you will miss me, I know that you will be angry that
I left you this way. But please understand:

I am not there with you, so that I will not be there with them.
Because while I was there, a living human girl on a living
human earth, I would never be free. I would never ever be free
of what happened, and what everyone knew had happened.

'Cause when I was here, with you, they could always always
get to me.

And that...moment in time, my terrible moment, the most
terrible moment of my life could never disappear.

It would always be there.

A click away.

For anyone who wanted to see.

And everyone, everyone wanted to see.

A click away a click away a click away.

At university, meet new friends, click, oh she's that girl,
wanting to write for the school paper, applying for a Mcjob,
click click, oh no, look at that, my first crush, click, oh she is
that girl? I don't think so; applying for scholarships, uh oh, uh
unh, and then maybe maybe someone does fall in love with
me despite it all but then at my wedding, there would be a
drunken nephew, click click look everyone look at the bride, on
her back...and then, imagine, my happiest moments, when I
have my first baby, new life nursing at my breast, nasty nurses
click click click, look at the mama back when, oh yes, I will
see it in their faces, their hating, hating faces, no escape, see,
no escape ever, when I am watching my daughter at soccer,
my son at ballet, click click, click click click. People with their
phones, jealous people, nosy people click, click click click,
when I am running for town council when I am a grandmother
sitting down to dinner with my grandkids, click, click, did you
see what Gramma did sixty years ago? Even on my deathbed,
my deathbed: click click, the cleaner will look me up, and click
click, do you know what happened to her? Always always
there for all the world to see, a vomiting ghost, haunting me.
This way, I will be forgotten, I will....vanish!

Vanishing is a beautiful thing.

SERENA walks into the water.

Scene 61

RAMONA reaches the pond. SERENA is motionless.

She wades in and lifts her, holding her in her arms. JAY, and FANTASIA and RILEY arrive, and they all stand in the pond and lift her up as high as they can.

She breathes.

Afterword

RAMONA: (*To audience.*) And she breathed.

I know, I implied at the beginning that she was dead, that she drowned herself. Well, we wanted you to have a happy ending. We wanted to leave you with hope.

Many families are not so lucky. Many of the children do end their lives. Many are doing so right now, as we speak.

     Music.

I am having that dream again: the dream where all the girls and boys who found it all too much to bear, where they arise.
Look.
They are rising from the dead!
They are here to show us
the way
to show us
how
to make a world in which this will never
ever
happen again.
We only have to
listen.

> *The cast all moves downstage to face the audience and each cast member states the name of a young person who has completed suicide, especially because of bullying. (NOTE: The permission of the families of these young people must be obtained before using their names. In the original production, the names included those of Amanda Todd, Rehteah Parsons, Henrik Helmers, and Shannon Hookimaw.)*

THE END

Resources

To get help for any situation:

- Kids Help Phone: https:kidshelpphone.ca
  (For immediate help, call: 1-800-668-6868.)

Help for LGBTQ2+ youth:

- Egale Canada: egale.ca/community-resources/
- School's Out UK: www.schools-out.org.uk
- Trans Lifeline: www.translifeline.org/about

For strategies to deal with bullying:

- Hollaback: www.ihollaback.org/resources/bystander-resources/
- Prevnet: www.prevnet.ca/resources
- Bullying Canada: www.bullyingcanada.ca/about-us/

Sexual health, pregnancy, rights, and justice:

- Advocates for Youth: advocatesforyouth.org
- Massey Centre: www.massey.ca
- Sex and U: www.sexandu.ca

Suicide Prevention:

- The Lifeline Canada: thelifelinecanada.ca/help/
- Honouring Life: www.honouringlife.ca